Shute

Shute

The Engineer who became a Prince of Storytellers

by

Richard Thorn

Copyright © 2017 Richard Thorn

The moral right of the author has been asserted.

Apart from any fair dealing for the purposes of research or private study, or criticism or review, as permitted under the Copyright, Designs and Patents Act 1988, this publication may only be reproduced, stored or transmitted, in any form or by any means, with the prior permission in writing of the publishers, or in the case of reprographic reproduction in accordance with the terms of licences issued by the Copyright Licensing Agency. Enquiries concerning reproduction outside those terms should be sent to the publishers.

Matador
9 Priory Business Park,
Wistow Road, Kibworth Beauchamp,
Leicestershire. LE8 0RX
Tel: 0116 279 2299
Email: books@troubador.co.uk
Web: www.troubador.co.uk/matador
Twitter: @matadorbooks

ISBN 978 1788032 575

British Library Cataloguing in Publication Data.
A catalogue record for this book is available from the British Library.

Printed and bound in the UK by TJ International, Padstow, Cornwall
Typeset in 11pt Aldine401 BT by Troubador Publishing Ltd, Leicester, UK

Matador is an imprint of Troubador Publishing Ltd

For Danusia, of course

Contents

Permissions	ix
Author's Notes	xi
Prologue	xii

Part 1 – Old World — **1**
1. Foundations — 3
2. University — 23
3. Aeroplanes — 30
4. Airships — 41
5. Success and Failure — 63
6. Entrepreneur — 79

Part 2 – Transition — **101**
7. Peace and War — 103
8. Home and Abroad — 125
9. Australia and Back — 146
10. Exasperation — 160

Part 3 – The Great Southern Land — **171**
11. A New World — 173
12. Flying a Different Flag — 185
13. The Future and the Past — 204
14. Novelist, Farmer and Racing Driver — 215
15. Armageddon, Conflict and Decline — 227
16. The Last Year — 242
17. Epilogue — 251

The Published Works of Nevil Shute	256
Selections from a Photo Timeline	259
Image Credits	269
Notes on Sources	271
A Select Bibliography	300
The Nevil Shute Norway Foundation	303
Acknowledgements	304
About the Author	306
Index	307

Permissions

Sincere thanks to:
Heather Mayfield and United Agents LLP on behalf of the Estate of Nevil Shute Norway, for giving permission to quote from the published books, unpublished writing and letters of Nevil Shute Norway.

Penguin Random House UK for giving permission to quote from correspondence between staff at William Heinemann Ltd and Nevil Shute Norway.

Karen Sharpe-Kramer for giving permission to quote from correspondence between Stanley Kramer and Nevil Shute Norway.

Thank you to the following individuals and organisations for allowing access to the papers and correspondence of Nevil Shute Norway:

Angela Groves
British Library, London
National Archives of Australia, Canberra
National Library of Australia, Canberra
The Nevil Shute Norway Foundation
Petersfield Museum, Hampshire
Portsmouth Museum, Hampshire
RAF Museum, Colindale, London
Random House Group Archive, Rushden
Harry Ransom Humanities Research Centre, University of Texas at Austin
State University of Victoria, Melbourne

Shute
Syndics of Cambridge University Library
Syracuse University Libraries, New York
Charles E Young Research Library, University of California, Los Angeles

Every effort has been made to obtain the necessary permissions for copyright material used. Any omissions to make appropriate acknowledgements will be corrected in any future editions.

Author's Notes

i) Norway or Shute?

As he was in full-time employment when his first book was published in 1926, Nevil Norway wrote under the pseudonym of Nevil Shute in order to protect his daytime reputation as an aeronautical engineer. Even when he became a famous novelist he usually signed his books N. S. Norway or Nevil Shute Norway. In this book I have usually called him Nevil Norway, only using the name Nevil Shute when referring to his books or specific activity as an author.

ii) Units of Measurement

Over Nevil Norway's lifetime, imperial units of measurement were the norm in the United Kingdom and Australia. Conversion of the imperial units used in this book to the metric-based International System of Units (SI) used by most countries today is shown below.

Length	1 foot (ft) = 0.3048 metres (m)
	1 yard (yd) = 0.9144 metres (m)
	1 mile (mi) = 1.6093 kilometres (km)
Mass	1 pound (lb) = 0.4535 kilograms (kg)
Area	1 square foot (ft^2) = 0.0929 square metres (m^2)
	1 square mile (mi^2) = 2.5899 square kilometres (km^2)
	1 acre (ac) = 4,046.8560 square metres (m^2)
Volume	1 Imperial gallon (gal) = 4.5460 litres (l)
	1 US barrel oil (bbl) = 158.9873 litres (l)
Velocity	1 mile per hour (mph) = 1.6093 kilometres per hour (km/h)
Power	1 horsepower (hp) = 745.6998 watts (W)
Temperature	°C = (°F − 32)/1.8

Prologue

An Unexpected Passenger
20 July 1950

At a quarter to five on a warm summer's afternoon in July 1950 the P & O liner SS *Strathnaver* left Tilbury Docks, London, bound for Australia. One of those on board was Nevil Shute Norway, better known to many around the world as the novelist Nevil Shute. Although like most of the other passengers he and his family were migrating to Australia to start a new life, Nevil Shute Norway was certainly not a typical 'ten pound Pom'. He was wealthy and leaving behind a lifestyle that most in England could only dream of.

He was 51 years old and had already experienced and achieved a great deal: as an aeronautical engineer playing a key role in Britain's ultimately ill-fated airship programme, as the joint managing director of a new aircraft manufacturing company, as a developer of secret weapons during the Second World War and now as a novelist.

Since the early 1920s, in parallel with his career in aviation, Norway had been writing. His first novel *Marazan,* written under the pseudonym of Nevil Shute, had been published in 1926, and by 1950 he had thirteen published books to his name, with three of them having been turned into feature films. The income from his novels and film rights meant that since 1938 Shute had been able to pursue a career as a full-time novelist, although this had of course been interrupted by the war. By 1950, he was living, with his wife and two daughters, on a 5-acre property on the popular holiday destination of Hayling Island, could enjoy his passions of sailing from a yacht moored at the end of the garden and flying his own aeroplane from the nearby Portsmouth Aerodrome. He had a lifestyle which would have been the envy of many in a country still suffering from austerity and rationing after the war.

It was therefore perhaps somewhat surprising that one of the most popular and successful novelists of the time was leaving England to settle in Australia, a country he had visited only once the year before and which the rest of his family had never seen. Although he would return to the country of his birth a number of times during the following years, he never returned there again to live. For the rest of his life Australia would become his home and, it could be argued, the inspiration for many of his best-loved and most enduring novels.

Nevil Shute was already dead when I first became aware of him. When I was growing up, my parents, sisters and I usually visited my aunt and uncle at Christmas. Crammed into their small but comfortably furnished living room, I was always drawn to a bookcase in the corner, the upper two shelves of which were lined with books from the Companion Book Club. To me at that time this seemed almost like a library. However, with their uniform styling, and aura of quality, the monthly selection from book clubs like this were very popular in Britain during the late 1950s and early 1960s. I can remember studying the rows of titles by authors such as Monica Dickens, H. E. Bates and Alistair MacLean, but as a teenager immersed in the world of Tolkien, most meant little to me. One, though, that always stood out during this annual review was *Round the Bend* by Nevil Shute; both the title and the name of the author, for reasons I did not understand, appealed to me. Of course, I did not get any further than looking at the spine of the book, but the name Shute remained with me.

A decade later in the early 1970s, as a poor engineering student looking for something to fill the time on a forthcoming train journey, I came across a copy of *Trustee from the Toolroom* in a second-hand bookshop in Bolton. This time I did go further than look at the title, and once I had started reading it, like countless numbers before me I was hooked.

I knew very little about Nevil Shute at that time. I might have read somewhere that he had a background in engineering, but I was certainly not aware that during the 1940s and 1950s he had been one of the most popular novelists in the English-speaking world; a best-seller of best-sellers, frequently referred to as a prince of storytellers. Like others of the era he has slowly drifted into obscurity, though less slowly than many as all his novels are still in print. There was, however, much more to Shute than his literary output, a great deal more. So who exactly was Nevil Shute, and what did he do?

Part 1

January 1899–April 1938
Old World

1

Foundations
January 1899–December 1918

Nevil Shute, or to give him his full name Nevil Shute Norway, was born in Middlesex at 16 Somerset Road, Ealing on 17 January 1899. He was the second son of Arthur and Mary Norway, with his rather unusual second Christian name coming from his paternal grandmother Georgina Shute, also a prolific author in her day.

Ealing was then on the edge of London, which, as the capital of the British Empire, was in many respects the centre of the world. The colonialist Cecil Rhodes summed up a common attitude of the time when he is reputed to have said: 'Remember that you are an Englishman, and have consequently won first prize in the lottery of life'.

At the beginning of the twentieth century, Queen Victoria's Empire covered over a quarter of the earth's land surface. It was the largest and richest in history, and getting bigger. With many of Victoria's children and grandchildren married into royal families across Europe, Britain's influence was continuing to spread.

Over a third of the world's trade went through London's docks. Key economic commodities such as cotton, wool, wheat and sugar were loaded or unloaded daily in London. Massive private trading companies, such as the East India Company, who had for so long controlled distant parts of the Empire on behalf of the British government, were now being dissolved and replaced by direct imperial rule.

In addition to political and economic power, the British Empire of course also had military might. For an island race this had traditionally manifested itself as naval power, which Britain had in abundance. Although the Royal Navy had a long successful history as the principal defender of the realm, its ships were now becoming dated, and countries such as Germany were already planning modern fleets to rival the British. The Royal Navy also performed an important second duty by ensuring the protection of the all-important sea trade routes. The first manned flight of the Wright brothers, and the beginning of the development of the aeroplane, which would ultimately redefine military capability, was still four years away. For the present, though, Britain still ruled the waves.

Of course, all was not perfect. The British Empire had its fair share of conflicts, especially at the outer fringes. For instance, the year Nevil Norway was born, the second Boer War began in South Africa. Although Queen Victoria had confidently asserted that 'we are not interested in the possibilities of defeat; they do not exist', reality turned out to be very different. It would prove a long and expensive war, and take the Empire three years and an army of nearly half a million men to finally reach a somewhat unsatisfactory conclusion against a much smaller opponent. This war, which was considered by many historians to be the 'last of the gentlemen's wars', brutally put into focus the difficulty of supporting an Empire that was spread across the world and the unsuitability of the army and its tactics for such conflicts. It was also a war in which newspaper propaganda was used in a major way for the first time to influence wavering public opinion. In spite of these weaknesses, for many, the British Empire, and in particular London, was still the place to be. It was into this world that Nevil Shute Norway was born.

Coincidentally, at the same time, but on the other side of the globe, the six colonies of Australia were nearing the end of negotiations that would lead to federation and the formation of the Commonwealth of Australia – a country which was also to play an important part in his future life.

Nevil Norway was born into a comfortable, upper-middle-class household that reflected the Victorian values of hard work, respectability, education and a keen interest in the wider world. His father, Arthur Hamilton Norway, was then 39 years old, with good prospects as a clerk in the Civil Service, having entered the Service via the competitive entrance examination on 6 August 1880. A position in the Civil Service was desirable to many at that time. It provided a permanent, well-paid career with a pension, and at the higher levels, status and recognition in the form of public honours. He was initially appointed as an assistant surveyor of taxes at the Inland Revenue in Liverpool, but in February 1883 he was transferred to the General Post Office and moved to London.

The days of entry to the Civil Service by patronage were over, and the entrance examinations were of university standard, requiring knowledge of a wide range of subjects, including the language and literature of England, France, Germany, Italy, ancient Greece and Rome, mathematics, the natural sciences and history. Although the system was described as open, it was still designed to heavily favour Oxford and Cambridge University graduates with a classics education. Although he was not from this background, Arthur Norway persevered, and with help from Mr Wren, a renowned Civil Service coach, he was ultimately successful in passing the entrance examinations. He clearly had both scholarly ability and a fierce ambition to succeed. In addition to his duties as a clerk in the secretary's office of the General Post Office, by the time Nevil was born, Arthur Norway had already had three books published by a mainstream publisher. These included travel guides of Yorkshire, Devon and Cornwall and a history of the post office packet service. The Victorians had a rapidly growing appetite for literature of all kinds.

Mary Louisa Norway, who had children rather late in life, was 38 when Nevil was born and from a strong military background. Her father, Frederick Gadsden, was then a retired major general from the Indian Staff Corps, who had spent nearly all of his working life in India. Following his retirement, the family had settled down in Ealing, also living in Somerset Road. Mary would have been used to living in different parts of the world, and she would have been well trained in running a household, managing servants and organising social events. Like her husband, she would later become a published author, writing a memoir on her experiences of the Irish Easter Rising in 1916. The young Nevil Norway was indeed fortunate to be in an environment in which both writing and travel, significant factors in his later life, were nurtured.

Nevil had one brother, officially Frederick but always Fred to him. Born three years earlier, Fred's arrival into the world had been proudly announced by his parents in the London *Times*; Nevil did not receive such an honour.

From an early age, Fred had demonstrated the same love for classical learning as his father, and so, in his parents' eyes at least, he was destined for great things and would be given every opportunity to achieve them. Although Nevil was very different to Fred, more content to build model aeroplanes out of wood and metal, and develop a knowledge of mechanics than studying literature and the classics, the two got on very well. While it would have been quite understandable if Nevil had been jealous of his elder brother, this was never the case and in many respects he idolised Fred. Sadly, like so many of his generation, Fred was to have his life cut short in the trenches in France during the First World War, and Nevil later poignantly wrote 'after nearly forty years it still seems strange to me that I should be older than Fred'.

At the end of the nineteenth century, Ealing was a rural urban town in Middlesex with a population of just over 30,000. Known as the Queen of the Suburbs, the urban district council was working hard to protect its image as a town for the prosperous middle class who worked in London. Somerset Road reflected this ideal, with a row of three-storey detached houses intended for professional families with servants. The Norway family at number 16 was typical of this, in that, like every house in the road, they employed domestic servants to support the smooth running of the household. In fact, at that time, Ealing had a higher number of female domestic servants than any suburb in London except Hampstead and Kensington.

Nevil and Fred therefore spent their pre-school years in a well-managed, secure environment in which they enjoyed the comforts of a modern urban home along with the many distractions of a country environment to stimulate their young imaginations. One of the young Nevil's earliest memories of life in Ealing was 'of seeing a balloon descend voluntarily about a mile to the south-west of Somerset Road'. For this event to be so clearly etched in his memory, and so vividly described in his autobiography over fifty years later, illustrates the fascination that aviation was already beginning to have on him.

As a young boy, Nevil could have best been described as rather plain. With brown hair and brown eyes, and a receding chin that always gave him a rather sullen look, there was little to make him stand out. The moment he opened his mouth to speak though, things were different – Nevil Norway had a significant stammer. This was an affliction which was to haunt him for the rest of his life and although it would bother him less as he got older it never left him.

As well as the stammer, Norway had to deal with a second problem: he was left-handed. This was something that was considered a social stigma at the time, and children were often punished for being left-handed and forced to write with their right hand at school. It has been suggested that the trauma associated with this may have caused Norway's stammer. However, while such a theory was widely believed up until the 1940s, there is now no medical evidence to support this. While the exact reasons for a stammer are still not clear, it is now recognised as being a neurological condition, rather than being caused by any trauma or shock. Whatever the reason, the stammer was to affect him to various degrees all of his life. There are no known audio recordings of Nevil Norway in existence.

In 1907, Arthur Norway was promoted to the grade of assistant secretary, and he became head of the General Post Office Staff Branch in London. This advancement was celebrated by moving the family to a new house. Still in Ealing, Corfton Road was a step up from Somerset Road, offering larger houses with bigger gardens.

The education of his sons would have been of high importance to Arthur. The expected education pathway for boys from the upper middle classes was preparatory school to be followed by a good English public school and university, preferably Oxford or Cambridge. It was thought by many that only public schools could provide the social, linguistic and sporting skills necessary for advancement in life. They also usually offered lifelong support in the form of the old boys' network. The Civil Service, of which Arthur was a lifelong part, was a great illustration of the importance of a public school education at that time. As late as 1927, 72 per cent of top-ranking civil servants, 80 per cent of the Indian Civil Service and 64 per cent of Dominion governors had been to public boarding schools.

Nevil's formal education began in 1908, at age 9, when he was sent to Colet Court, St Paul's Preparatory School in Hammersmith. He was not conforming to the norm for his social class and attending a boarding school, but instead still living at home and travelling to school each day on the recently electrified District Railway. Given Nevil's stammer and lack of confidence, it was most likely that his father's intention was that he would go on to the local St Paul's School, one of the few predominantly day schools in the prestigious 'Clarendon nine'. His brother was further along the expected education route and shortly to start as a boarder at one of the others in the Clarendon list: Rugby public school. Nevil's first experience of formal education was not a happy one. His stammer made him stand out, and he became an easy target for unsympathetic fellow pupils and masters alike. Already low on confidence, he became even more self-conscious, later describing that period as becoming 'so intolerable that escape becomes the only possible course'. He managed this by realising that the stop after Hammersmith on his daily journey would take him to the wonders of the Science Museum in South Kensington. He spent ten happy days there, absorbed, trying to understand the operation of the machines that had driven the industrial revolution, and fascinated by technology that would change the world in the future. He was particularly captivated by aeroplanes such as the Bleriot XI that had crossed the English Channel less than a year before. When his parents were alerted that he was not attending school, rather than send their son back to suffer at Hammersmith, they took a more far-sighted and sympathetic approach and sent him to board with friends in Oxford so that he could attend Oxford Preparatory School.

Norway, then 11 years old, joined Oxford Preparatory School (now called the Dragon School) in April 1910. It was colloquially known as Lynam's, after the Lynam family who ran the school at that time. The progressive headmaster, C. C. (Skipper) Lynam, promoted what was perhaps an unusual attitude for the period: the belief that children should enjoy school. The school had an informal ethos built around individual responsibility rather than regimentation. When he first arrived in Oxford, Nevil stayed with the Sturt family, whose head Henry Sturt was an old friend of Arthur Norway, and like Norway, a prolific author. The Sturts had three children, one of whom, Oliver, attended the same school as Nevil. Although Nevil only boarded with the Sturts for a term or two, he left his mark on the household by accidentally kicking the ear off a carved wooden fox which formed part of the central pillar of the family's ornate dining table. This became part of family history, with subsequent Sturt children often being reminded to not be like Nevil and keep their feet still while seated at the table during supper. The more relaxed atmosphere at school and the fact that he was boarding with an easy-going family allowed Norway to flourish, build his self-confidence, and with encouragement from the family develop a range of water interests such as swimming, boating and fishing which would remain with him for the rest of his life. He also nurtured his interest in mechanics by watching the teachers at school maintain their motorcycles. Motorcycles were still in their infancy, temperamental, and needed constant attention to keep them going.

Some of the Norway family's holidays during these formative years were spent in Trebetherick, Cornwall. Henry Sturt rented Shilla Mill in nearby Polzeath for six weeks or so every summer from about 1900 until 1915, to enable him to write while his children enjoyed the freedom of the rural surroundings. The Sturt and Norway children often found themselves in each other's company during these carefree summers. It is during this period that Nevil Norway also first met the future Poet Laureate, Sir John Betjeman. Although Betjeman was seven years younger than Norway, they shared holiday lessons, probably given by Henry Sturt at Shilla Mill. They would not be in regular contact again until near the end of Nevil's life, when he played a part in arranging a visit for Betjeman to Australia.

Back at Oxford Preparatory School, Nevil did not find his feet academically straight away, in fact finishing bottom of his form at the end of his first term. In truth he was never much of a scholar in the traditional sense, only improving his ranking marginally during his three years at the school. Perhaps much more importantly though, the more relaxed environment in which he now found himself was beginning to have a positive effect on him, and as a result his confidence began to improve. He ultimately won several school prizes for his holiday diaries – perhaps the first signs of a budding author. Just before leaving in April 1913, the boy with a stammer was third servant in a school production of *The Taming of the Shrew*, another sign of his growing self-confidence. Norway continued to stay in contact with the school in later years, writing a number of articles for the school magazine *The Draconian*.

On 17 August 1912 it was announced that, as from 1 October, Arthur Norway was to replace Sir Reginald Egerton as secretary to the Post Office in Ireland. However, this appointment was not necessarily the enviable one it might have first seemed, for a number of reasons – both personal and political. By 1912, Arthur had been one of the six assistant secretaries in the Post Office for just over four years. Given his age, experience and career progression at that stage, it is probable that he would have eventually been a strong candidate for the position of second secretary in London. While the position title of secretary to the Post Office in Ireland sounded impressive, the appointment in Dublin was in many ways a step to the side, in that it was at the same pay and a slightly lower level in status. However, Arthur was concerned about the health of his wife, who had recently undergone a serious operation, and his son Fred who had had suffered several periods of ill health at Rugby. He believed that a change to a more rural lifestyle would be beneficial to both, and so putting his family before his career he applied for the position in Dublin.

From a political perspective, Dublin in 1912 was part of a bitter crisis. In April of that year, the British prime minister had finally introduced the Third Home Rule Bill, which would give limited self-government to Ireland. Although there was fierce opposition to it among some parties, with the House of Lords no longer having the power to permanently veto a bill, devolved government was expected to become a reality for Ireland sometime during 1914. A part of the Third Home Rule Bill proposed that the Post Office and postal services within Ireland would be the responsibility of the new Irish Executive with revenue going to the Irish parliament, and therefore it was reasonable to expect that the secretary to the General Post Office would in future be an Irish national. Arthur's appointment was therefore intended as an interim one for a period of two years, although in practice it eventually lasted just over four. Arthur Norway described himself as 'a liberal of the imperialist school'. He believed strongly in the British Empire, had a history of setting high standards, expecting absolute loyalty from his staff but in return being just and loyal to them. However, perhaps not surprisingly, at a time when home rule was such a sensitive political issue, the appointment of an English Protestant to such a position was not universally welcomed. For instance, the nationalist *Sinn Féin* weekly described Arthur Norway's appointment as 'an insult to every Irishman in the Post Office'. Members of Dublin County Council were also not impressed by the appointment, especially when told by the postmaster general in London that 'the gentleman (Mr.

Norway) had been appointed for two years, with the view of enabling him to learn the duties of administration'. However, in spite of the controversy surrounding his appointment, in many ways this was to be the peak of Arthur Norway's career.

Along with a move to Dublin, Arthur Norway also needed to find accommodation appropriate to his new position. He leased South Hill House, a large country property set in 13 acres of grounds south of Dublin. Of course, the house and the social occasions associated with Arthur's position needed both domestic staff and gardeners to keep things running, but as a major general's daughter, Mary Norway was well used to dealing with such situations. Although Nevil was still at school in Oxford and Fred was now at Trinity College, Dublin reading classics in preparation for a career in the Consular or Civil Service, when they could be there South Hill offered a whole new range of country pleasures which they took full advantage of. Reflecting on this idyllic period in later years, Nevil Norway wrote of his parents: 'for two years until the first war they led a very happy life at South Hill ... I am glad my parents had that happiness while it was still there to enjoy'.

In May 1913, Nevil started at Shrewsbury School. While his brother Fred, and before that his grandfather Frederick Gadsden, had attended another famous public school, Rugby, for whatever reason, it was decided that Nevil should go to Shrewsbury.

At that time Shrewsbury School was led by the Reverend Cyril Alington, a young, forward-thinking educationalist and prolific author who had revitalised the school by his inspirational leadership and by appointing a number of bright young masters. However, the school day still followed a conventional Victorian/Edwardian public school pattern. A boy's life was completely controlled from waking at 7.15 am until 'lights out' at 10.15 pm, with a solid mixture of study, physical activity and plenty of chapel. Norway joined Oldham's House, whose idiosyncratic housemaster, J. Basil Oldham, not only funded the building of Oldham's House but was at Shrewsbury for the rest of his working life. During his three years at Shrewsbury, Norway did not excel in any of the usual areas and was certainly not seen by his housemaster as a being a luminary of either the house or school. In spite of the fact that Norway had made little impression during his time at Shrewsbury, in the 1950s, when Oldham was suffering hard times, and Norway was a famous and wealthy novelist, he still remembered his old housemaster. Norway generously opened and funded a bank account for Oldham to be used for holidays and whisky – two pleasures that Oldham could no longer afford. He also made other considerable loans that he did not expect to be repaid, and he paid for the publication of a specialist book on English leather bookbindings of the fifteenth and sixteenth centuries, which Oldham had devoted his later years to. In a typically understated view of his own work at the time, Norway observed that he thought it 'only fit that entertainment books should be bought in to assist more serious scholarship'.

After a somewhat hesitant start, Norway's time at Shrewsbury can best be described as sound but unspectacular. He ran, swam and rowed for his house, and won a number of minor prizes for academic achievement. His school record shows that he was good at physics and chemistry, but less good at mathematics (surprisingly for a future engineer), and very good at English (good for a future novelist!).

Though he was in the science rather than classics stream, Norway almost certainly cultivated his lifelong love of poetry at Shrewsbury. It was an age in which poetry was more mainstream reading than it is today. Many of the younger masters wrote poetry and boys were encouraged to follow suit. A few years later in 1916, a collection of poetry written by boys in the Fifth Form was published as a gift and tribute to their inspirational English teacher, Evelyn Southwell, who had enlisted to fight in France. He was subsequently killed at the Battle of the Somme. Although Norway was writing poetry by that stage, he himself later admitted that 'all of it was very bad', and none of his poems made it into the Fifth Form's book *VB Shrewsbury*.

At the deadline of midnight Central European Time on 4 August 1914, Britain had not received a response to their demand that Kaiser Wilhelm II respect Belgium's neutrality and withdraw his troops from the country. As a consequence, war was declared on Germany. The 'war to end all wars' had begun, and like millions of other families across the British Empire, the Norways would be permanently scarred by the conflict.

In spite of misgivings by some in Prime Minister Asquith's Cabinet, the decision to go to war was widely supported across the country, fuelled by the intense nationalism of the period. As *The Times* reported the following day, a large crowd had gathered outside the prime minister's office in Downing Street to follow events as the deadline with Germany approached. When 'news of the war reached the street, the crowd expressed its feeling in loud cheering'.

On the first day of the war, a serving military man, certainly the most famous in Britain at that time, Field Marshall Horatio Kitchener, Earl Kitchener of Khartoum and Broome, was appointed Secretary of State for War. At that time the British Army consisted of just under a quarter of a million men, about a half of which were already overseas supporting the Empire. Kitchener immediately despatched a British Expeditionary Force of about 100,000 men to France, but he realised that the army would be woefully understrength for the war ahead. Although the optimism on the streets suggested that it would all be over by Christmas, Kitchener believed (as it turned out rightly) that the war could go on for years and need millions of men. On 6 August, Parliament approved an increase of 500,000 in the army, which was also later shown to be a serious underestimate. On 11 August, Kitchener issued a call to arms for men to enlist for three years or the duration of the war. The response was overwhelming, with over one million men enlisting by the end of 1914 and 33,000 joining up during a single day in September alone. One man enlisting in Liverpool described seeing a queue over two miles long. There was a genuine feeling that this would be a quick war, and people did not to want to miss playing their part. A future prime minister, Harold MacMillan, who was then an undergraduate at Balliol College, Oxford, expressed the views of most when he wrote: 'The general view was that it would all be over by Christmas. Our major anxiety was by hook or by crook not to miss it'. Few could foresee the time the conflict would last or the horror that 'it' would become.

On the other side of the Irish Sea, on the first day of the war, Arthur and Mary Norway were at their home in Dublin. The position of Ireland was of course more complex than on the mainland. The *Irish Times* hopefully declared 'a few weeks ago it used to be said by English politicians that Ireland was two armed camps. Today it is a one armed camp, and its menace is directed against a foreign foe'. On 18 September, the Government of Ireland Act 1914 was finally approved. However, at the same time a Suspensory Act also became law, putting the issue of home rule for Ireland on hold for the duration of the war as far as the British government was concerned. However, the home rule problem was not that easily put to one side, and it would come back to confront the Norways before the war was over.

Like many others that day, Frederick, who was living with his parents in Dublin, probably saw the prominent banner in *The Times* calling for 'all young unmarried men to rally round the Flag and enlist'. The *Daily Express* was more blunt, demanding 'What are you going to do for your country? Stand by as a carping critic or do your duty?'. The age for enlistment at the start of the war was 18 to 30, so Arthur was too old and Nevil, who was still at Shrewsbury School, too young. However, at just under 19, Frederick was old enough and, like so many others, keen to do his duty. He had suspended his studies at Trinity College, Dublin having just completed two years of a Bachelor of Arts in Classics, no doubt intending to complete his degree once the war was over.

His initial application for a short service commission in the army was unsuccessful; he failed the medical. While he was recovering from an operation to correct this problem, his father decided that rather than enlisting through the short service route, he should apply for a regular commission. He would then at least have the option of a permanent career in the military when the war was over. Fred duly entered the Royal Military College, Sandhurst in October 1914. He completed the all too brief training on 17 March 1915, and by 29 April he was at the Western Front as a junior officer in the 2nd Battalion of the Duke of Cornwall's Light Infantry. Junior officers had probably one of the most unenviable roles in trench warfare, in that they were expected to lead their men 'over the top' from the front – often with just a revolver as a weapon.

Tragically, Second Lieutenant Fred Norway did not last long. Early on 13 June, in a trench near Armentieres, a German mine exploded, killing or wounding twenty-four of his platoon. Unhurt, but under heavy fire, Fred led men over the parapet to help comrades that had been buried by the blast. This time, he was badly wounded by a high-explosive shell. He was moved from the front line to No. 7 Stationary Hospital at Boulogne. On 15 June, Arthur Norway received a telegram from the War Office to say that his son was suffering from gunshot wounds, was dangerously ill and may be visited. Arthur replied immediately to say that Fred's mother would be on the overnight crossing to Boulogne. On 21 June he was moved to No. 14 Stationary Hospital, Wimereux suffering from the additional complication of scarlet fever. No. 14 Stationary Hospital was an isolation hospital for the Boulogne area, for men with infectious diseases. His mother was at his bedside when Second Lieutenant Frederick Hamilton Norway died of his wounds on 4 July 1915, aged 19. On 6 July, Arthur Norway received a telegram from the War Office confirming that his son was dead and noting that 'Lord Kitchener expresses his sympathy'. Obituaries appeared in both *The Times* and *The Weekly Irish Times*. His career in the army had lasted less than four months. A captain in his regiment said of Fred: 'He has proved himself one of the pluckiest youngsters and best workers I have ever come across ... He well deserves to be mentioned in Despatches'. Further up the chain of command, his colonel wrote: 'I have noted the good work done by your son and, when we are next asked to send in names, I shall forward his'. Even if this was ever done, Fred was never mentioned in Despatches.

He was buried in grave number 591, alongside thousands of others (including the Canadian physician and war poet John McCrae, author of the poignant 'In Flanders Fields' which helped enshrine the poppy as a symbol of sacrifice) in a cemetery at Wimereux, north of Boulogne. His death hit the family badly, and it is doubtful whether Arthur Norway, in particular, ever fully recovered from this. On the army medal index card for Frederick Norway there is a handwritten note that, in August 1921, A. H. Norway had applied for his late son's medals. Like millions of families across the country, the ubiquitous 1914–15 Star, British War Medal and Victory Medal were all there was ultimately to show.

Although still at school, life also changed for 15-year-old Nevil the day war broke out. Initially, the changes in everyday life may have seemed small, with some of the younger masters leaving the school to enlist and some boys who had recently left returning to show off their new uniforms. The school day carried on as normal, with chapel following 'First Lesson' in the morning. However, now the names of Old Salopians (as ex-pupils of Shrewsbury School were known) killed in action were read out by the headmaster Cyril Alington as part of the daily service. As 1914 moved into 1915, and it became clear the war was not going to be over quickly, the initial optimistic mood in the school (as in the country as a whole) changed. The numbers of those killed rose rapidly in 1915, with names read out being very familiar to the gathered assembly since they now included boys who had left the school only the year before – like Nevil's brother Fred, some were only 19 when they died. In 1915 alone, seventy-three Old Salopians were killed in action.

Like many public schools, Shrewsbury had an Officer Training Corp to which Nevil belonged. Junior Officer Training Corps were first formed in public schools in 1908 in order to help reinforce the ethos of duty to the country that public schools promoted and to provide a ready source of junior officer material should war break out. Weekly drills and exercises emphasised the importance of hierarchy and command in a well-ordered society in which they would soon be expected to play their part. While not all of the boys in the OTC would ultimately follow a military career, many of the characteristics being promoted would prove to be just as important to those aspiring to careers in the Civil Service or Colonial Service. However, after August 1914 all that changed. OTCs now took on a new reality, as boys minds no longer focused on life at university or a career after leaving Shrewsbury, but on when their time would come to enlist and whether their name would one day join the role of honour being read out daily at chapel. In accordance with their upbringing and public school indoctrination, duty prevailed, and enlistment became the norm for most. Such was the rush to join the army following Kitchener's call, in October 1914 most boys joined up rather than go to university. Of the fourteen prefects that year, twelve enlisted, with seven subsequently being killed. One of these, F. S. Nalder had been head of Oldham's Hall when Norway was a new boy. His brief school biography states: 'about to go up to Christ Church Oxford, when hostilities broke out, he joined the Kings Shropshire Light Infantry'. He was eventually promoted to captain but died on the Western Front in September 1918.

Meanwhile in Dublin, in the autumn of 1915, Arthur and Mary Norway moved from their country residence at Blackrock to the Royal Hibernian Hotel in the centre of Dublin. Although described in *The London Journal* as 'the most fashionable first class hotel in Dublin' this meant little to the Norways at that time. After the death of their eldest son, living at South Hill caused too many painful memories, and so they preferred to stay in the centre of the city until Arthur's temporary posting in Dublin was over.

Although there had been some significant opposition to Arthur Norway's appointment, once in the post he had overseen many improvements in the headquarters of the General Post Office, gained the trust and confidence of large numbers of his staff and it was later acknowledged that he had 'behaved in Dublin most impartially'.

During Christmas of 1915, Arthur took his wife and Nevil for a holiday to Rome and Naples. The very contained nature of the war at that stage somewhat surreally allowed life to go on as normal for many away from the front line. Arthur had a keen interest in Italy, having written a book *Naples Past and Present,* and perhaps the trip was intended to try and help the family take their minds off the common tragedy they had suffered that year. In order that he could be back in time for the start of school, Nevil had to travel back from Naples alone – another maturing experience.

Nevil next arrived in Dublin to stay with his parents over April 1916, and he ended up being caught up in one of the most important events in English–Irish history, the Easter Rising. The British government had believed that the issue of home rule had been reduced in importance in the minds of most Irish people once the First World War had started. For many this may have been true, since over 75,000 Irishmen had enlisted to fight on the Western Front in the first year of the war alone. However, a group of Irish nationalists led by the Irish Republican Brotherhood saw the diversion of the war as an opportunity to reach their political goal by use of force. The planning of the uprising can best be described as chaotic, with an expected arms shipment from Germany failing to reach them and the participation of the Irish Volunteers being confusingly cancelled at the last moment. Despite this, on 24 April 1916 – Easter Monday – a group of about 1,500 rebels occupied a number of key buildings in the city, with the General Post Office becoming their headquarters. Outside their headquarters, one of the rebel leaders, Patrick Pearce, read out a proclamation declaring the formation of an Irish Republic. At the time the rebels took over the General Post Office, Arthur Norway was in Dublin Castle, the centre of British administration, where he had been summoned to discuss rising tensions in the country with the Under-Secretary for Ireland, Sir Matthew Nathan and the army head of intelligence, Major Ivon Price. In light of intelligence reports about impending troubles, they were considering restricting telephone and telegraph services across much of southern Ireland. Nevil and his mother were on their way to meet Arthur for lunch, but realising what was happening, Nevil sent his mother back to the safety of their hotel. However, Arthur Norway and his colleagues were trapped inside the castle and spent a tense afternoon and evening there until a battalion of soldiers arrived from the Curragh in the late evening to rescue them. The British were initially caught badly off guard, heavily outnumbered, and bitter fighting developed in many parts of the city. The conflict worsened, and the number of casualties inevitably increased. At one point while out and about in the streets, Nevil risked his life by leading the lifting of a badly injured man over a rebel barricade so that he could be taken to hospital. Later in the week, Nevil joined a more formal ambulance service organised by the Royal Irish Automobile Club and spent much of that week as a volunteer stretcher bearer. For this service, he was later awarded a Certificate of Honour by the Chapter of the Order of the Hospital of St John of Jerusalem.

By Wednesday, significant British Army reinforcements and artillery had arrived from the mainland. The rebels were now heavily outnumbered and outgunned, and in the fighting that followed many buildings including the General Post Office were set on fire. By Sunday 30 April, seven days after the uprising had started, the rebels had surrendered and the insurrection was over. The General Post Office, which had been the rebels' headquarters, had been reduced to a ruin. The Norways particularly felt the loss of the treasured personal possessions of their son Fred, such as his books and sword. These had been stored in the safe in Arthur's office for protection and Mary Norway later emotionally wrote of the loss of these 'which we value more than anything else in the world'. During those seven days, over 450 people had been killed and nearly 2,600 wounded, many of them civilians caught up in the fighting. The British government reacted brutally to the attempted rebellion, taking just twelve days to try, sentence and execute fifteen of the rebel leaders. This blunt retaliation ensured that the issue of home rule would not be forgotten by the local population, and on a personal front, by the end of the year Arthur Norway had been replaced as secretary to the General Post Office by an Irish Catholic. In a function to mark his departure from Dublin, Arthur Norway's successor James MacMahon spoke of 'the impression which Mr. Norway had made on the Irish staff by his sincere and earnest devotion to their interests in the discharge of his responsible duty as chief of the most important department of State administration in Ireland'. Though his appointment had been controversial, it seems that in the end Arthur Norway had won many of his doubters over by his compassion and fair-mindedness.

While he was too young to fight in the war, during his time in Dublin that Easter Nevil Norway had witnessed killings, summary executions, snipers and many other atrocities. Describing this experience years later he wrote that 'I was far more comfortable and at home than my parents ... I was mentally conditioned for war; it was what I had been bred and trained for two years'. In May 1916, the Shrewsbury School magazine *The Salopian* published an article *'Easter Week in Dublin'*. Anonymous, and originally thought to be Nevil Norway's first piece of published writing, research has since shown that this was in fact written by another Shrewsbury boy, John Lowe Woods, who was also present in Dublin at the time. Mary Norway later wrote a short eyewitness account of the Easter Rising which was subsequently published (and which is still in print today). Ten years after he had retired, Arthur Norway also recorded his experiences of this dramatic period in his family's life. In the spirit of the service to which he had devoted his life, he did not intend the memorandum for publication but 'for the information of my family, and especially of any coming after me who may care to ask themselves what I did in difficult circumstances'.

Nevil Norway left Shrewsbury School quietly at the end of December 1916. Typical of his modest nature, his entry in the school's record simply reads 'N.S. Norway, VI. 1. Army Class; Cert. A.'. While Norway did not leave much of a mark on Shrewsbury during his time there, the school and some of its staff left a long-lasting impression on him. For instance, he used the hymn 'The Lord of Hosts Our King Shall Be', which was written by Alington, and would have been frequently sung at many chapel services, as an epigraph in his novel *In the Wet*; the housemaster Mr Scarlett of Shrewsbury School in his novel *Most Secret* is an affectionate portrait of Basil Oldham (interestingly he did not try to disguise the name of the school); and when he died forty-three years after leaving Shrewsbury, the school was a major beneficiary in his will.

Norway was almost 18 when he left Shrewsbury School and would soon be eligible for conscription. Nationally, the war had not been going well for some time, and the initial optimism for a quick win was long gone. Even though by December 1915 a staggering two and a half million men had joined the army since the day war had broken out, this was still not enough to meet the army's unimagined, insatiable demands. By the end of 1915, the total number of British causalities being officially reported by the government was 528,227 dead, wounded or missing. In a response to the perhaps not unexpected decline in voluntary enlistments, in January 1916 the government had finally introduced conscription for all single men between the ages of 18 to 41 (unless they were engaged in a reserve occupation, disabled, a widower with children, a minister of religion or a conscientious objector). By the end of the war the Military Service Act had been amended a further four times in order to dramatically widen the criteria of those eligible for conscription. In the end nearly anyone was eligible!

The period between leaving Shrewsbury School in December 1916 and finally joining the army in August 1918 was one of great frustration and torment to Norway; however, through no fault of his own the delay in joining up may have ultimately saved his life. Given his son's aptitude for science and interest in aviation and engineering, his father decided that Nevil should try for a regular commission in the Royal Engineers or Artillery, either of which required gaining entry to the Royal Military Academy, Woolwich (perhaps also recognising that with the training for a regular commission taking longer than a short service commission, his remaining son's chances of surviving the war would increase).

At the beginning of January 1917, Arthur and Mary Norway had returned to London. Arthur's temporary appointment in Dublin, although lasting over four years instead of the original two, had ended. Nevil was therefore able to live with his parents in London while he studied for the Woolwich entrance examinations. He successfully entered the Royal Military Academy in the summer of 1917, training as a gunner in the Royal Flying Corps. However, fate intervened again, and in April 1918, just as he was due to graduate, the aviation segments of the army and navy were merged to form a new independent service, the Royal Air Force. At that stage he was stammering badly, probably as a result of stress and overwork, and he failed the final medical at Woolwich. He reluctantly underwent further treatment for his stammer in order to try and get a commission in the new Royal Air Force, but as with previous efforts this proved unsuccessful.

On 1 January 1918, it was announced in the New Year's Honours List that, in recognition of his services during the war at the General Post Office, Arthur Hamilton Norway had been appointed a Companion of the Most Honourable Order of the Bath. The investiture by King George V on the morning of 9 February must have bought a short interlude of happiness and pride in what was a stressful period for the family.

By the middle of 1918, his parents finally accepted that despite everybody's best efforts it was unlikely that Nevil would ever get a commission in the Royal Air Force, and so in August, he joined the army. By the time Nevil enlisted, the old colonial military strategies based on men, horses and field guns were being forced to change – some may have said not before time. New technologies such as tanks (originally called landships) and aircraft were starting to play an increasingly significant role. As a consequence, ordinary civilians like Nevil's parents were now at risk. For instance, in mid-1917 the Germans had used Gotha aeroplanes to first bomb coastal towns and then London. On 13 June 1917, 162 people had been killed and 400 wounded in daylight bombing raids over the capital. The war was no longer limited to a foreign field.

Private Nevil Norway became a soldier in the First Reserve Garrison Battalion of the Suffolk Regiment. Although he had an interest in all things mechanical, his first posting was far more traditional. He was sent to the Isle of Grain in Kent, where he became part of a small force ready to repel any German invasion – no matter how unlikely that may have seemed. Like his much loved brother Fred, he was 19 when he joined the army, but unlike his brother he spent the remainder of the war in England – and survived.

While for most people in Great Britain the First World War ended on 11 November 1918, the loss of loved ones did not stop. The list of war casualties, printed by *The Times* newspaper each day since the start of the war, now included those killed by a new enemy – the Spanish flu. A relatively benign influenza pandemic, which had originally begun in the spring of 1918, had now mutated into a highly virulent strain which by the autumn was killing millions across the world. Healthy adults between the ages of 20 and 40 were particularly at risk, and so men being demobilised and returning from the Western Front were a prime target. Such was the high mortality rate, that for the last months of 1918, Private Norway was drafted into a permanent army funeral party on duty in Kent. In this grim and surreal world, he now had to consider the future and what he later described as 'a new, unknown and glamorous world opening before me'.

As for so many of his generation, the world had suddenly changed, from one in which death and destruction had dominated for the last four years, to one in which he now had to look forward and think about a future.

2

University
January 1919–December 1922

The 19-year-old Nevil Norway now contemplating his future was a very different person to the rather self-conscious 14-year-old who had started at Shrewsbury School. The Great War had been responsible for irreplaceable losses in so many families, but it had also often changed the personalities of those that had survived. In Nevil's case, while his spell in the army had been short, life as a private had noticeably improved his morale and self-confidence. He still stammered, but he was now beginning to accept that there was little he could do about it and that it was something that he would have to learn to live with.

Arthur and Mary Norway, on the other hand, had been numbed by the loss of their beloved son Fred. Nevil could never hope to fill Fred's shoes as the classical scholar that his parents had so badly wanted to follow in Arthurs's footsteps. He was now also the last of the male Norways. His father's only brother, now dead, had left three children but all were daughters.

As far as the immediate future was concerned, Nevil was still fascinated with the aeroplane and anything connected with it. He was happy enough to go along with his father's wishes and try to gain entry to university, but it had to be to study engineering and not classics.

It was still not the norm for someone, even from a public school, to go to university. If you did decide to go, it was usually a straight choice between Oxford and Cambridge; they were at the top of what was unashamedly an elitist structure. Few from public schools went anywhere else. For instance, while only 30 per cent of the eighty-nine boys who left Shrewsbury School in 1920 went to university, 85 per cent of those that did went to Oxford or Cambridge.

Relative to most other universities, Oxford and Cambridge were late in recognising engineering as a discipline for study in its own right. Cambridge had first offered an undergraduate degree in mechanical sciences in 1894, while Oxford did not establish the Honour School of Engineering Science until 1909. In line with the philosophy of its founding professor, Charles Frewen Jenkin, the Engineering Science degree covered a very broad range of topics: from structural design to gas engines and turbines. This was clearly not a course ideally suited to developing Nevil Norway's passion for all things aeronautical, but it seemed to be the best option available. Therefore, in late 1918 his father and Nevil agreed that he should apply for entrance to Oxford.

Having decided on Oxford and engineering, they then had to find a college that would admit Nevil. The post-war bulge would soon start to take effect with many looking for entry to university, so even with a public school education, this was not necessarily a formality.

Nevil and his father finally settled on Balliol College. By 1918 there had been twenty-four successful graduates in engineering science, fairly evenly spread over sixteen of the Oxford colleges. It is not clear why Balliol was chosen, maybe simply because it was the oldest. Whatever the reason, Arthur Norway wrote to the master of Balliol College, Arthur L. Smith, on 23 October 1918, asking if he would consider his son for entry. A few days later, Smith replied saying that this would depend on an interview and letters of recommendation from the headmaster and his housemaster at Shrewsbury School. While the references from Cyril Alington (who had now succeeded his brother-in-law as headmaster of Eton College) and Basil Oldham were supportive, though in Alington's case somewhat vague, they both mentioned what Oldham called 'his fearful stammer'. However, following a successful interview with the master, of which Norway later wrote he remembered nothing, he was offered a place and exempted from entrance examinations on the basis of his military service.

Nevil Norway therefore began his life as an undergraduate student at Oxford in February 1919.

The Department of Engineering Science was just beginning to become active again after the war, with staff gradually returning from military service. The head of department himself only resumed his appointment on 1 April 1919. Even though Norway started at the beginning of Hilary term, laboratory facilities were not up and running again until the beginning of the following term. He therefore had a less hectic start to university life than was usual.

In later life he considered his subsequent performance as an undergraduate as 'ordinary' and 'humdrum', having 'excelled at nothing'. Certainly the record shows that he did not leave his mark as a scholar on Balliol, even though he is now prominently listed on their website as a notable alumni. In reality, it is what he did outside of his formal studies and the people he met that really moulded his future life.

First there was sailing. Oliver Sturt, a friend from his Oxford Preparatory School days, was admitted to Queen's College (where his father had also studied) a few months after Norway in October 1919, also to study engineering. Before this, in the summer of 1919, they got a job as two of a three-man crew on *Aerolia,* a 28-ton yacht. An eventful cruise from her base in Southampton to the Scilly Isles and back not only taught Norway a great deal about seamanship, but it also instilled a passion for the sea and sailing which was to stay with him for the rest of his life and play a part in so many of his novels.

Then, perhaps more importantly, there was aviation. By the end of his second year at university in 1920, Norway began to think about his future career. Rather than spend the summer break sailing or travelling, he decided to try and gain experience in what was still a fledging aeronautical industry. He obtained a letter of introduction to the Aircraft Manufacturing Company (Airco) at Hyde, Hendon, from Professor Jenkin, who, as chairman of the Materials Committee of the Aeronautical Research Council, had many good connections in the aircraft industry. Airco was typical of the roller-coaster nature of the industry at that time. Formed in 1912 by the newspaper owner George Holt Thomas, the Company had prospered during the war, but now, like many other manufacturers, was experiencing a significant downturn following the cutback in military orders that had occurred since The Armistice. One of its greatest assets was the chief designer Geoffrey de Havilland, someone who would become an iconic name in the aviation industry for decades.

Following an interview at Airco with Charles Walker, Norway was taken on both as an unpaid assistant in the design office and to help with wind tunnel research. He saw and learnt a great deal about the reality of aeronautical engineering during the summer of 1920, as aircraft were conceived, designed, manufactured and tested in the same location. During this period he also first met another Airco employee, Alfred Hessell Tiltman, with whom he was to form Airspeed ten years later. He did not go back to Airco for the 1920 Christmas break, instead holidaying in the Italian Riviera with his parents, whose life had also been changing.

On 5 August 1920, at age 60, Arthur Norway retired as an assistant secretary of the General Post Office. His increasing deafness had no doubt influenced his decision to retire at the earliest opportunity. He had given over forty years of service, during which time he had 'discharged his duties with diligence and fidelity'. He was awarded an annual pension of £780, which was 50 per cent of his salary at that time, and a one-off payment of £2,381 12s. The average salary for a professional was then around £300 per annum, and so while Arthur Norway and his wife could look forward to a reasonably comfortable retirement, like many in their situation they would soon not be able to maintain the size of household they had been used to. The following year, the Post Office magazine *St Martin's Le Grand* contained a warm appreciation of Arthur Norway, the man and his career, and, probably what would have been most pleasing to him, his books. At an intimate farewell dinner organised by his colleagues, it was noted that 'formalities of all kinds, speeches and stereotyped valedictions included, were happily absent'. A cold appraisal of Arthur Norway's career might show that while he had achieved a great deal, often in difficult circumstances, he did not reach the very top positions of second secretary or secretary. However, he seems to have gained the great respect of his colleagues and, in keeping with his character, left the Service quietly and without fanfare.

Although he may not have realised it at the time, during his summer vacation in 1920, Norway had been working for a company that was about to fold. In common with many aircraft companies after the war, Airco had been finding it difficult to find new markets for its products. Therefore, by the beginning of May, Holt Thomas had sold Airco to the Birmingham Small Arms Company Ltd. They too soon realised that the business was not viable and placed it in the hands of a liquidator.

As a result, during the Easter vacation of 1921, Norway found himself working still unpaid, not with Airco but with the de Havilland Aircraft Company. Formed by Geoffrey de Havilland, with Holt Thomas now as a major initial investor, the new company was located at the premises previously owned by the London and Provincial Flying School, at Stag Lane Aerodrome, Edgeware. Such changes were very typical of the aeronautical industry after the war, with companies merging, being liquidated and reformed as something new, or just going out of business altogether. Many of Airco's previous employees had been transferred to de Havilland, with Tiltman now an assistant designer. During this period de Havilland also employed a pilot who was to play an important role in Norway's future career, Alan Cobham.

Norway continued his unofficial apprenticeship in aeronautical engineering again during the summer of 1921, taking on more responsible tasks and developing his skills in stress and performance calculations. As he later acknowledged, because of the small size of the company, it was an unparalleled chance to gain an insight into all sides of the business. By doing the 'hackwork' for two of the industry's best designers at that time and being a party to discussions on design, his work experience provided a golden opportunity that he took full advantage of.

Summer 1921 was also memorable for Norway in that he had his first experience of flying. It was common practice at de Havilland for the design office staff to be passengers on test flights. He marked his first flight in a D.H.9 biplane with poetry, which he still considered bad, but thirty years later he included it in his autobiography *Slide Rule*. This untitled poem is the only example of Nevil Shute's poetry that has ever appeared in print.

This wood, this metal to the touch
Stays solid, even though so much
Is changed, fantastic ...

Only this liquid element
That beats and clutches. One would float
Placidly, like a bottle dropped
From some swift-flying motor boat.

Only the sun, the sky, the air
   And mossy pincushions of trees
Upon the hazy picture there.
   Only the solid wings, and these.

(Nevil Shute, *Slide Rule*, 1954)

In comparison to the cutting-edge nature of work at de Havilland, life back at Oxford felt very different. Given his intense passion for, and now involvement in, aeronautics, he found it difficult to remain enthusiastic about some of the broader aspects of his formal studies such as the design of concrete structures or heat engines. However, he persevered, and in the summer of 1922 took his final examinations. Since he had been exempt from entrance examinations, his first experience of formal assessment at Oxford was also his last. He was one of twenty-seven finalists that summer, twenty-two of whom graduated. He was awarded a third class honours degree, which is equivalent to a 2:2 nowadays, as Oxford awarded fourth class honours degrees until 1967. Among those who also graduated in engineering science that year was his school friend Oliver Sturt, who was awarded a second class degree. Norway left Oxford 'with a deep affection for Balliol', perhaps more because of the experience and opportunities he had gained in aeronautics, and the many long-lasting friendships he had made, rather than the course itself. Reflecting this affection, Balliol College, like Shrewsbury School, was to become a major beneficiary in his will.

As far as his personal life was concerned, Norway had his first serious romance while at Oxford. Enid Fenton, whom he had first met during the war, was now at Lady Margaret Hall studying history. Like Nevil, she was from a family who considered education important. Her father, the Honourable William Fenton, was a high-ranking government official, ultimately becoming Financial Commissioner in the Punjab. Prior to going up to Oxford, she had been educated at Queen's College, Harley Street. By September 1919 they were engaged to be married, although Nevil later conceded that she was far more reluctant than him to commit to the relationship, and that he had essentially argued her into it. After a turbulent two and a half years, in spite of Nevil's best efforts to keep things going, the inevitable happened and she broke off the engagement. She graduated from Oxford with a first class degree, and after a spell as an organising secretary for the Women's Liberal Association in the Midlands, she married a lieutenant colonel in the British Army. Nevil never saw Enid again after she left Oxford, but the experience of personal rejection left a bitter mark on him.

On leaving Oxford, he had expected to start work straight away at de Havilland. Unfortunately, cash flow difficulties in the fledgling company meant that this had to be put on hold until the beginning of 1923. He therefore joined his parents, who were again holidaying in the Italian Riviera. Nevil spent the final months of the year exploring the country, learning a little Italian and, perhaps most important of all, beginning to write. During this period he wrote a short story 'Piuro'. This was never published, and once he became a published author, it was a form he rarely returned to.

As 1922 drew to a close, despite the personal setback of a failed engagement, Nevil Norway's prospects were looking promising. He had completed his formal education at a prestigious public school and university and secured a start in an industry he was passionate about. In spite of his father's example of what could be achieved in the Civil Service, Nevil had never really seriously looked further than the aviation industry for his future. A life as a full-time novelist must have certainly been one of the furthest things from his mind.

3

Aeroplanes
January 1923–October 1924

Having worked for them unpaid as a student, Nevil Norway joined the de Havilland Aircraft Company as a full-time employee in January 1923. He was employed as a stress and performance calculator on a salary of £5 a week, which was about normal for a recent science or engineering graduate at that time. He was joining an industry which, having endured many difficulties after the war, was now trying to look to the future. This in many ways mirrored the attitude in the country as a whole.

For many, 1923 was a time of hope rather than optimism. George V was now King of the United Kingdom, the British Dominions and Emperor of India, but his Empire was beginning to shows some signs of fracture. On 23 December 1920, nearly four years after Arthur Norway had left Dublin, the Government of Ireland Act had finally been passed, proposing the partition of Ireland into two autonomous regions, Southern Ireland and Northern Ireland. However, home rule could not be immediately established in Southern Ireland because of the ongoing Irish War of Independence. Finally, on 6 December 1921, the Anglo-Irish Treaty was signed, resulting in the establishment of the Irish Free State as a Dominion within the British Empire. Almost at once, Northern Ireland exercised its right under the Treaty to keep its status as part of the United Kingdom. Similar struggles for independence were also now starting in other parts of the Empire such as India, but this particular conflict was to last another twenty-five years.

Domestically there had been a major change to the suffrage system. Pre-war, those entitled to vote in a general election in Britain had been broadly limited to men meeting criteria of wealth or status. This meant that 30 per cent of men and 100 per cent of women in Britain were still not entitled to vote. Following the war such a policy could no longer be justified, the general view being that if you were good enough to fight and die for your country, then you should be entitled to vote. The Representation of the People Act, which had become law in February 1918, extended the right to vote to all men over 21, and women over 30 who were householders, married to a householder or a university graduate. Voting systems was a topic that Nevil Norway would have strong views on in later life.

On the home front, whether you approached 1923 with optimism depended to some extent on your social class and area of employment. On 1 January 1923, *The Times* reflected the optimistic view by noting 'rarely can business men have begun a New Year with greater hope of better things to come'. While on the other side of the fence, the *Daily Mirror* was more pessimistic, calling for the new government 'to retrieve the errors of their predecessors' and pronouncing 1923 the 'Year of Convalescence'.

One indication that life was beginning to return to normal was the disintegration of the coalition government. A general election in November 1922 had returned a majority Conservative government, with the Labour Party overtaking the Liberals to become Britain's second biggest political party. This was the first time Britain had had a single-party government since 1915, and it would have a lot to deal with.

The economy was in a fragile state. While unemployment had begun to fall from its post-war peak of 11.2 per cent in 1921, it was ultimately to remain high for the whole of the interwar period. Prices had begun to steadily fall, as did wages in many of the older manufacturing sectors. Key pre-war industries such as coal, textiles, heavy engineering and ship building shed jobs continuously as a result of structural changes in the economy and as they tried to match the efficiency of new competitors such as the USA. If you were middle class and had a job you could reasonably look forward to real gains in wealth because of a steady income and falling prices. If you were working class, you could probably look forward to losing your job or taking a drop in wages.

Nevil Norway was starting his career at a time of uncertainty and change, but in contrast to many others, he was entering a forward-looking industry full of entrepreneurial spirit, optimism and, of course, risk.

On 17 December 1903, Orville Wright is credited with having made the first manned controlled powered flight of a heavier-than-air craft when he piloted the Wright Flyer No. 1 a distance of 120 feet in 12 seconds. Orville and his brother Wilbur made a further three flights that day, finally achieving a distance of 852 feet in 59 seconds. Now, just twenty years since those rather hesitant first steps, powered flight had advanced beyond recognition. The First World War had perhaps been the single biggest factor for the tremendous advances made in aviation during that period, by supporting a huge expansion of the aircraft industry. By 1918 the British aircraft industry employed 268,000 people, who were producing 2,688 aircraft a month. Many new companies whose names would become legendary in the industry, such as Handley Page, Sopwith, Roe and Rolls Royce, had become established. Pre-war armourers such as Armstrong-Whitworth and Vickers had also seen the opportunities on offer and developed into prolific aircraft manufacturers.

Following the dramatic decline in orders for military aircraft at the end of the war, not surprisingly, many manufacturers went out of business. Mergers and takeovers were common. Although now smaller, military orders still represented a major part of the reduced market, and it has been argued that it was the Air Ministry who had saved the British aircraft industry from extinction after the war.

In this new era of peace, manufacturers were forced to look elsewhere for growth, with passenger transport, airmail services and cargo services being the main targets. Understandably, many people still only associated aircraft with military use and were yet to come to terms with what the real commercial possibilities might be. As a result, manufacturers who had been raised on designing for military applications were at first reluctant to produce aircraft designed specifically for new tasks such as passenger transport until they knew a market was there. In most cases, fledging airlines, such as the Instone Air Line, had to make do with aircraft originally intended for military applications. In trying to establish air services over European routes such as London to Paris and London to Brussels, these airlines were not only using aircraft which were not ideal, but also competing with existing train and boat services, and were at the mercy of the weather. Given all of these problems, it was not surprising that the government had to subsidise many of these new routes in order that they could remain in business.

Eventually, though, the manufacturers did start to focus on civilian applications. A good example of the capability of a new aircraft in 1923 was the Bristol Type 75, a single-engine biplane which had been designed specifically for passenger transport and had made its maiden flight in June 1922. This aircraft had a cruising speed of 110 mph, an endurance of 5 hours 30 minutes and could carry 2 crew and 8 passengers. Yet despite the many advances that had been made in aircraft design over the previous years, it was still not possible to see how such machines could be used to provide the increasingly needed transport services to the more distant parts of the Empire such as India and Australia. There was, however, an alternative which had already demonstrated the capability to cover large distances – the airship.

As early as 1909, the German company Deutsche Luftschiffahrts-Aktiengesellschaft (or DELAG) had been using rigid airships for commercial purposes. By 1919 they were running scheduled passenger services between Berlin and Friedrichshafen in southern Germany. The company was forced to cease operating in 1920, when its two airships were transferred to the Allies as part of the Versailles Treaty on war reparations. Other countries such as America and Spain were also taking airship development seriously. America had a large airship based on a Zeppelin design under construction, while Spain was considering the viability of an intercontinental airship passenger service between Europe and South America. The proposed service would allow 40 passengers to travel the 6,008 miles from Seville to Buenos Aires non-stop in 3 days 16 hours, and in what the promoters called the comfort of an Atlantic liner.

While the British government had supported the development of airships during the war, in peacetime, financial restrictions meant that they were unwilling to show the same enthusiasm. It would not be until 1924 that commercial airship development in Britain was restarted. The battle between the aeroplane and the airship had not yet reached a conclusion, and although he did not know it at the time, Nevil Norway was to play a part in both.

His first employer, the de Havilland Aircraft Company, had been registered on 25 September 1920, and two weeks later they moved into premises at Stag Lane Aerodrome. The new premises were far from luxurious, consisting of four poorly heated and poorly lit wooden huts. Two of these were used for aircraft overhaul and manufacture, one as a drawing office and one as the general office. In winter the huts became so cold that the chief designer, Geoffrey de Havilland, would insist on short sessions of exercise outdoors to keep people warm.

In the first days of the Company, the objective was purely financial survival. There was some work that had been inherited from Airco and the repair and reconditioning work of the many older de Havilland aircraft still in use. For instance, towards the end of the war over 4,000 D.H.9s and D.H.9As had been produced. A great many of these were now surplus to government requirements and so were being bought by foreign countries. Refurbishment and maintenance of these brought in much needed income. Always on the lookout for new opportunities, in 1921 the Company started operating an aeroplane hire service from the Stag Lane Aerodrome. This aviation taxi service took on a wide variety of assignments, from flying jockeys to races on the continent, aerial photography, transporting newspaper reporters to assignments and delivering the latest newsreel films to cinemas. In 1922, this service flew 126,000 miles in 1,500 hours, charging 2*s* 6*d* (12.5p) a mile, which was already considered competitive with road transport. Despite the unpredictability and difficulties of these early years, de Havilland survived what Edgerton called the 'shakeout' of the aviation industry, and by the early 1920s expansion was on the horizon. At the end of its second year of operation, not only had the de Havilland Aircraft Company survived, but they now employed over one hundred people and had made a profit of £4,667 on a turnover of £98,580.

Right from its formation, de Havilland had a strong belief in the future of civil aviation, and by January 1923, when Norway joined the Company, that belief was beginning to bear fruit. A new design, the D.H.34, which had made its first test flight in March 1922, with Alan Cobham as the test pilot, was now in service with two commercial airlines, Daimler Airway and Instone Air Line. The single-engine biplane, which had been specifically designed with the economies of civil aviation in mind, could carry ten passengers, two crew and had a range of 364 miles and a cruising speed of 105 mph. From these small beginnings de Havilland would grow by 1930 to become the largest British aircraft company devoted to the exclusive production of civil aircraft.

Having worked for both Airco and de Havilland as an undergraduate, Norway already knew many of the people he would be working with. He also obtained lodgings at Stag Lane and was able to walk to and from work each day. Settling in to full-time employment was relatively straightforward. He joined the aerodynamics and stressing team that was led by Charles Walker, who had originally interviewed him at Airco. He worked as part of a team performing design calculations on various elements of an aeroplane's structure as part of the process needed to take an aeroplane from the drawing board to production. In the days before computers made such things relatively routine, this work required meticulous attention to detail, with the same calculations often being repeated many times. Sloppy work or errors could put the safety of the aeroplane and ultimately peoples' lives at risk. In addition to his desk work, he took every opportunity he could to fly as a test observer or as what he later termed 'just plain ballast'.

By the spring of 1923, Arthur and Mary Norway had returned from holidaying in Italy and moved into a small house in Liss, a quiet village on the Hampshire/West Sussex border. At weekends, Nevil could now travel down to visit them in his newly acquired Morgan Three Wheeler. This car was considered to be one of the most fashionable on the road, but at around £150 it represented a significant part of his annual salary. Such a purchase demonstrated not only the 24-year-old bachelor's increasing self-confidence and belief in his future, but also what would be a lifelong taste for luxury. It seemed that his life was starting to move forward again. However, in addition to starting full-time employment, 1923 was a significant year for Nevil Norway for three other reasons – all of which to were play a part in his future life. He learnt to fly, he started to write novels and he met a woman called Flora Twort.

An important source of income for the de Havilland Aircraft Company in their early days was derived from teaching people to fly. The de Havilland School of Flying was opened at the Stag Lane Aerodrome on 1 April 1923. They had won one of the four contracts offered to train officers of the

RAF reserve using civilian flying schools, and in the first year they were allocated eighty pupils. In addition to training the RAF reserve, they also taught civilians to fly. Nevil Norway was an early pupil of a school which eventually trained such famous aviators as Amy Johnson and John Cunningham. Civilian pilots learnt to fly on one of three aircraft, depending on their ability. In Norway's case it was the popular and trusted Avro 504K biplane, which had been fitted with a 80 hp Renault engine. Whichever aircraft was used, this was not a cheap activity, especially when you were only earning £5 a week. Advertised fees for the Avro were £7 per hour when flying with an instructor and £6 an hour flying solo once qualified. For an additional £4 an hour, the would-be pilot was insured for damage to the aircraft and against third-party risk.

After nine hours of instruction, Norway successfully completed his first solo flight. Financial constraints would mean that it would take almost a year before he had gained enough flying experience to pass the test needed to obtain an Aviator's Certificate, the forerunner of the Private Pilot's Licence. He was duly issued Aviators' Certificate No. 7954 by the Royal Aero Club of the United Kingdom on 4 March 1924. This was a real milestone in his life, and he would remain an active pilot until ill health forced him to give up this activity when he was 52.

Now that his parents had moved to Liss, which was less than fifty miles from his lodgings in London, Nevil began to visit them increasingly regularly at weekends. The drive from Edgware took him along the historic London to Portsmouth Road, which had just been designated the A3 as part of the new road numbering system introduced in England. A few miles from Liss he would pass through the small market town of Petersfield. Here, like many other visitors to the town, he soon came across a bookshop situated on one side of the market square. The Bookshop, which since its opening in 1918 had developed a reputation as one of the best bookshops in the area, was run by three women, Hester Wagstaff, Maria Brahms and Flora Twort. In addition to selling second-hand books, the shop also sold paintings, pottery, textiles and jewellery produced by local artists, and so was also in many ways a cultural centre of Petersfield.

Flora Twort was five years older than Norway, and like him, her father was a high-ranking civil servant, and also like him she had lost a brother during the First World War. Born in Somerset, she had moved to London as a child where her father was employed as a tax inspector. During her childhood she had increasingly demonstrated an artistic ability and so on leaving school studied art at the Royal Drawing Society before moving on to the London School of Art, the London Polytechnic and eventually the Slade School of Art. Very much a free spirit, by 1919 she was living in Petersfield and part of the circle being encouraged by a local supporter of the arts, Dr Harry Roberts. Flora was also beginning to develop a reputation as a local artist, and she would eventually go on to exhibit regularly at the Royal Academy from 1927 until the start of the Second World War.

Following his first visit to The Bookshop in early 1923, Nevil became an increasingly regular visitor and not surprisingly became acquainted with Flora. Before long he was being invited to stay for tea, and slowly a friendship developed between the two of them. They started to take trips out together at weekends, he began to teach her to drive and by mid-July was inviting her to bigger events such as the George V Naval Review at Spithead. Sometime late in 1923 he wrote a short history of No. 1, The Square, Petersfield. This unpublished article shows that the place and, it is reasonable to assume, Flora were increasingly on his mind.

Soon after settling into his lodgings at Stag Lane in early 1923, Norway began writing in the evenings. While there was a history of writing in his family, with his grandmother, mother and father all having had books published, it is not clear what really motivated Nevil to begin along this path. Maybe it was boredom. As a single man living away from home on a modest income, and yet close to work, he would have had many free hours to fill each evening. Alternative forms of entertainment at that time were generally limited to newspapers and books. Radio was still a novelty, as the BBC had only begun broadcasting the previous November.

Whatever the reason, by the spring of 1923, Norway had completed his first novel, *Stephen Morris*. Given the short time it took him to write the novel, it is probable that some of it had been drafted the previous year during the time he spent with his parents on the Italian Riviera. It is unlikely that he could have written the 105,000-word manuscript in just a few months while also settling into a new job. Like many first novels it was substantially autobiographical, covering subjects and surroundings he was familiar with, in this case undergraduate life at Oxford, sailing, motorbikes, the struggles of the aviation industry to find a new direction after the war, and a failed engagement. By 27 April, confident that he had something worth publishing, he had applied to the Incorporated Society of Authors, Playwrights and Composers to become an associate member at a fee of £1 10*s* (£1 50p). In the letter accompanying his application he was clearly excited by his achievement, believing that he had succeeded 'in giving a picture of a bankrupt little industry that is of interest to the general public' and also convinced that 'This picture of contemporary aviation I think is the salient commercial fact about the novel, the thing that will sell the book'.

Following suggestions of potential publishers he had received from the Society, he sent the manuscript to three companies between June and September 1923, all of whom rejected it. Some replies were constructive and gave hope for the future. For instance, Bodley Head Ltd, while rejecting the manuscript, remarked that 'our reader, however, reports that it is a very promising work, but it is somewhat spoilt by the fact that you are prone to desert your story for moralising and discussion'. By September, his enthusiasm for the novel had subsided. In a letter to one of his father's publishers, Methuen & Co Ltd, he outlined how he had originally envisaged *Stephen Morris* being the first of a series of novels centred around aviation, but had now decided to put the manuscript aside, with the intention of rewriting it in a few years, and instead start work on a second novel. He never did rewrite the manuscript of *Stephen Morris*, considering it on later reflection 'a very poor book' and part of an author's learning experience.

In addition to Tiltman, another person who Norway worked with at de Havilland, and with whom he would collaborate professionally in later life, was Alan Cobham. Like Geoffrey de Havilland, Alan Cobham would have a long and distinguished career in the aviation industry, and he would gain international recognition for his long-distance flying exploits. For instance, in 1926, he would become the first person to fly from London to Cape Town and back, and then later the same year the first person to fly from London to Australia and back – a feat for which he received a knighthood. For now, though, he was simply employed by de Havilland as a pilot, taking on whatever flying task was required. In his memoir published in 1978, Cobham remembers 'four men from the Drawing

Office who got together for an evening's jollity and found that they could not raise as much as a penny between them'. The four young men were Ronald Bishop, who would become chief designer at de Havilland and be responsible for the design of the world's first jet airliner, Robert Hardingham (later Sir Robert), who would become chief executive of the Air Registration Board and play a key part in promoting the development of the 'black-box' flight recorder, Alfred Hessell Tiltman, who would become joint managing director and chief designer at Airspeed, and Nevil Norway. There seemed to be talent wherever you looked at de Havilland.

Having resigned himself to the fact that he would not find a publisher for his first novel, Norway shelved it, and in January 1924 he began work on a second. By April he had completed a draft of *Pilotage*. Like his first attempt, *Pilotage* was concerned with themes with which he was familiar, such as aviation, yachts and again a less than straightforward marriage proposal. He sent the draft manuscript to at least six publishers, including *Blackwood's Magazine*, in the hope of getting it into print, but in all cases it was rejected. It must have been hard for Norway to have found too many grounds for optimism with this second round of rejections. For instance, Cassell and Company thought the manuscript too short and wrote 'it hardly comes under the heading of a "full-blooded" novel – the writing is delightfully done, but it is not backed up by a sufficiently strong plot'. By the end of the year he had again shelved the novel, and he must have wondered whether life as a novelist was for him. After all, he now had an important new job with lots of new things to learn and plenty to keep him occupied. The manuscripts of *Stephen Morris* and *Pilotage* were found among his papers following his death. After some editing, they were published posthumously in 1961 in a single volume, probably because of the linked nature of the novels and with some characters appearing in both stories.

At de Havilland, he continued to gain experience in aircraft design. He became an Associate Fellow of the Royal Aeronautical Society in May 1924, and began writing a technical paper on the case for the revival of water channels, which was eventually published in November 1924. In spite of his relative lack of experience in the industry, he was ambitious and not content with his position. This state of mind had been reflected in *Stephen Morris*, where the main character writes a heavily mathematical paper on three-ply fuselages which he presents to his employer Captain Charles Rawdon (almost certainly based on Geoffrey de Havilland) with a request for a pay rise after only being in his job six months.

In *Pilotage* the character Peter Dennison applies for a new job in order to improve his prospects for marriage. In real life Norway was also beginning to think along similar lines, but he was finding it difficult to see any prospects for imminent promotion at de Havilland. Many of his seniors, though not that old, already had significant experience of this new industry. For instance, Norway's own manager Charles Walker, while not originally from an aviation background, had already accumulated ten years' experience in aircraft design and manufacture. As it turned out, Walker, who was a founding director of de Havilland, would be with the Company for the rest of his career.

Looking for alternatives, Norway heard that Barnes Wallis, who had experience of designing and manufacturing airships at Vickers Ltd, was now assembling a team to design and build a new rigid airship, a project in which Vickers was to be a major partner. Among the positions available was that of calculator. So in October 1924, Norway left de Havilland 'with some regret' to join the Airship Guarantee Company, a newly formed subsidiary of Vickers. As he later admitted, 'I knew nothing of airships at that time'. Life was again moving in a new direction.

4

Airships
October 1924–November 1929

Nevil Norway began his career with the newly formed Airship Guarantee Company (AGC) on 27 October 1924. Its formation had been far from straightforward, with the British government unable to decide whether the aeroplane or airship represented the best option for the future of civil aviation. In this climate, getting the Company established at all had been quite an achievement. Although he would later develop a reputation as a risk taker, it is doubtful whether even Norway really knew the risk he was taking in moving to AGC at that stage of his fledging career.

The Air Ministry's view at that time was that the aeroplane and airship could actually co-exist, the aeroplane being best suited to short distance, high speed applications and the airship to long-distance, load-carrying work. The capabilities of both had improved dramatically during the war, in many ways further accentuating their individual advantages. By 1918 the typical endurance of an aeroplane was 12 hours, while for an airship it was now 175 hours. As far as speed was concerned, however, the aeroplane was superior, with the de Havilland D.H.10a having a maximum speed of 128 mph compared to the German LZ120 airship's maximum speed of 82 mph. While there had been much debate about the best direction to take these competing technologies, there had been little action.

For many, as far as airships were concerned, Britain was falling behind in an area in which it had once been a leading player. Although the British government had actively supported airship development during the war, awarding military contracts to companies such Armstrong-Whitworth, Short Brothers and Vickers, since then it had shown little interest.

At the end of the war, Vickers Ltd, who had more experience of airship design and development than any other British company, were part way through a new design for the government, the R.80. Its co-designer, Barnes Wallis, was a 31-year-old engineer who had been with them since September 1913. The R.80 was intended to have a top speed of 70 mph and a range of 6,500 miles, thereby dramatically outperforming existing airships of a much larger size. Unfortunately, the construction of the R.80 was delayed, and when it was finally completed in 1921, it was no longer of interest to the military. Although Vickers then considered the R.80 as the basis of a commercial London–Rome passenger service, nothing came of this. So after briefly being used for training purposes by the US Navy, on 20 September 1921, what had been described as 'perhaps the most beautiful and efficient airship ever designed' made her final flight from Howden, Yorkshire to Pulham, Norfolk. As Vickers lost interest in airships and closed its airship department, Barnes Wallis, who also left the company at the end of 1921, must have thought that his days as an airship designer were over.

However, another champion for the commercial development of airships was emerging: Commander Charles Dennistoun Burney. Burney, who preferred to use his middle name, came from a naval family, had joined the Royal Navy at 15, and looked set for a traditional career in the service. He had, though, an entrepreneurial spirit which would lead him into a wide range of activities and industries during his career. From around 1910 he developed an interest in aeroplanes, and in particular in the use of seaplanes for submarine detection. He took part-time leave from the Navy a number of times so that he could work at Bristol Aviation to continue to develop his interest in this area. At the outbreak of the First World War he was given command of the destroyer HMS *Velox,* but in view of his expertise was quickly moved to the Portsmouth Torpedo School, HMS *Venon*, where he took responsibility for the development of the towed paravane for mine and submarine destruction. He retired from the Navy as a lieutenant commander in 1920 (later being promoted to commander when on the reserve list), having been awarded £350,000 for the government's use of his inventions. He then joined Vickers Ltd as a consultant and began to campaign for the development of a commercial airship service.

Understandably, Vickers was not that enthusiastic about supporting a new airship initiative. Although unemployment in Britain was starting to fall by January 1922, it was still high enough to make companies wary of investing in speculative schemes. As he was to prove many times, Burney was not a man who was easily put off, and eventually, on learning that the Shell Group had agreed to support the scheme, the Vickers board also agreed to support his proposal provided that the government also came on board.

On 22 March 1922, less than three months after Wallis had left Vickers, Burney formally presented his plan for the establishment of a self-supporting airship service to the Air Council. What became known as the Burney Scheme proposed the establishment of a commercial airship service, for both mail and passengers, between London and India and London and Australia. It was envisaged that the travel time to Australia could be reduced from the then four to five weeks to just eleven and a half days with three stops.

Burney's predictions may have been optimistic, but even allowing for this, the endurance advantage of the airship over the aeroplane was significant. In his record-breaking flight by aeroplane from England to Australia four years later, Alan Cobham had needed twenty-four refuelling stops to reach Darwin. The danger of needing too many stops in unstable parts of the world was also sadly highlighted by the death of his flight engineer who was shot and killed as they landed at Basra.

It was expected that the Burney Scheme would require £4 million working capital, to be raised through shares and debentures. Although no direct capital investment was required from the government, they were required to act as guarantor for the returns being promised to private investors over the first ten years. Under the scheme, six new airships would ultimately be constructed and operated by Vickers. Vickers and Shell had already agreed to acquire 100,000 shares each in the new venture.

The scheme was referred to the Committee of Imperial Defence, and in spite of some support from the Air Ministry and Admiralty, in practice little happened and the Burney Scheme was ultimately rejected by the then coalition government of Lloyd George on financial grounds. It would take another two years before the government finally approved an airship development programme. In this intervening period there were two general elections and yet more changes of mind about the Burney

Scheme. Finally, following discussions at Cabinet on 1 May and again on 7 May 1924, Ramsay MacDonald's Labour government agreed to what was to be called the Imperial Airship Scheme.

A week later, Lord Thomson, the Secretary of State for Air, outlined the new scheme in the House of Lords. The initial focus now was not on operating an airship service, but on research, design and construction of the airships themselves. The Labour government had replaced Burney's original privately financed scheme by a state and private sector collaboration, although it turned out to be more competition than collaboration. In addition to undertaking research using existing airships owned by the government, two new airships would now be built; the first, the R.100, would be built by a new Vickers subsidiary, the Airship Guarantee Company (AGC), managed by Burney and designed for commercial purposes. Lord Thomson had already made it clear to Burney that this airship should be designed by Barnes Wallis, who was now back at Vickers. Burney did not need any persuading, as he was also keen to have Wallis in the team. Wallis himself had no doubt about this opportunity as it meant that not only could he once again work on airships but also stay with Vickers and therefore be reasonably sure of continued employment should the project fail. In a letter to his future wife Molly Bloxam, Wallis was clear about his passion for airships, saying, 'Airships are the only thing I really care about. I've given up all my time and energy to them for the last ten years nearly, staked my future on them as it were'. The second airship, the R.101, would be designed and constructed by the government's Royal Airship Works at Cardington, and it would also be designed with regard 'to Service requirements, including naval reconnaissance'.

Finally, on 24 October 1924, the government awarded a contract to the Airship Guarantee Company for the design and construction of the R.100. Once constructed, the airship was to be delivered to the Air Ministry so that it could undergo trials, the first within the United Kingdom and the second a flight to India to test its performance under tropical conditions. If the flight to India was satisfactory then AGC would have the option to buy the airship back for £150,000 in order to establish an approved British Airship Transport Service. Included in the agreement was the normal clause, in such cases, excluding members of the House of Commons from benefiting from a government contract. It seems to have been overlooked that Burney had been Conservative MP for Uxbridge since November 1922!

Given that the state–private sector compromise was the initiative of a new Labour government, it is perhaps not surprising that the two airships were soon being popularly referred to as the 'Capitalist Ship' and the 'Socialist Ship'. The signing of the contract with AGC and the beginning of the Imperial Airship Scheme received a range of coverage in the national press. The conservative *Daily Express* had a banner headline on its front page proclaiming 'Our Wonderful Airship of the Future', with a leader boldly forecasting that 'Great Britain, after failures, half-hearted efforts, and long delay, has at last set to work in earnest to establish the world's greatest airship service'. The Labour-leaning *Daily Mirror* was more muted, with a short three-paragraph statement. Perhaps the possibility of luxury long-distance air travel was of less relevance to the majority of its readership.

Five days later, Ramsay MacDonald's minority government was defeated in a general election and replaced by a new Conservative government led by Stanley Baldwin. However, the new Secretary of State for Air, Sir Samuel Hoare, surprised some people by deciding to honour the contract with AGC. He believed 'it was better to proceed rather than once again throwing development into the melting pot'. Airship development in Britain was now underway again.

Although he did not know it at the time, the R.100 project would occupy six years of Nevil Norway's life. It would bring him rapid advancement and responsibility, contact with influential people in the aviation industry such as Lord Thomson, Burney and Wallis, but its outcome would also stay with him for the rest of his life, significantly colouring his views of government and government officials.

The R.100 had to be completed and delivered to the Air Ministry for trials by 30 September 1927. Given that the airship would have over twice the gas capacity, with significantly more lifting capability than anything then flying, this was quite a challenge. Although the R.100 and R.101 both had to meet the same technical specification (minimum gasbag capacity, maximum speed, maximum weight, passenger capacity and minimum endurance), there were two key differences in the projects: the budgets and the structure of the design teams. In approving the airship development scheme the Cabinet had set a maximum expenditure of £400,000 for the financial year 1924–25, with the same limit for subsequent years. The total cost of the R.100 was fixed at a maximum of £350,000, which included £50,000 for the purchase of the development site and plant at Howden. The R.101 team therefore had a budget of £850,000 over the proposed three-year development programme, but this was to include research on existing government airships, principally the R.33 and R.36.

The R.100 team was led by Barnes Wallis, who as chief designer wanted to be able to say 'I designed every part in that ship myself'. John E. Temple was the chief calculator at Vickers at that time. He had experience of airship development, having been chief calculator on the R.80 with Wallis, but he was about to leave the company, and so a replacement for this key position had to be found. Perhaps somewhat surprisingly, Wallis appointed the relatively inexperienced Nevil Norway as calculator. Wallis would have needed to be fully satisfied with Norway's mathematical skills before appointing him, since the role of Norway and his team of junior calculators would be to perform the many complex structural calculations required to validate Wallis's design. Wallis was also able to call on a range of specialists, all of whom he trusted, when required. However, Wallis was clearly the leader responsible for all major decisions. The chain of command was therefore simple and rapid – in theory; Wallis made the decisions as he saw fit, Burney looked after external relationships and Vickers supplied any short-term funding needed by AGC. Since soon after meeting him Wallis had said that 'I like Burney very much and shall love working for him', then a harmonious working relationship between the managing director of AGC and its chief designer seemed likely. Unfortunately, ultimately this did not prove to be the case.

In contrast, the R.101 team had more of a committee feel. The lead members were Group Captain (later Air Commodore) Peregrine Fellowes, the director of airship development; Squadron Leader (later Wing Commander) Reginald Colmore, deputy director, who would eventually take over from him near the end of the project in January 1930; Lieutenant Colonel Vincent Richmond, assistant director of airship development – technical (in effect Wallis's counterpart); Major George Scott, assistant director of airship development – flying; and Flight Lieutenant (later Squadron Leader) F. Michael Rope, assistant chief designer. Of these, only Richmond and Rope had airship development experience. Of course, there was a large pool of people at Cardington that could be called upon to provide advice, but it was difficult to say who owned and cared for the R.101 design in the way that Wallis owned and cared for the R.100.

As far as project management was concerned, it was stipulated that the two developments would be co-ordinated by an aviation board and a technical board, the assumption being that there would be information flow between the two teams. In practice they operated as totally separate entities – competitors not collaborators. Nevil Norway remembered that 'In the five years that were to elapse before either airship flew neither designer visited the other's works, nor did they meet or correspond upon the common problems that each had to solve. Each trod a parallel road alone, harassed and overworked'. Norway himself only made contact with his equivalent, Dr Harold Roxbee Cox, chief calculator on the R.101, towards the end of the project. This separation and increasing antagonism may well have fuelled some of the bitterness that later surfaced when disaster struck.

So Norway began his career with AGC on the R.100 project at Vickers House, Broadway, Westminster on 27 October 1924. He was initially appointed as calculator, working with John Temple, on a wage of £6 10s (£6 50p) a week. However, he would be ultimately expected to take on the role of chief calculator once a team of junior calculators was in place and Temple had left the Company. His first priority was to learn as much as he could about calculating stresses, forces and deflections in airship structures. Aware of public concern over the safety of airships following the R.38 disaster in 1921 in which the airship had broken up in mid-air killing forty-four of the forty-nine people on board, the contract for the R.100 specified in some detail the forces the airship should be able to withstand. The accurate calculation of forces and stresses on the airship structure were therefore extremely important. In addition to Temple, Vickers had employed two consultants to help Norway through this learning phase, Professor Leonard Bairstow, an expert on aerodynamics, and Professor A. J. Sutton Pippard, an expert on structures.

While Norway was learning about airships, elsewhere at Vickers Wallis was designing one. As, Jack E. Morpurgo, Wallis's biographer noted, 'In the last months of 1924 with very few excursions to the drawing board and none to the laboratory or testing-chamber, Wallis dreamed up an entire airship, complete in detail and rich in original features'.

By the end of 1924, three new junior calculators had been recruited, and Norway and his team were moved to the Vickers factory at Crayford. During the war the Vickers' Crayford Works had employed over 12,000 people manufacturing armaments and aeroplanes. A small village in what was then Kent (now part of Greater London) had been transformed into an industrial town by the construction of a housing estate and all the facilities needed to support the vast increase in population. The end of the war had bought a decline in the need for the factory's products, and despite a move to the manufacture of new products such as motor car parts, the workforce shrank dramatically to 3,500. In 1919, aeroplane production was moved from Crayford to Weybridge, leaving the factory at times close to closure and a shadow of its former self. It is therefore not surprising that Norway was to describe the new surroundings for him and his team as 'a derelict office in the depressing industrial suburb of Crayford'.

In early December 1924, Norway moved from lodgings at Edgware to new lodgings at Sidcup just over three miles from his workplace. So began a period of stability that lasted through 1925. He would travel by train to Crayford each day, work with his team, and then return home by train. Before Wallis's airship design could be constructed, a report had to be submitted to the government Airworthiness of Airships Panel showing the forces, stresses and deflections on every part of the airship's framework for a wide range of operating conditions. This was a daunting task for a structure which was described as being as big as an ocean liner: 709 feet long and with a maximum diameter of 133 feet. Norway and his team had to perform literally thousands of repetitive and complex calculations, which demanded immense concentration and a high degree of cross-checking. After all, mistakes could literally cost lives. The ability to pay such close attention to detail was a characteristic Norway would later become well known for in the construction of his novels.

In addition to the theoretical calculations, girders had to be tested in the laboratory to check that theory and practice agreed. To Norway, at times this heavily theoretical work with no semblance of an airship in sight must have seemed far removed from the world of aeroplane design and manufacture he had experienced at de Havilland.

Although Burney had finally obtained a long sought after contract with the government, it seems he was almost immediately looking to build a bigger venture. On 5 March 1925, AGC submitted to the prime minister a proposal for a mail and passenger airship line between Great Britain and Australasia. The Secretary of State for Air, Sir Samuel Hoare, was in no doubt what he thought of the new proposals. He concluded that 'the new proposals are founded upon a series of optimistic and untested assumptions' and that 'I have come to the emphatic conclusion that the new proposals should not be entertained'.

On 3 September 1925 the airship industry took a significant blow. The American airship the USS *Shenandoah* broke up in mid-air during a severe thunderstorm, with the loss of fourteen lives. One of the theories initially put forward for the accident was that the structure of the airship had not been designed to cope with severe weather conditions. Very aware of the damage that the calls from some quarters for all airship programmes to be scrapped could have on the Imperial Airship Scheme, Burney was quick to publicly respond to such allegations. He said 'the *Shenandoah* was a ten year old design' and that 'It was realised that present ships were not strong enough and care would be taken that the Empire airway service ships would be twice the present strength'. The *Shenandoah* disaster must have put into stark perspective the importance of the design calculations that Norway and his team were doing. It is perhaps therefore not surprising that for relaxation in the evenings Norway had begun writing again.

At weekends, Norway continued to visit his parents and meet up with Flora Twort. Now firm friends, they would spend time together boating, taking rides on a pony and trap and pondering over crosswords. While Flora considered Nevil a good friend, he obviously had a different relationship in mind, as on 26 September 1925, following their usual afternoon tea, he proposed to her. Her reaction was one of complete surprise. Reminiscing on this event towards the end of her life she remarked:

'I never realized he felt that way about me. We had never even kissed. I cried because I did not want to hurt his feelings. He was such a dear friend, but I did not love him, and you cannot marry without love, can you? I felt awful, but Nevil said I was not to worry. I would love him eventually – he would see to that.'

If Flora was shocked, it is difficult to imagine what the reaction of Nevil must have been. He came from a traditional and conservative Victorian/Edwardian upbringing in which the role of a man and woman were well defined. He was expected to get married and produce a son and heir, love did not really come into it. This was also the second time in his life he had been rejected.

Two days later, the normally reserved and rather private Norway wrote Flora a long, clearly heartfelt, very frank and at times rambling letter in which he talked in detail about his previously failed engagement, marriage, love, loneliness, companionship and what she meant to him. He was clearly very emotional, asking her, 'I want you to tell me about what to do, and not to be afraid of saying unpleasant things. But equally, don't say things "for my good", because I'm the best judge of that'. He also wanted her to continue their friendship, saying:

> 'I shall be alone in Town all the autumn with nothing what ever to do beyond my work. For two years you've been about the only intellectual friend, to whom I could talk about books and the things I'm keen on. Can we save anything of that friendship? Don't be afraid to say no.'

In spite of the fact that he had just proposed to her, perhaps reflecting the formalities of the time, the letter began 'Dear Twort' and ended 'Yours Shute'. Following a reply from her, he wrote again on 30 September. As before, he wrote with his heart on his sleeve. Accepting that her answer was still no, he was still keen that they remain friends, asking 'For two years I've been a friend to you. I can carry on like that: the difference will be that you know that I love you and that I am satisfied that you can't marry me. Can we carry on in that way?' Although he had given up for the time being, he would try again the following year.

By the spring of 1926, after over a year of intensive effort, all preliminary calculations for the R.100 had been completed and the results passed to the Airworthiness of Airships Panel. It was now time to put the theory into practice and start construction. The site that had been chosen for the construction of the R.100 was a now disused airship station at Howden in East Yorkshire. RNAS Howden had been a thriving airship station during the war, but following its closure in 1921, the 1,100-acre site had now fallen into a poor state of repair with much of its structure and facilities having been dismantled or sold off. Its main attraction was No. 2 airship shed, which at the time of its construction in 1919 had been the largest in Britain. Having been saved from demolition by falling metal prices, the shed was in poor condition but big enough to house the R.100 during construction.

Even though a team from Vickers had been trying to clean up and renovate the site during 1925, the new place of work was still in a pretty miserable state. Even though Crayford had not exactly been the best working environment, the Howden site was a big shock to Norway when he arrived there with the rest of the main workforce in April 1926. The largely flat rather harsh landscape surrounding the airship station was very different to the environments he had been used to in London or Oxford. The nearest community was the village of Howden, three miles to the south. Although Norway did not appreciate the beauty of the area immediately, the local inhabitants were more than happy to see the new arrivals. The airship project would bring many opportunities for local employment to both men and women in an area that had been depressed since the war; indeed, the General Strike was only a month away. As well as Norway and his team of calculators, Barnes Wallis and many people from the Vickers Shipbuilding Works at Barrow-in-Furness moved to the new Howden site. Among these was Major Philip Teed, a chemist with expertise on the production of hydrogen. He was to become an increasingly important member of the team. Perhaps most importantly to Norway though, for the first time since leaving de Havilland's, he was part of an engineering community again.

On-site accommodation was limited to a number of rather basic, uninsulated bungalows with corrugated iron roofs. These were reserved mainly for senior personnel. Barnes Wallis, his new wife and two-month-old son lived in one of these, but like many others, Norway lived in Howden a few miles away, where he moved into new lodgings at 78 Hailgate.

Visiting his parents or Flora at the weekends was no longer as easy as it had been. He therefore had to find new ways to entertain himself. He initially tried country pursuits such as shooting, but very soon he came across the Yorkshire Aeroplane Club, one of the many private flying clubs that had started to flourish up and down the country. The Yorkshire Aeroplane Club was one of the oldest of these, having been established in 1909. Situated twenty miles west of Howden, the club had recently moved to the Sherburn-in-Elmet Aerodrome, which had been disused since the war. It was therefore relatively easy for Norway to reach, which he did increasingly frequently at weekends. He took every opportunity his time and finances would allow to increase his solo flying experience. The club owned two D.H.60 Moths and had a membership approaching 250, with many of these owning their own aeroplanes.

In 1926, John Temple left Vickers, and Norway was promoted to the position of chief calculator. Not only did this provide an increase in salary, but it was also a position of significant status and responsibility for someone just over 27 years old. Perhaps this encouraged him to once again ask Flora to marry him. Again the answer was no, and this time he seems to have accepted it. Flora Twort never married, but she and Nevil Norway remained very good friends for the rest of his life. Frequently corresponding, she became a godmother to his second daughter Shirley, but despite promises to do so, she never did visit him in Australia.

In spite of the disappointment of having had his first two novels rejected for publication, Norway was not put off and continued to write. He not only displayed a tenacity not to be beaten, but he also believed that occupying his mind with writing in the evenings allowed him to forget the issues of the working day which had just ended and start the following day with a refreshed mind. He started his third novel *Marazan* towards the end of 1924 and by the end of 1925 had a finished manuscript. This took him longer to write than his earlier attempts, with the whole thing being written twice and some parts being written three times. He was clearly determined to learn from the feedback he had been given on his previous novels.

By the mid-1920s the market for literature in England was changing. Recognising this, many publishers had moved from the nineteenth century practice of basing their book catalogues largely on classics and ecclesiastical literature to one with an increased interest in popular fiction aimed at all social classes; books were becoming commodities. The profile of authors, though, was changing more slowly. Published British authors in the first quarter of the twentieth century were still most likely to be male, from a professional background having been educated at a public school and Oxbridge – in fact, a good description of Nevil Norway.

Defining who was reading what was an altogether more difficult question to answer. There were no best-seller lists at that time, and publishers' sales figures were not disclosed. There was no common literature across the social classes, but 'the preponderant literature of the period culturally and politically was middlebrow. This was so because the middlebrow literary canon included not merely sensational novels or romances or a good read, like J. B. Priestley's novels, but also "political" novels, novels of conflict ... or novels of social engagement'. Looking at the summer holiday list of a major publisher of fiction of the period, such as Hodder and Stoughton, showed new books in a wide range of genres, from the traditional areas of romance and westerns, through to newer reading interests such as crime and espionage. Recently published titles in great demand included some authors still in print today, such as Edgar Wallace and Zane Grey and many others now long forgotten.

Norway had obviously learnt from his earlier attempts, since on 23 February 1926 he received a letter from the chief book editor of Cassell and Company offering to publish *Marazan*. It seemed that the subject matter and style of his manuscript was now more in line with what publishers were looking for in a modern popular novel. As in the unsuccessful *Stephen Morris* and *Pilotage* novels, Norway kept to themes he was familiar with, such as aviation and sailing, but in *Marazan* these were now part of a more adventurous plot with elements such as an escaped convict, drug smuggling and murder. The principal character, Philip Stenning, who had also appeared in *Stephen Morris*, reflected Norway's early intention to write a series of novels with an aviation theme and perhaps some common characters. Such a practice was often used at the time, one of the best known examples being *The Thirty-Nine Steps* and its four sequels, a series of novels John Buchan wrote around the adventures of Richard Hannay. Although it is clear why Norway used an aviation theme in his early novels – it was a subject he knew about – it is not clear who his literary influences were. Much later in life he was to say that he read a great amount, however 'anything and everything but novels – I don't suppose more than two or three novels a year. Technical journals and weeklies dealing with current events are my main literary diet'. The only clue to his taste in fiction at that time was the A. P. Herbert novel he read before a flight to Canada; not an obvious influence for aviation adventure stories.

The offer from Cassell was an advance of £30 and a royalty starting at 10 per cent for the first 3,000 copies sold. Cassell and Company were a well-regarded publisher, having been in existence for over seventy-five years, and with a catalogue which included some of the iconic writers of the period such as Sir Arthur Conan Doyle and G. K. Chesterton. Norway should have been proud of his achievement but almost ended his career as a novelist before it had begun! Maybe overdoing advice he had obtained from the Society of Authors, Playwrights and Composers, he returned the provisional agreement to Cassell, objecting to nearly every clause! The response from Cassell was perhaps predictable; they returned his manuscript believing that business with the aspiring author would no longer be possible. Realising the error he had made, Norway contacted Ronald Watt, who he had known at Balliol College, to try and recover the situation. Ronald now worked for the family company A. P. Watt & Son, the oldest and one of the most respected literary agents in England. The company represented many major authors such as Thomas Hardy, Rudyard Kipling, P. G. Woodhouse and H. G. Wells, but it was by no means certain that they would take on an unknown author, especially one who appeared to be somewhat difficult to please. However, following a nervous wait, Watt agreed to help, and Cassell accepted the terms of the standard agreement used by A. P. Watt & Son as a basis for publication. Norway learnt from this episode, and as he later wrote, 'Since then I have never done any of my literary business at all, but I have left it all to Watt. I could not have a better agent, or a more loyal friend'.

As a result of Watt's intervention, on 17 August 1926 *Marazan* was finally published. The author however was not N. S. Norway but Nevil Shute. Norway, conscious that writing novels was still very much a hobby, decided to write under the pseudonym of his two forenames, thus protecting the developing reputation of Mr N. S. Norway aeronautical engineer.

He did not see the publication of *Marazan* as much of a milestone in his life, treating it in a more or less offhand way. In a letter to his old headmaster at Oxford Preparatory School, he wrote that 'It had been written simply for my own amusement – I had quite given up hope of getting anything published'. It seems he also got bored with the book towards the end, as he also added, 'As for the end, I had got fed up with it by that time and the previous love scenes had been so awfully difficult that I couldn't face another one, and so left it there, and that's the bare, unvarnished truth'.

Like many debut novels, *Marazan* was not selected for review by the major newspapers or magazines, although it did get a mention in some of the less-well-known regional newspapers. For instance, the book reviewer of the *Aberdeen Press and Journal* noted that 'This first novel reveals a flair for telling a story'. Not a high-profile start to a literary career, but the reviewer had noted something that many others would ultimately agree with. *Marazan* eventually sold around about 1,200 copies. It then remained out of print until 1951, when Norway's publisher William Heinemann Ltd reissued it as part of a uniform series of his books. Despite the modest sales of his first novel, Nevil Shute was now a published author.

As far as his day job was concerned, the R.100 was now being built from scratch inside the big airship shed on the aerodrome. It is sometimes difficult to imagine just how big an undertaking this really was. The airship frame itself was enormous, 138-foot high and 709-foot long. To put this into perspective, the ill-fated RMS *Titanic* had only been marginally bigger with a height of 175 feet and length of 882 feet The required completion date for the airship specified in the contract was now less than eighteen months away. For a project with so many new technical hurdles to overcome, this was never likely to be a realistic deadline, and so it proved.

Wallis's design for the framework of the airship consisted of sixteen 16-sided transverse frames, with tensioned wires running from each junction on the frame to the centre of the structure, likes spokes on a bicycle wheel. The transverse frames were joined together using longitudinal girders to form fifteen individual compartments, each of which would house a gasbag. The gasbags were held in place in each compartment by a wire mesh carefully designed to allow effective transmission of the lifting force from each gasbag to the airship framework while at the same time constraining its movement as pressure and gas volume changed. The design was novel and resulted in a number of patents, some of which rather generously showed Burney as co-inventor. The framework was constructed from Duralumin, an aluminium alloy, with the required tubing being manufactured on site from metal strips, using a machine specially designed by Wallis. He even specified the direction rivets being used to join the tube should be inserted during the manufacturing process. This was an example of Wallis's desire to be involved in every part of the process, with no detail being too small for his attention. Burney on the other hand was interested in the broader picture, keen to keep pushing things forward, and so, perhaps not surprisingly, tensions between the two soon began to develop.

In addition to the design and construction of the framework and internal wiring, accommodation for passengers and crew had to be designed, engines had to be chosen, gasbags sourced, and the whole structure covered in a stretched fabric skin. The hydrogen needed to inflate the gasbags had to be produced on site, and finally the complete airship had to undergo a range of preliminary trials in the shed before being released from the construction bay and a Permit to Fly issued. The design and construction of the R.100 has been described in detail in a number of books – see for example those by Anderson and Deacon.

Norway was now spending increasing amounts of his free time at the Yorkshire Aeroplane Club. He began participating in club races and quickly became part of the club community. Like other flying clubs in the country, there was a somewhat happy-go-lucky attitude among the members. For instance, an excerpt from the Yorkshire Aeroplane Club weekly news report published in the magazine *Flight* in 1927 records that 'Saturday: Mr Beck with Mr Weaver as passenger flew over to Beverley, where they landed on the racecourse. After an excellent lunch at the Beverley Arms they returned to Sherburn', while later the same year the news from the club says 'The less we dwell on the club report this week the better. Sunday: Gale, resulting in Mr Norway almost being successful in effecting a roll on our Renault Avro while taxiing in'. However, along with the fun there was always the risk. Sadly, in September of that year a private owner at the club crashed, severely injuring himself and killing his passenger. Deaths in the private flying community were still not an uncommon event.

In addition to flying activities, the Yorkshire Aeroplane Club also organised social events such as air pageants and dances. It was at one of these, around 1927, that Nevil Norway first met his future wife. Dr Frances Heaton was a newly qualified doctor, then working at York County Hospital as a house physician. Three years younger than Nevil, she came from a family with strong Anglican roots in which service to the Empire had played a big part. Her father Bernard, like Nevil's father, belonged to the Civil Service. When Frances had been born in India in 1902, he was principal of the Calcutta Civil Engineering College. The fourth of six children, Frances studied medicine at the University of London, at a time when this was still not a common thing for women to do, and was registered as a doctor by the General Medical Council in January 1927. Although they may have not known it when they first met, Nevil and Frances had a lot in common, indeed both their families were living in Ealing when the 1911 census was completed.

Even though his days and weekends were busy, Norway continued writing in the evenings. By the end of July 1927 he had completed the first draft of his next novel, having spent a week of his holiday on Lundy, an island off the coast of North Devon, to achieve this. He initially wanted to title the novel *Renegade* but then discovered that Cassell and Company had recently published a novel by Arthur Friel with the same name. The alternatively titled *So Disdained* was published in the summer of 1928, again by Cassell and Company. Aviation still played a prominent part in this novel, with Stenning and Morris again present but this time as minor characters. In this novel, the adventure element of the plot concerns espionage, rather than drug smuggling, with Norway venturing into areas with far bigger social implications.

A First World War pilot who has fallen on hard times, believing England has failed him, feels he has no alternative but to move to Russia to get worthwhile aviation work, and ultimately he ends up spying for the communists. This time, in addition to publication in the United Kingdom, Ronald Watt negotiated an agreement for the book to be published in America by the Houghton Mifflin Company. A condition of that agreement was that the book be retitled to *The Mysterious Aviator* for the American market. Although Norway did not like the proposed change, he reluctantly agreed. Arguments with publishers over titles was to be a reoccurring problem over his career, but this was one of the few times that his mind was changed. The book was not widely reviewed in

America. *The Saturday Review of Literature* was particularly unimpressed, wondering 'why the author spun out to full novel length materials which could have as readily fitted into half that space', and concluding that 'though the tale is not badly written, we saw slight justification for writing it at all'.

In Britain, *So Disdained* was noticed by more reviewers than Shute's first novel. In addition to reviews in the regional newspapers, this time the novel was reviewed by a key journal in the literary world, *The Times Literary Supplement*. Although only receiving a paragraph in the Short Reviews section, it was still an important step forward for the aspiring novelist. While he was still learning his trade as a novelist in the evenings, during the day, work on the R.100 was now reaching a critical phase.

By 30 September 1927, the original delivery date for the airship, work was well behind schedule. Construction had suffered from a host of delays due to factors such as the late ordering and delivery of material, changes in mind about the design, and difficulty in getting skilled workers. Always the optimist, Burney believed that that the airship would now be ready by mid-1928, and was as a result constantly pressuring for faster progress. Burney's optimism was treated with scepticism by some at the Air Ministry; indeed the Secretary of State for Air himself was later to observe that 'so far, no single one of Commander Burney's estimates for completion of the airship have been realised, and I see no reason why we should accept his latest estimate without examination'. Burney's push for a fast completion conflicted with Wallis's methodical approach to the project and certainly did not help improve the working relationship between the two.

To some extent, Norway was caught in the middle of the increasing rift between Burney and Wallis, both of whom he admired. Reflecting on these two large personalities over twenty-five years later, he described Wallis as 'the greatest engineer in England at the time, and for twenty years afterwards', while he considered that Burney 'had the keenest engineering imagination of anyone that I have ever met, coupled with a great commercial sense'.

Despite the many problems, the construction of the airship moved slowly forward, but by late 1928, the relationship between Burney and Wallis had reached breaking point – with hostility from both sides. From Wallis's perspective, Burney did not understand the engineering issues, while from Burney's, Wallis would not accept discipline and was constantly undermining his right to manage the project. The gulf that had grown between the two can be illustrated by a memorandum Burney sent Wallis in October 1928, in which he gave his chief designer a humiliating reprimand, stating:

> 'I have frequently expressed my opinion that you do not go around the Drawing Office at frequent enough intervals with the result that not only is there a considerable waste of Drawing Office time, but also, as in the present instance there is waste in the shops. I should be glad if you would make it a constant rule to go round the Drawing Office at a fixed time every day, so as to prevent a recurrence of instances of this character.'

Not only had the relationship between Wallis and Burney broken down, but that between their wives seemed no better. In a letter to an old school friend, Mollie Wallis complained that 'Mrs Burney is staying here and she's been sitting in here all morning telling me how to bring up my children'. In a later letter she described how she sat in the kitchen with most the house in darkness, the front door locked and the doorbell disconnected, 'all to keep Burney out'.

With the design and construction of the airship frame largely complete, Wallis was keen to find a way out of his current predicament. In November 1928, following a number of meetings between the two, Wallis was called to the Vickers factory at Weybridge by the chairman, Sir Robert McLean, and offered the position of chief designer at Vickers Aviation – a move from airships to aeroplanes. The only condition was that Wallis did not leave Howden until after the R.100 gasbags had been inflated (expected to be spring of 1929) and remained available to AGC to help with any major problems until the end of the project. In order to compensate for the fact that Wallis would increasingly be unavailable, Norway was promoted to the position of deputy chief engineer. In many ways, for some time he had been seen as the person to go to by many of the construction staff whenever a problem needed discussion, so was already suited to his new position. He was also helping to promote the project through events such as lectures at the local branch of the Royal Aeronautical Society. He would ultimately take full responsibility for technical aspects of the project once Wallis had moved to Weybridge permanently. This was quite an achievement for someone who was not yet thirty. With the increased status and salary, living in shared lodgings in Howden no longer seemed appropriate, and so Norway moved in to the St Leonard's Club in York, travelling by car to work every day. Living in York, he was also nearer to Frances Heaton, whom he was now seeing regularly.

During 1929 Burney wrote a book on the future of aviation with the rather ambitious title *The World, the Air and the Future*. Norway had been asked by Burney to contribute a chapter on heavier-than-air craft, perhaps a mark of Burney's growing respect for Norway. In it, Norway considered in detail the future of the what he called the 'Land Aeroplane' and the 'Flying Boat'. His best guess was that it would be fifty years before the aeroplane matched the airship in terms of endurance. Even though it was Norway's chapter, Burney still added a footnote at the bottom of the page on which Norway had made this prediction, stating he disagreed with it! Ever the optimist, he thought the timespan would be shorter, and this time he was right. There was also a chapter on airships in this book, but Wallis was not asked to contribute – perhaps intended as a final snub to the departing chief designer. However, whatever Wallis might have thought of the book, Burney saw it as an opportunity to promote his cause, and with the completion of the R.100 on the horizon, the timing could not have been better.

A general election was held in the United Kingdom on 30 May 1929. The Conservative Party led by Stanley Baldwin, which had been in government since the airship programme had started in late 1924, was replaced by a minority Labour government led by Ramsay MacDonald. In the new Cabinet, Lord Thomson once again became Secretary of State for Air.

The 1929 election was also a time of change for Burney. He had been a Conservative MP for Uxbridge since 1922 but retired at the May election. By June he had become Sir Charles Dennistoun Burney, having succeeded his father, becoming 2nd Baronet Burney of Preston Candover.

Another change to the R.100 team during 1929 was the appointment of an old colleague of Norway's, A. Hessell Tiltman from de Havilland, as a designer in October of that year. Tiltman would play a key part in the next stage of Norway's professional career.

On 14 October 1929, the R.100's sister ship the R.101 completed its maiden test flight. This achievement was announced in a blaze of publicity. *The Times* printed dramatic photographs of the airship passing over famous London landmarks such as St Paul's Cathedral and Hyde Park, while the influential aviation magazine *Flight* devoted three pages to the event. A week earlier, the same magazine had allocated over half of its issue to the triumph of the R.101, even before it had flown! Marketing and publicity of the R.100, which was in essence really just Burney, could never hope to compete with the government marketing machine used to promote the R.101. Although this was not really meant to be a competition, the news must have dampened spirits at Howden.

Dampening the spirits of many others at that time was the Wall Street Crash, which started on 24 October. At one stage the American stock market fell by over 24 per cent in just two days. Although this did not have an immediate effect on the airship programme, the economic collapse and resulting depression would be one of the factors that helped finally end airship development in Britain. However, for now, the work continued, and by late October the R.100 was finally complete and ready for shed trials, which were to be supervised by Wallis and Norway. For these trials, engines had to be run continuously at cruising power, with the airship's gasbags inflated with hydrogen and the airship still in its shed. Given the small clearance between the airship's propellers and the ground, and the airship and top of the shed, it is not surprising that the sight of the airship lurching up and down in the air currents generated stayed etched in Norway's memory. A small error would have meant complete disaster. Fortunately, all went well, and after some final finishing touches, on 8 November, Burney informed the Air Ministry that construction of the R.100 was complete. Tests were performed to check the balance and assess the lifting capability (and therefore the passenger capacity) of the fully inflated airship. Finally, although the lift was slightly less than the minimum that had been specified in the original contract, on 25 November 1929, a temporary Permit to Fly was issued by the Air

Ministry. This permitted official flight trials of the airship G-FAAV (the R.100) to be carried out within Britain and Northern Ireland, and it was valid until 28 February 1930.

So, more than two years late, and after periods of frustration and disappointment, the R.100 was finally ready to realise the hopes that so many had in her. For Nevil Norway, it had been a period of huge change; he had started as a calculator and was now deputy chief engineer of a major national aviation project – a considerable advancement in just over five years. There was now light at the end of the tunnel, but in many ways the real test was still to come.

5

Success and Failure
December 1929 – November 1930

Following the issuing of the temporary Permit to Fly on 25 November, there was a short but nonetheless frustrating period before the R.100 could finally take to the air. This was due to a combination of logistics and the unpredictability of the British weather. Under the agreement with the government, once construction of the R.100 had been completed, a crew supplied by the Air Ministry would take command of the airship and fly it to the Royal Airship Works at Cardington for flight trials. Although now under the command of Air Ministry employees, the airship would still remain the property of AGC until flight trials had been successfully completed.

Previously used methods in which an airship was tethered to the ground when docked often resulted in damage in high winds. Given the size of the R.100 and R.101, mooring towers were now considered to be the only safe option. A mooring tower was typically a 200-foot-high steel-framed structure designed to withstand a force of thirty tons in any direction, with the airship being tethered to a movable pivot on the top of the tower so that when docked it would always be in the direction of the prevailing wind. Passengers and cargo entered the airship through its nose, via a lift or stairs in the tower. Unfortunately, at that time the only mooring tower in the country was at Cardington, and it was currently occupied by the rival R.101. Eventually, on 30 November, the high winds over Bedfordshire dropped enough to allow the R.101 to be detached from the mooring tower and put back safely into her shed. Sadly, the weather at Howden was still not calm enough to allow the R.100 to be taken from her shed. No mooring tower had yet been built at Howden, and so once the R.100 had been taken from the shed, it had to start its flight.

While Norway thought the publicity machine of AGC limited in comparison to that available to the government-led R.101, by November the progress of the R.100 had really caught the public's imagination. Newspapers up and down the country were full of rumours and predictions of when the airship would finally make its maiden flight. As early as 26 November the *Western Morning News and Courier* in Devon speculated that the R.100 would not leave Howden until 28 November, while a week later at the other end of the country the *Courier and Advertiser* in Dundee was confidently predicting that 3 December would be the day.

Finally, after another two weeks of waiting and increasing tension for all concerned, predictions from the meteorological office indicated that the blustery winds which had been present over northern England had at last subsided and that 16 December would be calm enough for the R.100 to finally leave her shed for the first time and make her maiden flight. The time to put Wallis's design to the test had finally arrived.

In the early hours of a frosty but clear December Monday, the normally quiet roads around Howden were crowded with vehicles and people. There were coaches and lorries taking the handling party of 500 soldiers from barracks at nearby York, Beverley and Pontefract to the aerodrome, and cars of both local and national reporters keen to record what had become a big media event. There were also the local residents, who had travelled by bicycle or foot from the surrounding villages, eager to be part of one of the biggest days the area had seen in living memory. As one local reporter had observed, the first of the sightseers had arrived at around 1.00 am and that 'at 6 o'clock there were thick clusters of people at many points of vantage'. Some local coach operators had even been offering tours to see the launch.

On its inaugural flight, the airship was to be flown by a crew, which had been appointed by the Air Ministry, and led by Squadron Leader Ralph Booth, assisted by First Officer Captain George Meager. Both were experienced airship pilots and had been at Howden for a number of months fully familiarising themselves with all aspects of the airship and its controls. Although Booth was officially captain of the airship, also on board was Major George Scott, Assistant Director of Airship Development (Flying), who was responsible for flying operations of the overall airship programme and had already piloted the R.101. In addition to the crew, the passengers consisted of two representatives from the Royal Airship Works, one from Rolls Royce (whose engines were being used on the airship), two from the Royal Aircraft Establishment at Farnborough and eight representatives from AGC, including Burney, Wallis and Norway. Wallis, who was now suffering from severe symptoms of stress, had moved temporarily into the Cairn Hydro Hotel in Harrogate. It was more luxurious than the cramped bungalow on the aerodrome, but he was still easily accessible when a decision about the date of the maiden flight was made. It is perhaps surprising that so many people with so much airship knowledge and experience were all travelling together on what was after all still a test flight. Wallis, recognising that this trip would not be without risk, had written his will the previous evening.

Many newspapers later carried reports from those who were at Howden that day to witness the launch of the R.100. Few, though, could have been more personally felt than the brief but vivid first-hand account Norway himself wrote over twenty years later:

'It was a wonderful, moonlit night, clear and frosty, without a cloud or a breath of wind. We opened the doors of the great shed for the last time, slunk into dark corners to keep clear of the reporters, and stayed waiting for the dawn. In the shed the crew were running their engines slowly to warm up.

The first light of dawn came at last, and at 7.15 we got on board through the control car in the growing light, and the ship was finally ballasted up. Then the order was given to walk the ship aft. A centre line had been painted on the floor and extended out on to the aerodrome and plumb bobs were suspended from the bow and stern; keeping her straight in this way the handling party walked her out. It was all over quickly. Inside the ship we could not see when the ship was clear of the shed, but a great cheer from the crowd told us when the bow had passed out on to the aerodrome.

There was very little to be done. Major Scott had her walked out to a safe distance from the shed, swung her round to point her away from it, and checked the ballasting again. I am told that her enormous silvery bulk was very beautiful in that misty blue December dawn. Scott completed his ballasting arrangements and climbed on board.

The take-off was simple. From the control car Booth emptied a half-ton bag of water ballast from the bow and another one from the stern and, leaning from one of the windows of the car, he shouted, 'Let her go'. Inside the ship we heard the cheers and saw the ground receding, and we set about our job of finding out our mistakes.'

There were no mistakes, and at 7.53 am on 16 December 1929, the R.100 finally left Howden, never to return. Once the airship had risen to about 500 feet, the engines were started. The silence was replaced by the drone of the propellers slowly moving the ship forward. The airship did a circuit of Howden while the crew became accustomed to its feel. This gave the vast crowd below a last chance to marvel at what was a great source of local pride. To them this was a Yorkshire airship. At a time of great economic difficulty, in which the manufacturing sectors of the North of England were suffering, the *Hull Daily Mail* captured the mood of many of the crowd:

> 'To us who have, literally speaking, seen the growth of the R.100 from a mere mass of tangled metal into a luxurious vessel, an object of pride and a monument to British craftsmanship, today is indeed one to be remembered… it reveals to the country, and will eventually reveal to the world, the fact that despite all this modern talk of lost skill and craftsmanship, the North can still use its hands and brains and produce, if need be, a creation which maintains past traditions and renews old-time envy.'

After spending about half an hour above Howden, the airship set a north-west course for York, where it did a circuit above York Minster before heading south to Cardington. Although Scott had originally planned a much more ambitious first flight, passing over major cities such as Sheffield and Leeds, he eventually settled for a shorter flight, probably keen to minimise the risks on what was the first time in the air for the R.100. The airship arrived at Cardington just after 11.00 am and was met by a large crowd, keen to see one of the symbols of the new era in civil aviation. Major Scott, who had decided to take over the responsibility for landing the airship, found that this was not straightforward, and it took a number of approaches before the airship was safely attached to the mooring tower. At 1.40 pm the maiden flight was over; the airship had been in the air for 5 hours 47 minutes. No difficulties had been encountered, apart from a minor problem with a ventilator in the outer cover and small mechanical issues with two of the engines. Although the airship had not been flown at maximum speed, Scott seemed pleased with the airspeed of up to 55 mph achieved using just four of the six engines and everybody was confident that it would be capable of the 70 mph specified in the contract.

The R.100's achievement was prominently reported in a host of national and local newspapers, with many containing impressive photographs of the airship in flight or tethered to the mooring mast at Cardington. Sadly though, not everybody got the credit they really deserved. *The Times* named the airship's designer as Mr V. N. Walles, while the *Daily Mirror* decided the designer was Sir Dennistoun Burney.

The following day, the R.100 made a second flight from Cardington around the London area. This was used to gain a greater understanding of the manoeuvrability of the airship, see how it performed at higher speeds, and check the fabric on the underside of the hull which had been seen flapping during the first flight. After 6 hours 49 minutes in the air the airship returned to the mooring tower, this time managing the docking operation in 32 minutes, although again not without some difficulty. The following day, the R.100 was disconnected from the mooring tower, pulled down to earth and guided into No. 2 Shed, next to her sister ship in No. 1 Shed. With the maiden flight over, Norway could at last take a proper break. It had been a busy five years, with periods of high stress, but he could now take a holiday with a sense of pride and great relief. The R.100, of which he was now a major part, had cleared its first hurdle, all in the spotlight of public gaze and without incident. He later remarked that the skiing holiday he took in Switzerland was in many ways the best of his life.

Wallis, who was exhausted, suffering from migraines and insomnia and, in danger of a nervous breakdown, also took a much needed break at his wife's family home in Hampstead. He was eager to move permanently to his new career in aeroplane design at Weybridge, but he was also concerned that the success of the R.100's first flights may result in this arrangement being altered or even terminated. However, he need not have worried. Sir Robert McLean was sure that in the event of AGC being awarded a contract to build further airships, others could found to implement the design principles which had been devised by Wallis. Therefore, on 1 January 1930 the contract to transfer Wallis to Vickers Aviation was signed, and his role as chief designer on the R.100 project effectively came to an end.

Under the conditions of the contract with the Air Ministry, the R.100 was required to successfully complete four flights of increasing duration, before undertaking a long-distance flight to India. In fact, by the end of May 1930, the R.100 had successfully completed six flights, clocking up a total of 110 flying hours. Burney and Norway were passengers on all of these flights. Although generally more than meeting expectations, there had been a problem with excessive forces on the tailpiece of the airship which resulted in the need for modification to the shape of the airship's tail. Somewhat surprisingly, these modifications were undertaken by staff at Cardington, who were now officially responsible for the airship, rather than the AGC staff at Howden, who had designed and built her. The airship sheds at Howden were now largely deserted. Most of the workers had been laid off, with a skeleton staff of designers being kept on, pending the outcome of the trials.

On 26 July, the newly modified R.100 completed a final 24-hour test flight and was now ready for its maiden long-distance flight, only the destination was now to be Montreal in Canada rather than India as originally intended. It had been decided by the Air Ministry that because the R.100 used petrol engines, rather than the diesel engines used by the R.101, the risk of fire in a hot climate was too great. If successful, the R.100 was now destined for use on colder transatlantic routes. For the present, the airship was ready for its first passenger flight across the Atlantic Ocean and back – a test of whether it really was a future ocean liner of the skies.

The R.100 left the mooring tower at Cardington at 3.45 am on 29 July, bound for Montreal. The departure had been delayed a little because of the reports of poor weather over the Atlantic Ocean. As with all her previous flights, the airship was under the command of Squadron Leader Ralph Booth. The command structure was again slightly complicated by the presence of Major George Scott, Assistant Director of Airship Development (Flying), on board. It was, however, agreed in writing prior to the flight that Scott would be acting in the capacity of an admiral, offering advice on matters such as the route, but that Booth would still be captain of the airship and not be bound to necessarily take any advice given.

In addition to the thirty-seven officers and crew, there were six passengers for this first overseas flight, very much below the capacity of one hundred. These included Burney and Norway, but not Wallis. Sir Robert McLean, who clearly had strong views about where Wallis's (and maybe the Company's) future lay, had overruled his wish to go on this trip, saying quite bluntly that 'Wallis could kill himself if he so wished, but in one of the aeroplanes he was going to build, not in this airship contraption'. It seemed that the Air Ministry were similarly cautious, as they required all passengers to sign an indemnity form stating that no claim for compensation would be made in the event of any accident or death! Somewhat surprisingly, given the opportunity that the trip would give for national and international publicity, there were no representatives of the press on board.

The Secretary of State for Air, perhaps wary of Burney's habit of looking for opportunities for publicity and making policy statements on the run, made it quite clear that 'Sir Dennis Burney is simply a representative of the board of the Airship Guarantee Company who has taken an active part in the construction of the R.100, but he has no official position or official backing of the Air Ministry'. He would not be allowed to make statements to the media while he was a passenger on the airship.

There was also no absence of entrepreneurial spirit among some of those on the flight. Reports suggested that someone was being paid by a dealer to carry one hundred philatelic covers, presumably for stamping in Montreal and resale back in England. Others, though, saw the flight across the Atlantic as a rare opportunity to further their research. Dr Dillon Weston, a mycologist from Cambridge University, was interested in knowing whether fungal spores could be carried across the Atlantic Ocean by the winds. To aid this research, Booth and members of the crew collected samples of spores in the atmosphere by simply holding a glass dish out of the window of the control car at three-hourly intervals

Norway kept a detailed diary of the airship's maiden international flight, which was published the following year in the *Journal of the Royal Aeronautical Society*. This gave a first-hand account of life on board during the three-day flight, illustrating some of the advantages and shortcomings of airship travel. Norway, who had reasonable experience of travelling by aeroplane, thought the comfort of the flight 'almost staggering'. Life on board seemed to be more like that on a cruise ship, with a cocktail party in the saloon, and the opportunity to 'sleep all night in bed, get up, shave in hot water, dress and eat a normal breakfast'. There were of course also some limitations, like the ban on smoking, the need for good heating and ventilation, and the condition of the lavatories towards the end of the flight! However, it was assumed that these could be overcome with further development. Burney also wrote an article on the R.100's flight to Canada, but this was very much a statement of personal opinion rather than a record of the flight. It concluded that while the R.100's flight had proved the concept and design, an airship of around twice the cubic capacity and higher top speed would be required for a transatlantic service to be commercially viable. There seemed to be little technical basis for these estimates, but as always Burney was looking to the future and trying to prepare the ground for his next big venture.

Nearing Montreal, the airship ran into severe winds and then a thunderstorm, exposing the limitations of the airship in poor weather conditions. At one point, the changes in the airship's normal serene stately progress was so sudden and great that the supper which had been laid out in the saloon 'shot off, down stairs, up the corridor, till some of it reached frame 2'. Of far greater concern, though, was the fact that what were by no means an unusual series of weather events during the flight had caused a number of large tears and holes in the airship's fabric, some of which had to be repaired during the flight. Norway described one hole in the airship's lower surface as being 'large enough to drive a bus through'.

The R.100 appeared in the sky over Montreal in the early hours of Friday 1 August, finally completing the docking process at 5.33 am. The flight of 3,353 miles had taken 78 hours 49 minutes, at an average speed of 45 mph. Although the flight had taken longer than expected, because of the need for in-flight repairs, changes of route and adverse weather conditions, it was still the best ever done by an airship and justified its reputation 'as the fastest airship as well as one of the two biggest airships in the world'.

The airship's arrival at St Hubert was a major national event, with VIPs and the media out in force. The 1 August edition of the *Montreal Gazette* was typical of the immense interest being shown, covering the event from every possible angle: from biographies of the officials and officers though to details of the menu on board and a large map of how to get to the R.100. Businesses were taking every opportunity to incorporate airships into their advertisements, and there were of course many companies offering tours to see the R.100 in comfort. At the aerodrome, hundreds of stalls selling food and memorabilia of every kind had appeared, from the usual badges and postcards to sheet music and records of commemorative songs – the R.100 was a big celebrity. A circus had even established itself just outside the aerodrome, keen to take advantage of the large crowds. It is estimated that 70,000 people came to see the R.100 on its first day in Montreal. The initial enthusiasm did not diminish, and over the next twelve days at least 600,000 people (approximately 6 per cent of Canada's population) came to see this new wonder of the modern age.

During the stay in Canada, Norway was kept very busy: organising repairs, taking special guests on tours of the airship, accompanying Burney to a series of meetings to discuss proposals for future schemes and fitting in sightseeing where he could. By the time he left for home on 13 August, he had gained a very positive view of Canada, writing with some feeling:

> 'I would have never had believed that after a fortnight's stay I should be so sorry to leave a country. I like this place; I like the way they go about things, and their vitality. The tremendous physical health of everyone. I am going home, and sorry to go; though I am leaving this country for a little time I cannot believe that I am leaving it for good.'

The R.100 left Canada on the evening of 13 August. The number of passengers for the return journey had grown from six to sixteen, with this time nine of them being from the press. The trip was certainly going to be well covered, but, because the flight was largely uneventful, after the initial enthusiasm for life on board, many struggled for things to write about. For instance, *The Times'* special correspondent used many column inches describing the food on board and the dramatic change in menu that occurred when a rainstorm caused the electricity on board to be switched off. Breakfast had gone from a luxury full English to sardines, bread and butter, and beer or lime juice and 'tea was a tragedy being tea without tea'. Since the flight going east was wind assisted, the R.100 docked at Cardington just before noon on 16 August, 57 hours 36 minutes after leaving Montreal. In contrast to the reception they had received in Canada, the welcome at Cardington was rather an anti-climax. Although Lord Thomson was there to lead the official welcoming party, the crowd was small, and Norway was disappointed. One possible reason for the small crowd may well have been that England were playing Australia at cricket that day at London's Kennington Oval, and Bradman, arguably one of the best cricketers of all time, was batting imperiously! The following day, the R.100 was taken down from the mooring tower and stored in the shed at Cardington. It would never fly again.

Back in its shed, the R.100 could now be properly examined to determine the effect the transatlantic crossing had on the airship. While the trip itself had been an undoubted success, particularly with the public in Canada, it had also highlighted some shortcomings in the airship's design and construction. The strength and durability of the outer covering was certainly a problem. The first officer of the R.101, Lieutenant Commander Noel Grabowsky-Atherstone, visited the R.100 shortly after her return from Canada and noted in his diary: 'Found a large hole in the outer cover at the bottom of the ship ... with three petrol tanks hanging out of it'. For his part, Norway was still enthusiastic about the potential for airships but acknowledged that the materials used, particularly the fabric covering, needed improving, and that to some extent in the flight to Canada they had 'got away with it'. On the positive side, the R.100 had certainly demonstrated its potential to provide a transatlantic passenger service, living up to its reputation as a cruise liner for the skies. After all, the aeroplane still did not seem to have anything like the ability to convey large passenger numbers non-stop over long distances in comfort. For the time being, the airship still had a future. What lay ahead for the R.100 and Norway himself now depended on the flight trials of its competitor.

During this period of waiting, Norway and what was left of the design team at Howden utilised their time examining potential improvements to their airship and considering alternative designs. It must have been difficult to remain motivated as nobody knew what the future would be once AGC's contract with the Air Ministry expired at the end of November.

In this time of uncertainty, Norway was sure of at least one thing: he was going to be married. On 13 September, *The Times* announced the engagement between Nevil S. Norway of the St Leonard's Club, York, and Frances Heaton, MB, BSc, of Bromley, Kent.

After a failed engagement and two unsuccessful proposals, it can only be imagined what had been going through Nevil's mind when he asked Frances to marry him. He was now 31 years old, and he came from a background in which it was often almost seen as an obligation to marry. Five years earlier, in a letter to Flora Twort following his first unsuccessful proposal to her, Nevil had talked of his keenness to have children, not because he was wanted to keep the family line going, but for the children themselves. He dreaded being a lonely bachelor in old age, and by then he was already sure that he would only marry for one thing – companionship.

Nevil and Frances were both independently minded people who had to some extent succeeded against the odds. They were from the same social class, liked flying and travel, and so on the face of it they looked a reasonable match. Of course only time would tell.

The 1930 Imperial Conference was scheduled to take place in London between 1 October and 14 November. This gathering of the government leaders of the Colonies and Dominions of the British Empire was an ideal opportunity to promote the Imperial Airship Scheme and, at a time of depression, seek financial support for its establishment. The Secretary of State for Air therefore intended to join the conference having just completed a successful flight to India and back in the R.101. It seems that as early as July 1930 he was insisting that the airship was ready for her flight to India by the last week of September. Most of those involved were conscious that failure to meet this deadline could put the future of the Imperial Airship Scheme, and maybe even their jobs, in jeopardy.

Although the R.101 had made its maiden flight two months before the R.100, it was in the shed undergoing major modifications at the time of the R100's flight to Canada. Right from the start, flight tests to the R.101 had shown that it was significantly overweight and under-powered, and therefore only capable of lifting a much smaller load than originally expected. Despite making every attempt to reduce its weight by removing any superfluous equipment and changing the gasbag harnessing system to allow the gasbags to be inflated to a larger volume, the disposable lift was still well below that required. In the end the drastic decision was taken to increase the lift of the airship by increasing its length by 45 feet so that an extra gasbag could be inserted. This was a major change to the design, which could possibly also have significant effects on the airship's handling, but the pressure was on to get the airship ready for an overseas flight.

The modifications to the R.101 were finished on 26 September, and a recommendation to issue a Permit to Fly obtained via telephone. On 1 October the newly extended airship left Cardington for its first and only test flight, as preparation for its flight to India. It can be questioned whether a 17-hour flight over the east of England, in good flying conditions without ever running the airship engines at full speed, was really adequate preparation for a long-distance flight in unstable weather and tropical conditions. *The Times* described the proposed trip to India as 'essentially an experimental flight with a new airship over new territory, assisted by a meteorological organisation which will be serving a long flight for the first time'. Nevertheless, the decision to go ahead with the flight to India was made, and two days later, early on a Saturday evening, the R.101 left its mooring mast at Cardington, cheered on by a crowd of around 3,000, and bound for India. Indicative of the fast pace at which things were moving, the Certificate of Airworthiness was only handed to the captain on the morning of the flight. The bureaucracy took rather longer to catch up. A note confirming that this had taken place was added to Air Ministry files on 13 October 1930 – nine days after the airship had crashed. The written report required to support the issuing of a Certificate of Air Worthiness, which the Air Ministry would have normally have used to inform its decision, was in fact never completed.

Surprisingly, given the fact that this was still in many ways very much a test flight, there was a small but elite group of twelve passengers on board. These included Lord Thomson, Secretary of State for Air; Sir Sefton Brancker, director of Civil Aviation; Major Percy Bishop, chief inspector of the Aeronautical Inspection Department, and the complete R.101 leadership team of Wing Commander Reginald Colmore, Major

George Scott, Lieutenant Colonel Vincent Richmond and Squadron Leader Michael Rope.

The flight did not begin smoothly; the departure had been slightly delayed by problems with a starter motor. The wind was beginning to gust with rain approaching. One journalist watching the departing airship thought it 'seemed strangely heavy and unwieldy' and 'did not rise as on each other occasion I have watched her cast off'. Nonetheless the airship made steady progress towards France and by 11.36 pm was crossing the French coast at Pointe de St Quentin, travelling towards Paris. At midnight, Cardington received a wireless message from the airship that all was going well: 'After an excellent supper our distinguished passengers smoked a final cigar, and having sighted the French coast have now gone to bed to rest after the excitement of their leave taking. All essential services are functioning satisfactorily. The crew have settled down to watch-keeping routine'. Unusually for a vessel containing so many large gasbags filled with extremely flammable hydrogen gas, the R.101 had a smoking room. The floor and ceiling of the room were made of asbestos and metal while the walls were the fabric used on the rest of the ship. This was not considered a hazard.

The airship reached the small city of Beauvais at around 2.00 am just as the watch was changing. The weather was stormy, and eyewitnesses later recalled that the airship appeared to be struggling in severe gusts of wind. However there were no communications from the airship's wireless operators to suggest that anything was wrong.

A few minutes later the airship suddenly started to dive, the change being so abrupt that crew were thrown off balance and furniture slid towards the front of the airship. This dive was corrected, but it was almost immediately followed by a second dive. This time it was not possible to recover, and a few seconds later the R.101 hit the ground just south of Beauvais. Almost immediately the airship burst into flames, and the fire quickly became an inferno fuelled by the hydrogen in the massive gasbags. All twelve passengers on board were killed, and only eight of the forty-two officers and crew survived, two of these dying of their injuries shortly afterwards. The R.101, one of the biggest and most luxurious airships in the world, which many had seen as the future of long-distance air travel, was now a smouldering skeleton of twisted metal in the countryside of northern France.

At around 6.00 am on Sunday 5 October, the prime minister, Ramsay MacDonald, who was staying at his country residence Chequers, was informed of the crash. He arranged to return to London straight away, to take charge of the aftermath of the disaster. The following day, most newspapers had blanket coverage of what was now being called Britain's worst air disaster. The Air Ministry announced that a public inquiry into the disaster would be set up immediately. There were published messages of sympathy from King George V and many leaders from around the world.

By Wednesday the bodies of the dead had been transported from Beauvais to Westminster Hall to lie in state. A steady procession of people passed by the draped coffins day after day, and by the time the doors of the Hall were closed after midnight on Saturday, it is estimated that over 90,000 people has paid their respects. The victims were honoured by a memorial service at St Paul's Cathedral on 10 October. The service was broadcast by the BBC, and the huge congregation included the Prince of Wales, relatives and personal friends of the deceased, the prime minister and members of the Cabinet, a host of foreign dignitaries, and representatives from public bodies and companies. While Sir Trevor Dawson was present representing the Vickers-Armstrong company, neither Burney, Wallis or Norway had been invited. At the same time as the memorial service at St Paul's Cathedral was being held, Catholics were holding their own requiem Mass at Westminster Cathedral, to mourn the four Catholic victims of the disaster.

Finally, on the morning of the 11 October there was a full ceremonial procession of the coffins from Westminster via Whitehall and the Strand to Euston Station. All along the route, large crowds had gathered to pay a last tribute to the dead, as the procession, which was almost two miles long, passed by – a solemn Nevil Norway was one of these onlookers. The coffins were then taken by train to Bedford, before being transported to the small village cemetery of St Mary's church at Cardington for burial with full military honours in a common grave. The following year, a memorial tomb was erected at the burial site inscribed with the names of the forty-eight victims. The official mourning was over. It was now time to focus on the causes of the disaster, and the effect that this would have on the future of airships.

A public inquiry into the causes of the R.101 disaster, led by Sir John Simon, opened just over three weeks after the crash on 28 October. It sat for a total of thirteen days until 5 December, interviewing forty-two witnesses, including all six survivors. Nobody from AGC was called as a witness, but Norway later admitted it was doubtful if anyone from the Company could have contributed much to the inquiry.

As far as the future of the R.100 and its design team was concerned, the news was not good. Burney had meetings with the Air Ministry in late October to try and agree a future development plan and secure funding. There was now a new Air Member for Supply and Research, Air Vice-Marshall Hugh Dowding. One of his first decisions in his new role had been to recommend the issuing of a Certificate of Air Worthiness for the R.101's trip to India. In later years he was to say that this was a decision he regretted and that he should have insisted on more extensive tests before issuing the Certificate. Dowding now made it clear to Burney that AGC would receive no more money until the results of the inquiry were known and the government had made a decision regarding future airship policy. With no new funding possible, Burney had little alternative but to inform Norway that as from 30 November AGC would cease operations and that all staff would lose their jobs. Norway made one last attempt to keep the design team together by advertising their services overseas, but this came to nothing. On 11 December, the R.100 was deflated and stored in the shed at Cardington until a decision could be made about her future.

Sir John Simon's Report on the R.101 Inquiry was published at the end of March 1931. The Inquiry concluded that the immediate cause of the disaster was a sudden loss of gas from gasbags in the front of the airship, probably as a result of a large tear in the outer covering at the top of the airship. There was no criticism of any individual, although, touching on areas on which Norway was later to express even stronger views, he observed that 'It is impossible to avoid the conclusion that the R.101 would not have started for India on the evening of October 4 if it had not been that reasons of public policy were considered as making it highly desirable for her to do so if she could'.

The prime minister made a statement to the House of Commons on 14 May 1931 on future airship policy, and although a proposal to continue the development of airships was agreed, by August this had been reversed as part of cuts proposed in a National Economy Bill.

At a Cabinet meeting on 31 August 1931, it was reluctantly agreed that in order for the Air Ministry to achieve economies asked of them, airship R.100 would be scrapped and the Royal Airship Works at Cardington closed. An airship which had cost around £450,000 (equivalent to £25 million in 2016) to develop, and which had at one time been a proud symbol of the future of long-distance air travel, was finally broken up and sold as scrap for just £450 (equivalent to £25,000 in 2016).

Norway, perhaps closing his part in what he later described as 'the airship venture', wrote to *The Times* on 17 November putting on record what he saw as the many achievements of the R.100 and concluding that 'it is a great pity that she had to go'. Government development of airships had finally come to an end. Norway was later to say that 'the decision to abandon development was right, though whether it was taken for the right reasons I rather doubt'. Although it could not have been foreseen at the time, it would not be many years before the rapid development of the aeroplane would have made the airship obsolete.

At the end of November 1930, Nevil Norway found himself unemployed. He had come a long way in the last six years, and although he could probably have found some alternative employment in the aviation industry, he was not that keen to return to a lower level position or the drawing office. He enjoyed making decisions and managing, but the country was still in an economic depression and so companies offering opportunities such as this were rare. He had been aware for some months that AGC did not have a future, and so he had already started thinking of what to do next. Now though, he had not only himself, but also a future wife to consider.

6

Entrepreneur
December 1930 – April 1938

December 1930 was not a good time to be without a job in Britain. There were nearly two and a half million unemployed and this would get worse over the next few years, particularly in key industries such as heavy engineering and manufacturing. Nevil Norway had just spent six years of his life gaining experience in an airship industry which the government would effectively close in the coming year. His prospects certainly did not look promising.

At the beginning of 1930, George V was in the twentieth year of his reign, but neither Britain nor its Empire were what they had once been. Domestically the country was in crisis. Having struggled with the economic consequences of the Great War, the Wall Street Crash in America in October 1929 now added further difficulties. Exports, which had already been declining with increased competition from other parts of the world, fell further and more dramatically. Sectors such as coal, steel, textiles and shipbuilding, which for so long had been the backbone of industrial Britain, were now producing products that few in a globally depressed world wanted. With exports down, unemployment up and growth in gross domestic product negative, the country was in recession.

The rapid rise in unemployment did not affect all industries equally. Traditional sectors suffered most, and as a result the North, Midlands and Wales were hit badly in comparison to the South of the country. For instance, by 1931, unemployment in the shipbuilding, cotton and iron and steel industries was 51.9 per cent, 43.2 per cent and 45.5 per cent respectively. With no other employment options, and few opportunities to reskill or relocate, many breadwinners in the family were facing a bleak future. Whole regions of the country were plunged into poverty, from which it would take years to recover.

In comparison London and the south-east of England suffered less badly, with unemployment around 12 per cent. This may well have been because many of the newer industries such as cars, chemicals, electricity and, importantly for Nevil Norway, aviation were predominately located in this part of the country.

Given the dire state of the economy, it is perhaps not surprising that many of the New Year messages for 1931 were gloomy. The prime minister, Ramsay MacDonald, called for the need for goodwill to get through critical times, while *The Times* predicted that 'the one fact about 1931 which is already certain is that it is bound to be a year of difficulties'. MacDonald's Labour government had come to office in June 1929, although as a minority government and needing the support of Lloyd George's Liberal Party to pass legislation. The Labour Party had pledged in its election manifesto to 'deal immediately and practically with unemployment'. Whatever the government's plans, they had little immediate effect, as unemployment continued to rise throughout 1930.

By January 1931 the Cabinet were already admitting that proposed schemes such as the introduction of relief work would be unlikely to have much of an effect on unemployment numbers because of the rate at which they were growing. They now did not believe that any government would be able to reduce unemployment for at least twelve to eighteen months. The patience of large numbers of Labour's core voters was being sorely tested. Many were beginning to draw analogies with 1914 and calling for a government of national unity in order to deal with the crisis that the country was facing. While this may have been an unreasonable comparison, 1931 would turn out to be a pivotal year in the country's economic history.

In the six years that Norway had been absorbed with airship design and development, both the aeroplane and the aeroplane manufacturing industry had also moved on. By 1930, in spite of the Depression, aeroplane manufacturing in Britain was beginning to grow again. While the military still played a significant part in many companies' order books, civil aviation and private owners were now becoming increasingly important markets.

Commercial civil aviation had experienced a stumbling start after the war, with fledgling companies unable to attract enough passenger traffic throughout the year to support a viable operation, even with state subsidies. Finally, the government decided that if Britain were to have a commercial airline it would need to be bigger and seriously subsidised by the state. As a result, in March 1924, four private airlines had been merged to form Imperial Airways, a private monopoly with a state subsidy guaranteed for ten years. Soon, Imperial Airways had one of the largest route networks in the world, carrying passengers, mail and freight to a wide range of destinations in Europe and the outer reaches of the Empire.

Despite the growth in passenger numbers, the chairman of Imperial Airways still firmly believed that airmail was the priority for the company. Not surprisingly, the aeroplanes used by the airline, such as the Handley Page HP42 biplane, were built for load-carrying capacity rather than speed, and technologically were not much of an improvement on the Handley Page bombers that had been used in the First World War. In comparison, overseas airlines such as TWA and KLM would soon introduce modern monoplanes such as the Douglas DC-2. Such aeroplanes would make the biplanes and flying boats being used by Imperial Airways seem like something from another age.

At the beginning of 1930 there were twenty-six aeroplane manufacturers in Britain and the number of people employed in the industry had grown to 20,000. The next decades were to be one of stability for this industry; indeed, 'no major firms left aircraft or engine production between the mid-1920s and the 1950s'. It was, though, also very difficult for new entrants to join, as Air Ministry contracts could only be bid for by companies on the approved list.

Norway's first employer de Havilland was a good example of the trials and tribulations faced by a company focusing on new markets. By the early 1930s they employed around 1,500 people and produced a range of aircraft from the D.H.66 Hercules seven-passenger airliner, which had been built for Imperial Airways and West Australian Airways, to the iconic single-engine D.H.60G Gipsy Moth, which became a great favourite of private owners and flying clubs. As was common at that time, most aircraft designs for the civil sector were bespoke for specific applications or owners and did not often result in big production runs. De Havilland had associated companies in Australia, Canada, India and South Africa, a well-established flying school and had just moved to a new aerodrome at Hatfield. Even so, the Company was still struggling to break even, and at the annual general meeting in 1930 it reported that for the first time in its history it would be reducing the dividend paid to shareholders. De Havilland was in no way unique in the problems it was facing in what was a worldwide recession, and as the chairman noted somewhat bitterly, 'we have had a long period now of depression in business, and although during that period much discussion by politicians and others has taken place as to the most likely remedies, England is still suffering as much from lack of policy and uncertainty as to future plans as anything else'. If companies such as de Havilland were finding things difficult, then starting a new aeroplane manufacturing business was certainly not for the faint-hearted. However, this is exactly what Nevil Norway and Hessell Tiltman were planning to do.

Norway had advanced significantly in experience and responsibility during his time on the R.100 project, and as he later wrote, he 'had become a big frog in a little puddle, too big a frog to be easily absorbed back into the aeroplane industry as it was in those days'. He was keen to start his own aircraft manufacturing company, and he found a willing partner for this venture in Hessell Tiltman.

Alfred Hessell Tiltman was eight years older than Norway, and they had known each other since Norway had joined Airco as an unpaid undergraduate during the summer of 1920. Hessell Tiltman preferred to be known by his middle name, probably in order to avoid confusion with his father, also Alfred Hessell. Like Norway, he came from a middle-class background in which education was important. However, unlike Norway, it was a household in which finances were far more of a problem. His father was an architect, whose practice seems to have struggled for many years before his early death in 1910. His younger brother John had been offered a place at Oxford University when he was only 13 but could not take this up because of the change in the family's financial circumstances following his father's death. John Tiltman would however go on to develop a highly successful career in military intelligence in both Britain and the United States, achieving the rank of brigadier and being described 'as the greatest cryptanalyst of his time'.

Hessell Tiltman could also not afford to attend university full-time and so had to take whatever opportunities were available, while working, to advance his education. This included part-time study at Coventry Technical College and Montreal Technical Institute. He eventually completed a BSc in Engineering with the University of London as an external student in 1919.

After a short spell with the Daimler Company, in 1911 he left England for Canada, where he joined the St Lawrence Bridge Company. They had been awarded a contract to construct a bridge across the St Lawrence River near Quebec, following the disastrous collapse of the first design in 1907. He joined the design team, gaining experience of the design of steel structures. This second design was also not without its problems, thirteen men being killed when a span of the bridge gave way in 1916. When it was finally completed, the St Lawrence Bridge was the longest cantilever bridge in the world.

Following the outbreak of war, Tiltman returned to England. Being unfit for military service, he joined Edward Wood and Company, a firm specialising in the design of iron and steel structures. Then, in 1916, he took his experience of structural design into the aircraft manufacturing industry by joining the design office of Airco at Hendon. When Geoffrey de Havilland formed his own company in 1921, although still only 30, Tiltman was invited to join the new venture as an assistant designer. He stayed at de Havilland for eight years, before following in Norway's footsteps and joining the Airship Guarantee Company in October 1929. By this time, the R.100 project was nearing its end, and for these last months he took on the responsibility for running the drawing office and acting as chief designer.

By 1930 he had accumulated twenty years' experience in structural design, with nearly half of that being in the aviation industry. He now also had a reputation for meticulous and elegant design, Norway describing Tiltman's designs as 'both beautiful and efficient'. It seemed that combining Norway's management experience and his experience of flying many different types of small aeroplane with Tiltman's design flair would be just what was needed to lead the new company.

Though AGC did not effectively shut down its operations until the end of October 1930, Norway and Tiltman had already been discussing and planning starting a new company for a few months before this. In fact, in Tiltman's case, he had been thinking about branching out on his own as early as 1928.

Like all new companies they needed three things: a product to sell, a board of directors and financial backing. As far as the product was concerned, Norway and Tiltman had identified the small two- or three-seater aeroplane aimed at the private owner and flying club as the best starting option. Such aircraft were still generally made from wood and so did not require expensive tools and equipment, or a high capital cost to produce. They estimated that £40,000 would be sufficient to finance the start-up of such an activity.

Therefore, on 22 October 1930, Tiltman had written to Sir Alan Cobham, whom he had known since his days at Airco, telling him about the probable demise of AGC and the light aeroplane scheme that he and Norway were proposing. He asked for assistance, though was not very specific about what that assistance might be. A fortnight later he followed this up by sending a general arrangement drawing and sketches to show the versatility of the biplane AS.3 they were proposing.

At the same time, Norway, who was still living in York, made contact with Lord Grimthorpe, a Yorkshire landowner, banker and racehorse breeder. Ralph Beckett, the 3rd Baron Grimthorpe, was a director of the Leeds Bank, Beckett and Company and chairman of the custom coachwork builders, Eustace Watkins Ltd. He had a good knowledge of the financial and manufacturing sectors and was well placed to suggest potential backers for the new company. More importantly, he was interested in aviation. A keen private pilot, he most likely first met Norway through the Yorkshire Aeroplane Club of which he was then the president.

Lord Grimthorpe agreed to invest £3,000 in the new company and take on the role of chairman once it was formed. Despite numerous letters from Tiltman (many handwritten in the distinctive green ink he often used, and on AGC headed notepaper!). Cobham seemed reluctant to formally commit to the company. Finally, on 7 December 1930, in order to try and force a decision on the matter, Norway wrote to Cobham formally offering him a directorship on the board of the as yet unnamed new company, suggesting a payment of 2½ per cent of gross profits for his services. Still this did not bring a decision. The initial optimism of Norway and Tiltman was now beginning to fade; obtaining financial backing was proving to be very hard indeed.

Norway was still living at the St Leonard's Club in York but spending a lot of time in different parts of the country following up leads for finance. It was hard and dispiriting work as most meetings came to nothing. In the evenings, he continued to write, and during the winter of 1930 he started work on what would become his third published novel, *Lonely Road*.

While Norway continued the search for financial support and premises for the new company, Tiltman was reassessing the options of what the first product should be, maybe in an attempt to increase the interest of potential backers. In his mind there were three choices: to continue with the biplane as originally planned, to redesign the biplane as a monoplane, or to buy an existing design from another company. After a detailed analysis, it was decided to continue with the original option.

The year 1931 started on a positive note, as, after a great deal of persistence from Norway and Tiltman, Sir Alan Cobham finally agreed to join the company as a director. His apparent reluctance to make a decision may well have been due more to the number of projects Cobham was developing at the time, rather than any worry about the feasibility of Norway and Tiltman's proposal. Norway now began working even harder, starting the development of a company prospectus, while continuing the search for finance. The company now also had a name – Airspeed Limited. Norway had wanted an impersonal name beginning with A, so that it would appear near the front of trade directory listings. It was Tiltman's wife Miriam who came up with the suggestion of Airspeed.

Cobham also suggested that the company should seriously consider adding gliders to its product list. He believed there would be a great expansion in gliding as a hobby in the coming years, and as a product it would be cheap to produce and help get the company's name known among the aviation community. Tiltman therefore started on the design of a high-performance glider, the AS.1 Tern.

During the early part of 1931, Norway and his fiancée experienced moments of both extreme sadness and extreme happiness. On 14 February, Frances' younger brother Arthur committed suicide by walking in front of a train on the Southern Railway main line near his home in Bromley. Frances had to endure both a coroner's inquest and a funeral just three weeks before her planned wedding.

However, on 7 March the wedding went ahead, and Nevil Shute Norway married Frances Mary Heaton at the parish church in Bromley. Although Frances was working and living in York, Bromley was where her parents lived and so for all intents and purposes was still her family home. The newly married couple left for a honeymoon in Switzerland with Nevil taking with him calculations needed to support the design of the new Tern glider. The pressures of starting a new company and finding an income were beginning to mount, and not even a honeymoon could get in the way. As if that were not enough, Frances broke a bone in her ankle, and so the new bride spent part of her honeymoon partially incapacitated.

Now that he was married, Norway could of course no longer continue to live at the St Leonard's Club, so on their return to England, Mr and Dr Norway rented a flat at 7 Clifton in York, both close to where Frances worked and to Airspeed's recently acquired offices in Piccadilly Chambers. It had long been decided that the new company would initially be located in Yorkshire, though at one stage Hull rather than York had been a possibility. Of the prospective members of the board, only Cobham was really well known outside of the area.

Finally, on 13 March 1931, Airspeed Limited was officially registered as a public company and a formal prospectus issued to raise finance. The company was now seeking nominal capital of £50,000 in £1 shares, with at least £7,700 required for the company to trade. The minimum five directors required by law were named as Lord Grimthorpe, Sir Alan Cobham, A. E. Hewitt, Norway and Tiltman. Hewitt, a well-known local solicitor in York who Norway had met through the St Leonard's Club, was also appointed the company solicitor. The closing date for subscriptions was set as 25 April. As far as roles within the company were concerned, Grimthorpe was made chairman, while Norway and Tiltman became joint managing directors – an unusual arrangement which is often resisted by organisations because it does not make clear who has ultimate responsibility for decisions. However, in this case their individual roles soon evolved to suit their skills and personality. Norway, with his determined nature and appetite for risk, was soon taking the lead as far as all business matters were concerned while Tiltman's more meticulous nature and natural artistic ability was better suited to lead on the design side. Tiltman somewhat modestly later stated that 'Norway was the inspiration behind all of this, I merely trailed along behind him; he had infinite imagination and courage'. However, without Tiltman's elegant and imaginative designs, Norway would have had no product to sell. While it had been a lot harder to attract interest in the new company than they had initially expected, it was hoped that now a final prospectus had been issued, things would improve.

The local press in Yorkshire were more optimistic, with the *The Yorkshire Post* on 24 March confidently stating 'Aircraft Works for York'. However, the text below the headline illustrated much of the uncertainty that still existed, with phrases like 'definite prospect that aircraft manufacture will be commenced at York', 'at present the Company have not yet definitely selected the site of their factory' and 'when the business expands ... it is hoped to acquire a site for an aerodrome in the neighbourhood'.

At one of the new company's first board meetings on 17 April, Cobham mentioned an idea he had to establish an Aviation Day enterprise. This would tour the country giving as many people as possible the chance to experience the joys of flying. In order to support this he was looking for a ten-passenger airliner, which would be suitable for use in small fields, provide good views for all passengers and be easy to maintain. He was proposing to order two of these aeroplanes from Airspeed if they could produce designs which met his requirements.

While such offers were of course welcome, there were more immediate problems. It was soon clear that the public subscription was a disaster, and that by the end of April they had only received applications of around £6,000. This was below the minimum subscription required and certainly not enough to support the development of a powered aeroplane.

The Tern glider now became a priority, even if for no more of a reason than to give the struggling company some breathing space. The assumption was that if they could produce a good product in the Tern, this would generate more interest and the capital investment needed to produce a powered aeroplane. In a letter to Cobham on 22 April, Norway was clearly becoming anxious about this strategy, noting, 'I am a little uneasy that the further capital might not be as easy to find as we have thought, and I think we must have some pretty definite prospects of the additional capital required – about £10,000 – to put towards the meeting on Tuesday'. In reality they had few alternatives but to keep going and hope for better things.

Following the failure of the initial public offering, they formally applied to the Register of Companies to operate with a lower authorised working capital than had been specified in the prospectus, finalised an agreement to rent part of a vacant bus garage in York, employed staff and started construction of the AS.1 Tern glider. Airspeed Limited was now in business, but only just.

Cobham was good to his word, and in June he placed a formal order for two 10-passenger airliners. Norway estimated that the difference between the cost of construction and the agreed contract price was only about £250 per aeroplane, so there would not be a great profit in this order. In addition, the aeroplanes had to be ready for the opening of Cobham's National Aviation Day enterprise in mid-April 1932. This was an extremely tight schedule, but at least it was work and would give them experience of designing and building a powered aeroplane, and hopefully it would enhance the reputation of the company in its intended market. Tiltman duly started work designing a three-engine, ten-passenger biplane which would meet Cobham's requirements. The essential characteristics of the design was summed up 'as having a large cabin and small petrol tank'. Airspeed's second product, the AS.4 Ferry was underway.

Meanwhile, the first Tern glider was completed in early August, and after a number of test flights a programme to attract publicity by attempting to break a number of British gliding records was devised. Typical of this was the flight from Stoupe Brow, Ravenscar to the beach at Scarborough on 24 August which broke the record for the longest flight made by a British-built glider – although admittedly this was still only a distance of fifteen miles in thirty-eight minutes. Such events drew good crowds, and the increased publicity also attracted high-profile reviews of the new company in respected industry journals such as *Flight*. However, although the number of small investors in Airspeed increased, the expected surge in orders for the Tern did not materialise. While not particularly cheap at £248, it seemed the market for high-performance gliders that Cobham had anticipated was just not yet there.

In the end only two gliders were sold, with parts of a third being sold unfinished. While they did not expect to make much money from manufacturing gliders, Norway later described the few they did build as 'a dead loss'. Although at the time it seemed that the work on gliders had been wasted, the successful development of Airspeed Horsa during the Second World War would show that this was not in fact the case.

Despite the massive workload involved in trying to establish a new company, and with a new wife, Norway still continued to write in the evenings. In many ways this must have been a strange experience for Frances. After working all day, for her new husband to shut himself away and write for a few hours three or four nights a week would perhaps not seem the most obvious way for their married life to begin.

With the completion of *Lonely Road* in the summer of 1931, Norway finally decided to stop writing novels for the foreseeable future. The pressure of work was now intense, the lack of money to support the business was a constant problem and at times it was a battle just to keep the company afloat. There were of course four other directors, but as the managing director responsible for business development, Norway took much of this stress. He felt an obligation to all those who had invested in the company (including family and friends), as well as to those they now employed, to put all his energy into trying to make Airspeed a success. The overdraft at the bank was still growing, and the fledging company's future was still far from certain. With the AS.4 Ferry off the drawing board, Norway and Tiltman now had to immediately start thinking about what the next product could be.

While considering the idea of a monoplane for five or so passengers suitable for the growing small airline market, Tiltman read about the Model 9 Orion which had recently been introduced by Lockheed in America. This fast single-engine wooden monoplane could carry up to six passengers and had a retractable undercarriage, allowing a faster top speed and increased fuel efficiency. It was the first airliner in the world to have such a feature. Norway was convinced that Airspeed had to display similar innovation if it was to survive. The reliable Tiltman quickly came up with a design for an elegant single-engine low-wing monoplane, capable of carrying five passengers and with a top speed of 150 mph. It had a retractable undercarriage but this did not retract fully, allowing the aeroplane to land with the undercarriage still up in an emergency. Airspeed's third product, the AS.5 Courier, had been born. The year ended with Airspeed Limited still in existence, but with its outlook far from secure. Norway would soon have even more to think about, though, as Frances was now pregnant, with a baby expected the following May.

The spring of 1932 saw the publication of Nevil Shute's third novel *Lonely Road*. As with his two previous books, it was published in the United Kingdom by Cassell and Company. However, this time Ronald Watt managed to secure a contract with a different American publisher, William Morrow and Company in New York. This was the beginning of a long and happy working relationship, as Morrow would remain the American publisher of Nevil Shute's novels for the rest of his life.

Understandably, while learning his trade Shute had stuck to subject matter he felt comfortable with. In *Lonely Road* he finally started to break away from the aviation theme that had been so prominent in his previous novels. Set in the 1930s, *Lonely Road* is centred around what was a topical subject at that time: politics and the potential for a communist uprising in Britain. However, this novel was far more than a standard comic-book style espionage story with an overlying romance. The central character, Commander Malcolm Stevenson, is a lonely and bitter man, obsessed with a tragedy of the past, while the heroine Mollie, who offers an unexpected chance of happiness, dies from wounds sustained while helping him to foil a gun smuggling operation. The hero settles scores with those he believes responsible for Mollie's death before resuming his lonely life, ahead of his own early death. A pessimistic novel, it reflects the disillusionment and lack of hope that so many people were experiencing in Britain at that time. Many believe this was the first novel to really show Shute's emerging powers as a compelling storyteller. As far as reviews were concerned, in Britain these were again confined to the regional newspapers. Typical of these was the *Aberdeen Press and Journal*, which in a positive review noted that 'with the action of the thriller and realism of the character study – that "Lonely Road" is in a class practically by itself'. On the other side of the Atlantic, Morrow had managed to get the novel reviewed by none other than *The New York Times*. While they thought the ending of the book the weakest part, they also concluded that 'Mr.

Shute writes in a simple austere style that harmonizes perfectly with the rather pleasing melancholy of the tale, and his characters are etched with a delicate and discerning hand'. It seemed that the part-time novelist was beginning to be noticed.

Back at Airspeed, the first AS.4 Ferry was complete and ready for its test flight in March 1932. It had taken only nine months to move from Tiltman's concept to a finished aeroplane. This was a remarkable achievement given that at the same time Norway and Tiltman were still assembling the nuts and bolts of the company, building an organisational structure and of course looking for more work.

The testing of the AS.4 Ferry was a critical hurdle in the company's survival. With no other orders on the books at that time, failure would have been catastrophic. Testing took place on 5 April at Sherburn-in-Elmet Aerodrome, still the home of Norway's local flying club. The Yorkshire Aeroplane Club also provided another service, its chief pilot. Captain Harry Worrall was employed for the day to test the aeroplane, since at that stage Airspeed's resources did not stretch to being able to afford a full-time pilot. Fortunately all went well, and on being granted a Certificate of Airworthiness, Airspeed's first powered aeroplane (Registration G-ABSI) joined Cobham's National Aviation Day touring show in early May. The second aeroplane was delivered a month later. The AS.4 Ferry proved to be perfectly suited to the needs of Cobham's air show, and by the end of the tour's first season in October the two aeroplanes had provided the experience of flying to 92,000 passengers – without a single fatality. The National Aviation Day toured Great Britain from April to October for four years, typically visiting a new town nearly every day. Cobham estimated that by the end of the venture they had given over 12,000 air displays and carried over a million passengers on joyrides. While the sale of two AS.4 Ferries to Cobham was not a great success financially, the promotion that the Airspeed name received from National Aviation Days was priceless. Two more AS.4 Ferries were eventually built for Midland and Scottish Air Ferries. However, like many of the small national airlines at that time they did not stay in business very long. The AS.4 Ferry had been designed to meet the very specific needs of the National Aviation Day tours, and was therefore less well suited to more general applications. Very soon, other aeroplane manufacturers were producing passenger aeroplanes that were more attractive to small airlines. The AS.4 Ferry had helped keep Airspeed afloat in the short term, but it had no long-term future.

By early May, Cobham had submitted a provisional order for an AS.5 Courier, but in order to keep the company afloat they needed other business. One such venture was the construction of an aeroplane for the design partnership of William Shackleton and Lee Murray, who, like Norway and Tiltman, were trying to start an aeroplane company, but as Tiltman observed they 'were more interested in selling than in building'. This short-lived collaboration resulted in the Shackleton-Murray SM.1, a two-seater monoplane aimed at the private flying club market. Just one aeroplane was ever built, and it was the only time that Airspeed built aeroplanes that they had not designed themselves.

Again the Norways experienced the full range of human emotion in the summer of 1932. On 31 May, Nevil became a father for the first time with the birth of his daughter Heather Felicity. Less than a month later, on 11 June, he experienced the other end of the life cycle with the death of his mother Mary Louisa Norway at the age of 71. In many ways the least publicly known member of the Norway family, her published memories of the Sinn Féin rebellion clearly illustrated not only her strong character but also her unflinching support for her husband and Nevil.

Even though Airspeed was still in its infancy, it was soon very clear that the use of half a bus garage as a location for manufacturing was far from ideal. Tiltman and his new assistant A. E. Ellison (an old colleague from de Havilland) were working in a single room on the other side of town, while the testing of any aeroplanes meant a trip by road to a local aerodrome. Such an arrangement would clearly not support any serious growth, and so, almost immediately after the formation of the company, Norway began the search for new premises. By September 1932 he had secured an agreement to move Airspeed to a newly opened municipally owned aerodrome at Portsmouth. The local council were keen to attract new business to the area and so offered Airspeed very generous terms. They proposed building a large new factory, with 14,000 square feet floor area, for an upfront payment of only £1,000 and a nominal ground rent, with the balance payable over ten years. For a company with very limited finances, this offer was just too good to turn down; Airspeed Ltd was beginning its transformation from a somewhat makeshift affair to a properly equipped aeroplane manufacturing company.

In the spring of 1933, Airspeed moved to its new factory at Portsmouth Aerodrome. Although the company had bright new premises, money was still a problem, and so while employees willing to move south would keep their job, there was no money available to pay removal or travelling expenses. By that stage Airspeed had about one hundred employees, half of whom decided to move to Portsmouth. The company was now at last all under one roof, and work could continue on the AS.5 Courier, which was now near completion.

The Norways also moved south. Leaving their flat in York, they found a house more appropriate for a family in the small town of Bishop's Waltham. Unfortunately, it seems this did not suit them, since within a few months they had moved again, this time to a house in Craneswater Park, Southsea. Their new home was pleasantly situated only a short walk to the sea front and around a mile away from the new company. Though now not writing on a regular basis, Norway occasionally wrote short stories, most of which were never published. An exception to this was 'The Airship Venture', a short story which, although very much a factual account, was published under the name of Nevil Shute in the monthly *Blackwood's Magazine* in May 1933. This told the story of the R.100, and it began to show the maturing of a style which would become so familiar in his future novels. Much of this story was to be reused forty years later in his autobiography *Slide Rule*. By then he was not afraid to express strong personal opinions on the shortcomings of the Imperial Airship Scheme.

At Airspeed, the test flight of the first AS.5 Courier had taken place from Portsmouth Aerodrome in early April. The advanced design had generated a lot of interest, with the increase in top speed that could be achieved with a retractable undercarriage being clearly demonstrated. The board of Airspeed underlined its faith in the new design by sanctioning the construction of six more AS.5 Couriers, although a further purchase of shares by the chairman and a number other shareholders was needed to ensure that the cash flow was there to support such a move.

Cobham had ordered an AS.5 Courier for a heavily advertised, proposed non-stop flight to Australia, which would utilise an in-flight refuelling technique he was developing. Originally planned for 1933, this was eventually rescheduled to 1934, with the destination being changed from Australia to India.

December 1933 ended on a positive note for both Norway and Airspeed. On 12 December he was elected a Fellow of the Royal Aeronautical Society. Still not quite 35, this was a significant recognition of achievement by his peers. Tiltman was also elected a Fellow at the same time. More importantly for the future of Airspeed, the company was admitted to the Society of British Aircraft Constructors as an associate member. While only full members had the right to bid for government contracts, this was a further step along the road to respectability for Airspeed. However, another end of year financial loss certainly helped to keep everybody's feet on the ground.

As it turned out, 1934 was to be a pivotal year in the life of Airspeed. Money was still the major issue, and despite the advances the company was making technologically, the overdraft kept increasing. Tiltman had started on the design of a larger two-engine version of the AS.5 Courier, which was to become the AS.6 Envoy. However, without a further cash injection into the company it was considered unlikely that any further developments would be possible. After discussions with a number of potential partners, an agreement was finally reached with Swan Hunter and Wigham Richardson Ltd, the long-established Tyneside shipbuilders. Like many shipbuilders in Britain, they were a big organisation facing uncertainties in their traditional markets and looking for a foothold in one of the new industries. Norway and his fellow directors were faced with a dilemma; on the positive side, Swan Hunter and Wigham Richardson were able to offer solid financial stability to Airspeed, but in return they would have the controlling interest in an industry they knew little about – in effect it was a takeover.

The directors of Airspeed Ltd finally agreed, and on 24 July the prospectus for a new company, Airspeed (1934) Ltd, was published, with the old company going into voluntary liquidation. The preparation of the prospectus had not been without stress or drama. Not only did Norway have to take most of the responsibility for its preparation, but he also had to try and ensure that Airspeed's prospects and assets were valued at the highest price possible. In many ways he had to curb his natural ability to tell a story, aware that there was a fine line between the boundless optimism so often associated with the founder of a new company and misleading potential investors. The penalties for crossing this line could be severe, and Norway himself later admitted that he was beginning to gain a reputation for 'reckless and unscrupulous optimism that came close to dishonesty'.

The new company would now have eight directors, with the five Airspeed directors being joined by three nominees of Swan Hunter and Wigham Richardson. Lord Grimthorpe would remain chairman, Cobham would become a director of sales, while Norway and Tiltman would keep their jobs as joint managing directors for five years on a salary of £1,000 per year plus 5 per cent of profits. Although the new company would acquire all Airspeed's assets, it would also take responsibility for their liabilities. The share offer was expected to raise £78,000 and unlike Airspeed's first efforts was well oversubscribed. Clearly, the city set great store in the interest taken by Swan Hunter and Wigham Richardson.

After the subscription was closed, Norway found himself in the newspaper headlines for the wrong reasons. An irregularity had been found in the issue of allotment letters, and although Norway and all others in the company were ultimately found to be innocent of wrongdoing, the experience of the care that was needed when preparing a company prospectus and dealing with financial markets remained with him and provided material for his next novel.

On 22 September 1934, Alan Cobham's long-proposed, non-stop, long-distance flight finally began. However, recent interest from both the Royal Aircraft Establishment and Royal Air Force in this venture had resulted in the destination being changed from Australia to Karachi, India. While the in-flight refuelling technique was successfully demonstrated, the attempt had to be eventually abandoned at Malta because of a simple problem with the aeroplane's throttle. In addition to the frustration of not being able to complete the flight, Cobham also suffered a personal tragedy. One of the refuelling aircraft that had been used in an earlier part of the flight had crashed on its way back to England, killing all four people on board – all were part of Cobham's National Aviation Day operation. In spite of this setback, in-flight refuelling would remain a key interest for

Alan Cobham during his lifetime, and it would result in the formation of Flight Refuelling Ltd, which still exists today as Cobham plc.

The flotation of Airspeed (1934) Ltd provided some welcome capital reserves for the company, even though it was still not making a profit. Some of this was used to start the Airspeed Aeronautical College, an operation which was championed by Norway. Although not a unique concept (de Havilland had been running an Aeronautical Technical School since 1928), the Airspeed venture was nonetheless newsworthy enough to receive publicity in *Flight* and provided training in aeronautical engineering for many students during its lifetime.

Like many other aeroplane manufacturers, Airspeed was caught up in the frenzy of the England to Australia air race during the later part of 1934. At the end of the previous year, the Australian confectionary manufacturer Sir Macpherson Robertson had announced that he would provide prize money and a trophy to support an air race between London and Melbourne as part of the celebrations to mark the centenary of the founding of Melbourne. With a prize of £10,000 (equivalent to about £600,000 in 2016) and a cup valued at £500 (equivalent to about £32,000 in 2016) for the first across the line, it was not surprising that many of the best known pilots from across the world (including Sir Alan Cobham, Sir Charles Kingsford Smith and Amy Johnson) expressed an interest in taking part. By the time the race started on 20 October the field had been reduced to twenty, ranging from purpose-built racers such as the de Havilland D.H.88 Comet to converted old bombers like the Fairey Fox. The King and Queen visited the aeroplanes taking part in what was being called 'the greatest race in the history of aviation', with Queen Mary seeing the inside of an aeroplane for the first time in her life when she stepped inside a Douglas DC-2. Nearly 60,000 crammed into Mildenhall Aerodrome to see the start of the race. Airspeed was represented by two entrants. Squadron Leader David Stodart and his nephew, a pilot in the RAF, flew an Airspeed AS.5 Courier and finished a creditable sixth across the line (fourth on handicap), taking 9 days and 18 hours to reach Melbourne. The other competitors had an altogether less happy experience, withdrawing with brake trouble at Athens and then subsequently unsuccessfully suing Airspeed for supplying a defective aeroplane! When the case finally reached the High Court, it produced more publicity for Airspeed, although not the type they would have necessarily appreciated. Sitting observing proceedings in court did though provide more background material for the budding novelist.

Airspeed was in the headlines again in December. A modified AS.6 Envoy had been bought by the Australian aviator Charles Ulm in order to test the feasibility of an air service from San Francisco to Sydney. Unfortunately the crew lost their way on a flight between California and Hawaii and disappeared never to be seen again. Transcripts of their last desperate radio messages were printed across the front pages of the popular press, with a *Daily Mirror* headline proclaiming 'Radio Drama Then Hours of Silence'. The company could not be blamed for the accident, but again this was not great publicity.

Tiltman, in particular, was convinced that producing one-off aeroplanes for racing or long-distance record attempts was not a viable basis for a business proposition. Sadly though, Airspeed was still making a loss, and they would need to rely on these one-off specials to supplement income for a while yet.

What had been a difficult year ended on an optimistic note for the Norway family. Frances was again pregnant, with the family due to increase the following spring.

The next three years were a period of stability and yet paradoxically increasing frustration for Nevil Norway. On 6 March 1935, Frances gave birth to a second child, another daughter, christened Shirley Anne. In 1936 they moved to 14 Helena Road (today known as Norway House), a large semi-detached property just off the sea front in Southsea. The move not only reflected the needs of a growing family, but also the increased financial security Norway was now receiving from both Airspeed and his writing. In addition to royalties from book sales, Ronald Watt had also managed to sell the film rights of the novel *Lonely Road* to Associated Talking Pictures; quite an achievement for the third novel of an unknown author. Nevil was invited to Ealing Studios in his old home suburb to see the film being made, and no doubt would have felt some satisfaction in seeing his name being displayed in the film's opening credits when it opened in London in August 1936.

As far as developments at Airspeed were concerned, progress was in the right direction. The AS.6 Envoy was becoming increasingly popular with civilian operators, and having gained full membership of the Society of British Aircraft Constructors, Airspeed could now bid for military contracts. Since 1935 the government was financing serious expansion of the Royal Air Force in order to counter the significant growth in German air power, and so military contracts were soon again to be a key part of most aeroplane manufacturer's activity. In response to an Air Ministry invitation to submit, Tiltman produced a modified version of the AS.6 Envoy. This would become the AS.10 Oxford, a standard twin-engine training aircraft for the RAF, and ultimately one of Airspeed's most well-known aeroplanes.

In March 1937, Airspeed received the ultimate seal of royal approval when it was asked to supply a special aeroplane for The King's Flight. The King's Flight had been formed in 1936 to provide an air transport service solely for use of the royal family. Up until 1937 the service had used a D.H.89 Dragon Rapide personally owned by the King, but this was now to be replaced by an AS.6 Envoy which would be owned and maintained by the state. G-AEXX was delivered in June 1937, and it would subsequently be used to convey the new King George VI around the country. It was no doubt a source of great pride for all those associated with Airspeed.

While the support of Swan Hunter and Wigham Richardson had bought financial respectability (although not yet profitability) to Airspeed, it had also gradually changed the character of the company. Lord Grimthorpe had stood down as chairman, being replaced by a Swan Hunter and Wigham Richardson director in 1936, and some of the original Airspeed employees were also now being replaced as the growth in the company took it outside of their level of competence. Norway, a natural entrepreneur and risk taker, was becoming frequently frustrated by what he saw as the now conservative attitude of the board of directors. Disagreements were becoming increasingly common.

Since 1931, Airspeed had been the constant focus of Norway's time and energy, often to the detriment of his wife and young daughters. With the company gaining increasing credibility and orders, by 1936 he started to reorganise his work-life balance to 'try to behave more as a father and husband should'. Somewhat contradicting this, he also began writing again in the evenings. In October 1937, *Blackwood's Magazine* published a short story that owed much to his experience of Alan Cobham's National Aviation Days called 'Air Circus'. He had also started work on a new novel, *Ruined City*, which with its themes of a declining shipbuilding industry, company acquisitions and raising corporate finance in times of an economic depression, drew on much of what he had learnt during the takeover of the original Airspeed company. By the end of 1937, though he perhaps did not fully realise it at the time, Nevil Norway's eventful career in the aviation industry was coming to a close.

The deteriorating relationship between Norway and the board of directors was also having an effect on other members of the management team, most notably Tiltman. By the spring of 1938 the sensitive Tiltman was so unhappy with the working atmosphere in the company that he sent a letter of resignation to Lord Grimthorpe. Although no longer chairman of the company, Grimthorpe was still a director, and one of the first people Tiltman had written to when he and Norway were forming Airspeed; he would have expected an understanding response. He was somewhat shocked therefore when rather than receiving a sympathetic reply, it was one which was highly critical of his action. Grimthorpe made his feelings clear in no uncertain terms, stating, 'I am profoundly upset by your attitude and consider that you have badly let down your backers amongst whom I include myself, as I was the first to support you. I hope it is not yet too late for you to reconsider your attitude and for the managers of Airspeed to resume their former happy relationship'. Whether Norway or Tiltman were to blame for the situation that the company now found itself in was not really clear, however it was now obvious that the two were no longer capable of working together – one of them had to go.

After Norway had overcome 'the first shock to my pride' when he realised that the board of directors would prefer him rather than Tiltman to leave, their reasoning being that good aeroplane designers were harder to find, he accepted the decision willingly. It may have seemed surprising that he did not put up more of a fight. After all, Airspeed had occupied most of his waking hours for eight years, often to the detriment of his wife and family. However, the company had made him a generous financial offer. He had just delivered the manuscript for his next novel *Ruined City* to Watt and there was the serious chance that somebody would buy the film rights for this. Norway had the chance to try something new, and so he decided to move on.

Although Norway did not formally resign from Airspeed until 9 November 1938, he played no further part in the company after April, being sent on leave until his resignation took effect. In November 1938, at the fifth annual general meeting of Airspeed (1934) Ltd, the chairman George Wigham Richardson was able to report that for the year ending 31 July 1938, the company had made a profit for the first time. The size of orders the company was now receiving from the government for the AS.10 Oxford had required an increase in workforce and an extension to the factory. Largely as a result of the impending war, the company was finally on the road to sustainability, but it was no longer the risk-taking, entrepreneurial organisation that Norway and Tiltman had started eight years earlier. Hessell Tiltman remained with the company as a managing director until 1942, but the broken friendship with Nevil Norway was never repaired.

As far as Airspeed was concerned, in 1940 de Havilland bought Swan Hunter and Wigham Richardson's shares in the company, finally taking full ownership in 1951. At that point the Airspeed name finally disappeared from the aviation industry. Somewhat ironically, a company which had been started by two ex-employees of de Havilland ended up back at its roots.

The year 1938 marked the end of an era for Nevil Norway. He had spent just over fifteen years working with many who were to become legends in the British aviation industry. He had experienced the highs and lows of airships, and together with Hessell Tiltman he had started an aeroplane manufacturing company during one of the worst economic periods of the twentieth century. Aviation had been his life, but now he was contemplating something completely different. His career in aeroplane manufacturing was over and a new one as a full-time novelist about to begin – or at least that was the plan.

Part 2

May 1938–July 1950

Transition

7

Peace and War
May 1938–December 1944

If leaving Airspeed was a decision not altogether of Nevil Norway's choosing, deciding to become a full-time novelist certainly was. For a family man with two young children, many might well have considered this to be a foolhardy move to make. With war an increasing possibility, most aviation companies would soon have more work than they could handle and men with Norway's experience would be invaluable.

He was, though, not one to worry too much about what might have been. As he had already shown a number of times in his career, once a decision had been made, he didn't look back, he just got on with it.

Having agreed a settlement with Airspeed, Norway estimated that he and his family now had enough money to live on for five or so years. He found himself in the unfamiliar position of having no deadlines to meet and no work to do – this must have been quite a strange feeling after the almost constant pressure of the last eight years. He and Frances therefore decided to take a holiday so that they could think through the options for the future. For a destination, they finally settled, somewhat at random, on the picturesque town of Saint-Claude in eastern France.

While there, Norway received more good news. Watt had sold the film rights of *Ruined City* to the American film studio Metro-Goldwyn-Mayer for $35,000 (equivalent to $574,000 in 2016). Not only was Nevil Shute beginning to gain a reputation on the other side of the Atlantic, but the financial reserve in his bank account had now grown from five to ten!

MGM listed *Ruined City* as part of its schedule for production and release during the 1939-40 season, and the film correspondent of *The Observer* confidently reported in early 1940 that production of *Ruined City* starring Robert Donat was about to start. In reality, Donat had already decided not to take the part, and the film was never made.

The Norways returned to England in the early summer of 1938, where Nevil settled into his new life as a full-time author in Southsea. Having spent his working life so far leading or working as part of a team, and immersed in engineering, it must have seemed a strange existence at first to find himself spending his working day alone, with just a typewriter to keep him company. He began a daily work routine that, apart from the war, he would follow for the rest of his life. He was not an author who believed in the technique of waiting for inspiration to strike but instead wrote regularly every morning from nine o'clock until one, seven days a week. He later described this as 'a fixed and invariable rule'; to him writing was now a full-time job and needed to be treated as such.

Of course Frances was around, but she soon understood that one of her key duties was to keep everyone away from her husband's study while he was working. Although still registered as a general practitioner, she did not work again during peacetime. Now a married woman with two young children to look after, as was normal for the upper middle class at that time, she was not expected to work.

While they had been away in France, Nevil Shute's fourth novel was published by William Morrow and Company in America. Released under the title of *Kindling* at the end of May 1938, it was then published as *Ruined City* in Britain by Cassell and Company a month later.

In this novel Shute continues the move away from the aviation and adventure themes that had characterised his earlier work, the central character in *Ruined City* being a banker. Set in the early 1930s, it tells the story of Henry Warren, who has built a successful career in London by never making financially risky loans no matter how worthwhile the cause might be. Although wealthy and successful, he has a deteriorating marriage and increasingly fragile health. He decides to take a walking trip in the North of England, where one day alone on the road he falls seriously ill. He is taken to a hospital in a small shipbuilding town where he sees at first hand the effect that the Depression is really having on so many communities. He resolves on his return to London to help this town by buying and reopening its main source of employment, a shipyard. However, in order to accomplish this he has to resort to shady financial dealings, for which he eventually goes to prison. He accepts this as the price he has to pay to help the 'ruined city' regenerate, and at the same time he finds new love and a new reason for life. The elements of shipbuilding, the difficulties of starting a company in the Depression and the workings of the financial sector clearly owed much to the knowledge and experience Norway had gained establishing Airspeed.

William Morrow made a big effort to promote *Kindling*, saying at one point, perhaps with a degree of marketing exaggeration, that 'it was planning to feature it as one of the most important novels it had ever brought out'. In spite of this enthusiasm from his American publisher, the author was still reluctant to reveal his true identity, believing 'that coming out from under his pseudonym would hardly do his firm any good' – he was still technically an employee of Airspeed at that time. *Kindling* was prominently reviewed in many of the major newspapers in America, and although some thought the story a bit far-fetched, it clearly caught the public's imagination, selling 20,000 copies within six months. The royalties on these sales alone more than matched the annual income he had been receiving at Airspeed. In Britain, it was also well received, being reprinted twice during the first month of publication. *The Observer's* respected literary critic and novelist, Frank Swinnerton, urged readers 'who look for new talents to note the name of Nevil Shute' confident that 'if he can maintain the standard of "Ruined City" he will be distinguished hereafter'. If Nevil Norway was wondering whether a full-time career as a novelist was a viable proposition, it seemed the answer was yes.

While Norway was settling into his new career during the latter part of 1938, the country was stumbling towards war. Most of the British public still supported the government's policy of appeasement; there was little appetite for conflict. Unemployment had fallen from the post Wall Street Crash high of 3.4 million in 1932 to 1.8 million, and the bank rate had now been maintained at 2 per cent for nearly six years, a financial record. After so much pain there was a steady current of rising prosperity, and most did not want to jeopardise this. On his return from the Munich conference at the end of September, bringing with him what *The Times* called 'peace with honour', the prime minister Neville Chamberlain had been cheered by waiting crowds. Among the dignitaries present to welcome and congratulate him were Cabinet ministers, high commissioners for the Dominions and high-ranking diplomats from France, Italy, Hungary and, surprisingly, Germany – it seemed there were many interested in preserving peace.

Away from the public spotlight though, there had been increasing concern about Germany's growing military power. While Winston Churchill had regularly and loudly made speeches from the backbenches of the House of Commons warning that Hitler was a threat and rearmament was essential, reflecting the public mood, few in the government listened, considering Churchill a warmonger. However, by 1935, even the Cabinet had become nervous, with the Secretary of State for Air, Ramsay MacDonald, calling for expansion of the Royal Air Force in order to reach parity with the Luftwaffe. It would still take a while to convince everyone that war was coming. For instance, in February 1939, one of Norway's ex-colleagues, George Wigham Richardson, the chairman of Airspeed, was saying that 'he considered the possibility of war was not so great as some thought'. It was, though, now generally recognised that if war came, air power rather than sea power would be a deciding factor, and unlike in the First World War, significant numbers of the civilian population would become a target.

In a letter written the day before he died, Norway reflected on the novels he had written over his lifetime and classified them into two groups: the first written for pure entertainment and the second written with a particular purpose in mind. He did not expect the second group to be financially successful but considered it the role of a novelist to occasionally raise 'subjects which ought to be discussed in public and which no statesman cares to approach'. He now started work on his fifth novel *What Happened to the Corbetts*, which had an original working title of *Overture*. This would be the first to be written with a particular message – in this case the future war in the air. The plight of civilians in war would provide the subject which Nevil Shute would use to show that popular fiction could be used for purposes other than pure entertainment.

Sometime in late 1938, Nevil Shute made what was a major decision for any author: he decided to change his publisher. Cassell and Company had published his first four novels in Britain, but for reasons not recorded he decided to move to William Heinemann Ltd. Heinemann was a well-respected publisher with a high-profile international author list, including some of the best-selling English novelists of the day, such as J. B. Priestley, Graham Greene and Somerset Maugham. However they did not offer Shute greatly different terms to those Cassell had been giving, and so it may be that Shute (or Watt) believed that the higher profile of Heinemann would be better for his future career. The decision proved to be the right one, because Shute remained a Heinemann author for the rest of his life.

Christmas 1938 was a time of sadness rather than celebration for the Norway family, as on 25 December, following a heart attack, Nevil's father died. He was 79, and in recent years since the death of his wife had lived near his son, while still making trips to his much loved Italy whenever he could. Arthur Hamilton Norway was buried five days later at Longcross Cemetery, Dartmouth alongside his wife. In spite of his relatively humble beginnings and lack of a public school or university education, he had achieved much, both within the Civil Service and as an author and historian. The obituary in *The Times* (which was also published in *The Irish Times*) poignantly reflected that 'His departure from the Post Office under the age limit in 1920 left his colleagues with a feeling that a man of real distinction had disappeared from the service'. Arthur Norway had reached the rank of assistant secretary in the Civil Service, but even so he was not a particularly wealthy man, and did not own any property when he died. His son was the sole beneficiary of his estate of £3,626.

Nevil Norway was someone who always believed that his private life should be just that, rarely mentioning his family in public. There can however be little doubt that he would have missed his father. He had been a constant source of advice during his formative years, for example helping with his admission to Balliol College. While Arthur Norway never got over the death of his first son Fred, who he had hoped would follow in his footsteps as a classical scholar, he must have had a quiet pride in seeing his less promising second son developing a reputation as an established author.

What Happened to the Corbetts was published in Britain in February 1939. It tells the story of totally unexpected air raids on Southampton at the beginning of an unannounced war. The growing effect that these nightly attacks have on a local resident Peter Corbett and his family, as essential services start to fall apart, is described in harrowing but detached detail. Very soon there are food shortages, disease and lawlessness on the streets. Realising that things are well out of control, Corbett decides to defy government regulations on movement and use his small boat to escape with his wife and children to safety overseas before returning alone to fight for his country.

By this time, most people in Britain believed that a war with Germany was inevitable, and so Shute's novel would have been extremely relevant. Despite the public image of diplomacy being the answer to the crisis, the government had been preparing the country for an invasion by air. A year earlier the Home Office had printed a booklet *The Protection of Your Home Against Air Raids* which it intended to distribute free to every household in Great Britain. However, as far as Norway was concerned it focused too strongly on the use of gas as a weapon and too little on what he considered the main threat from any air raid, the destruction that would be caused by high explosives. While in this prediction he was ultimately to be proved correct, like the government he did not foresee the damage that would also be caused by fire. *What Happened to the Corbetts* contains a blunt and perhaps rather opinionated epilogue to the people of Southampton in which Shute is unconcerned about upsetting any of the city's officials, believing that 'if I have given to the least of your officials one new idea to ponder and digest, then I shall feel that this book will have played a part in preparing us for the terrible things that you, and I, and all citizens of all cities in this country, may one day have to face together'. In order to help spread Shute's message, Heinemann gave away 1,000 free copies of the book on the day of publication to Air Raid Precautions personnel. Maybe it was a topic that many people did not want to think too much about, but whatever the reason, despite reasonable reviews, the book did not sell as well as his previous novel in Britain.

In America it was a different story. Published under the title *Ordeal*, less than a month after publication Morrow was reporting that they had printed 142,000 copies. It was number eleven in *The New York Times* Best Sellers list, and, importantly for an aspiring popular novelist, was a selection for the Book of the Month Club for April.

Founded in America in 1926, the Book of the Month Club sent a book automatically every month to each of its members, unless they elected to replace it with an alternative selection. The monthly selection, which was chosen by a panel of literary critics, was aimed at a middlebrow market but gave a good indication of what the average American was reading, or what the panel of experts thought they should read. At the time *Ordeal* was chosen as the Club's monthly selection, this would have meant the book reaching an audience of hundreds of thousands, something of an achievement for a relatively new author.

A prominent review of the novel in *The New York Times* called it 'an astonishing performance for the author of last year's best-seller *Kindling*'. The review also contained an unattributed sketch by Flora Twort of Shute somewhat incongruously dressed in full flying gear gazing into the distance. For the moment at least, it seemed that he was more popular in America than his home country.

On 25 March 1939, Norway boarded the ocean liner RMS *Ascania* at Southampton for a trip across the Atlantic arranged and hosted by his American publisher. Although the trip was solely connected with his activities as a novelist, it seems he still did not believe that this was really now his full-time occupation, as on the passenger list for the outward and return passages he was listed as N. S. Norway, Engineer. He travelled first to Halifax, Nova Scotia and then on to Cape Cod in order to research a region which would play a key part in the next novel he was planning. He spent the rest of his trip in America, where the main objective of his publisher was to promote *Ordeal*. William Morrow had arranged a hectic schedule for their increasingly popular author: attending parties, being interviewed on the radio and speaking at functions. A large photograph of Nevil Shute even appeared on the front cover of *The Saturday Review of Literature*, the first of three occasions this was to happen.

The schedule would have probably been a strain on an experienced public speaker, but for someone with a stammer, who was wary of publicity and was doing many of these things for the first time, the pressure must have been considerable. Following an evening of wining and dining at the Rainbow Room in the Rockefeller Center near the end of his trip, he experienced a major health problem which was to plague him for the rest of his life. He later described that it felt like being shot, and that it was difficult to walk or breathe. The diagnosis by a local doctor in New York was that he had strained his heart. It is unclear whether in fact he had suffered a minor stroke, heart attack or a pancreatic attack. Whatever the cause, it took many weeks for the pain to disappear completely.

A somewhat fragile Nevil Norway finally left America on 6 May, travelling in comfort on the Cunard White Star liner MV *Britannic,* and arriving back at Southampton on 14 May. While no doubt relieved to be reunited with his wife and children, he was increasingly aware that the predictions he had made in *What Happened to the Corbetts,* and talked about frequently during his trip, were nearer to becoming reality.

Although now ostensibly a full-time author, the engineering part of Nevil Norway did not completely wither and die (in fact it never did), and in 1939 he began to collaborate with Sir Dennistoun Burney again. Since the closure of the R.100 programme, Burney, ever the inventor and entrepreneur, had been involved in a number of ambitious projects. First there had been the formation of Streamline Cars Ltd, which had produced a futuristic car which incorporated many of what were then advanced concepts, such as independent suspension and hydraulic braking. Despite generating a lot of interest, the car was a failure commercially and the company closed in 1936. More recently, Burney had been trying to interest the Air Ministry in a new design of engine that he called the Chordal Turbine engine, and which it was claimed would generate higher power for a given size than conventional petrol engines. With typical enthusiasm, even before a single prototype had been built, Burney was planning mass production of the engine for use in a diverse range of applications from aeroplanes to submarines. The Air Ministry did not share Burney's optimism, and right from the start they made it clear that all initial development had to be at his own expense. In the end, no engine was ever made, and the Air Ministry finally lost interest in the project.

Not a man to be put off by a simple refusal, Burney then suggested another ambitious scheme. This time he proposed developing four new weapons which, given the war, he thought would have appeal. These were an air-launched gliding torpedo (the Toraplane), an air-launched gliding bomb (the Doravane), a gliding mine (the Octaplane) and a device for vertical bombing (the Diving Doravane). Of these, only the Toraplane and Doravane were of immediate interest to the government, but in order to enhance the credibility of his proposals, he needed someone with a formal engineering background as part of the project team. As a result, Nevil Norway became an unpaid consultant to Burney, while Nevil Shute continued to write novels.

Following his trip to Canada and America, Norway had settled back into life at home and during the late summer started work on his next novel, which he promised to deliver to Heinemann by January 1940. Having just finished a book about the war, and with the country now focusing on the possibility of another conflict, Shute wanted to write something that would take both his and other people's minds off war. He therefore started *An Old Captivity* while continuing to collaborate with Burney on the Toraplane.

Although Britain had been working hard on the diplomatic front to avoid a war, the government had also been building up military forces and preparing the population more generally for conflict with Germany. Parliamentary approval of the Emergency Powers Act in August 1938 and the Military Training Act in April 1939 had paved the way for a host of special measures thought necessary to defend the nation, including calling up military reservists, the mobilisation of Air Raid Precautions (ARP) volunteers, and of course, eventually, conscription.

By 2 September 1939, the British government's patience with Adolf Hitler had run out. At 4.15 pm on a Saturday afternoon, the Cabinet was in emergency session in order to decide the time limit on an ultimatum that had been made to Germany to withdraw troops from Poland. After much discussion it was agreed that Germany be given until midnight 2/3 September, although, following consultation with the French government, this was eventually extended to noon Central European Time on 3 September. At 11.15 am the following day, the prime minister Neville Chamberlain made his now famous radio broadcast to the nation from the Cabinet Room at Downing Street, announcing 'that this country is at war with Germany'.

Nevil and Frances Norway were sailing in the English Channel when war was declared, taking a last opportunity of enjoying their recently acquired yacht *Runagate*. It would be many years before they could repeat the experience, as this time nobody was predicting that it would all be over by Christmas.

While the first air raid siren sounded over London less than half an hour after war had been declared, Chamberlain's announcement did not immediately change the day-to-day life of everybody in a big way unless you were a man of fighting age or a family with young children. Parliament immediately passed an Emergency Forces (Armed Services) Act which required all men between the ages of 18 and 41 to register for military service, but as in the First World War, young single men were the first to receive their call-up papers. For the present, Norway would have been considered too old, and in any case the work he was doing with Burney may well have been classed as a reserved occupation. One other decision the British War Cabinet made at its first meeting was to introduce petrol rationing – a topic which would become something of a fixation of Norway's after the war.

From 1 September 1939, even before war had been declared, the government began the implementation of Operation Pied Piper (a name Shute would use for a future novel), the mass evacuation of children from areas the enemy were expected to target, such as London and Manchester, to more rural locations. Children under the age of five were evacuated with their mother, while those of school age were evacuated with their school, accompanied by teachers. In his first report to the War Cabinet, the Minister of Home Security, Sir John Anderson, recorded that between 1.5 and 1.6 million children had been relocated in less than a week. He also concluded that the billeting of mothers with young children had proved more difficult than unaccompanied schoolchildren, and that perhaps in future the evacuation of adults requiring billeting should be avoided. Evacuation was not compulsory, and wealthy families could make their own private arrangements, something that the Norways would eventually do.

Portsmouth was not initially classified as an evacuation area, but as 1939 progressed, Norway became increasingly concerned that the family home in Southsea could become an unintended casualty of any bombing raid on nearby military targets such the Portsmouth Dockyards and Airspeed factories. As a result, in late 1939, he and his family moved a few miles along the coast to the Old Mill at Langstone, which had been bought as a holiday retreat by Flora Twort. Norway then bought nearby Langstone Tower as a new home for his family. Unfortunately, Langstone Harbour was soon being used as a bomb decoy to lure enemy bombers away from Portsmouth, so perhaps this was not the best thought out of moves.

For the rest of 1939 and into 1940, Norway continued his double life working with Burney and writing. In the spring of 1940 his sixth novel *An Old Captivity* was published. On this occasion, it was released with the same title in both Britain and America. Having used his previous novel to promote discussion of a social issue he was passionate about, in this one he returned to pure escapism. Using background he had gained from his recent visit to Canada and America, it is set in the 1930s and tells the story of Donald Ross, employed by an Oxford academic to fly a survey mission from Scotland to Greenland. The objective of the trip is to search for traces of the early Viking explorer Leif Erikson, thought to be the first European to have reached North America. In addition to taking the academic, Ross is also forced to reluctantly take the academic's daughter Alix, who is very much against the whole venture. Ross has to resort to taking increasing numbers of sleeping tablets during the later stages of the expedition to help cope with stress. Falling into a coma bought on by an excessive number of tablets, he starts to dream that he and Alix, whom he has become increasingly fond of, are slaves Haki and Hekja aboard Erikson's ship on its voyage to Greenland. In one part of the dream the two slaves leave a stone with their names carved on it in the foreign land. Awake, and continuing the survey trip, Ross recognises some of the landscape from his dream and eventually finds the stone with the name of the two slaves from long ago carved on it. The theme of reincarnation was one Shute would return to in a later novel, *In the Wet*.

The book was received with guarded enthusiasm in America, perhaps because it did not use a standard chronological story structure, instead mixing dreams of the past with reality. *The Saturday Review of Literature's* book reviewer concluded that 'the great fault of the book is that it does not hang together well' but also that 'its parts offer excellent entertainment, varied and unusual'. Many were not convinced by the authenticity of the mystical theme in the novel or the lack of a link between the psychiatrist introducing the story and the ending of the book.

Others, though, thought differently, as *An Old Captivity* was chosen as the 'Monthly Selection' by the Literary Guild of America Book Club for March 1940. Again, this would help the name of Nevil Shute spread further across the country.

In Britain, where people were looking for something to take their mind off the war, the reception was also mixed. While *The Sunday Times* reviewer was engrossed by a credible novel, concluding that 'the characters were agreeably real and Mr. Shute's quiet writing highly effective', the book reviewer in *The Observer* thought that the dream sequence was less successful. It seemed that, in the eyes of some, Shute's novels were still not quite the finished article.

The development of the Toraplane and Doravane were typical examples of the turbulent process many engineering projects must have experienced during this period, as Britain moved from peace to war. Initially, the development of the Toraplane was championed by the Admiralty, with the state-owned Royal Aircraft Establishment (RAE) at Farnborough assisting. However, once war had been declared, and the First Lord of the Admiralty Winston Churchill had taken an interest, then in order to try and ensure greater co-operation between the different branches of the armed forces and government departments, a Toraplane and Doravane Development Committee was formed. Norway, who must have thought that his days of dealing with bureaucracy were behind him, found himself attending meetings with very high-ranking military and government officials and being named in the minutes of these meetings as 'Assistant to Sir Dennis Burney'. His skill for observing people would have given him a great deal of material for many of his future war novels. In the end, in spite of some successful trials, the Toraplane was found to be too unreliable and work on it finally abandoned in the spring of 1940. While he did not know it at the time, the highs and lows of working on military projects was something Norway was going to gain a lot more experience of in the next few years.

Having delivered his manuscript of *An Old Captivity* to Heinemann and Morrow, Shute then immediately started work on his next book. Once writing became his principal source of income in 1938, as you would expect from someone with an engineering background, he approached his new profession systematically. Usually taking around nine months to complete a book, he averaged one novel a year for the rest of his life. He never seems to have suffered from writer's block.

The Lame Ducks Fly, which he intended to be his seventh novel, was started sometime in early 1940 and was concerned with a topic which now dominated the thoughts of so many: the outbreak of war. Set in Singapore, the story tells of a plan to fly two squadrons of bombers back to England at short notice. However, how the plot then develops will never be known, as having completed the first chapter Shute stopped work on this novel, never to return to it. The unpublished chapter, along with a single page detailing the distances and stopping points an aircraft could follow on a flight between Singapore and England are all that remain of this work. Having abandoned *When Lame Ducks Fly*, he moved on to *Landfall: A Channel Story* (originally titled just *A Channel Story*). This story was also set at the beginning of the Second World War but this time starts in England. The beginning of the novel has no similarity to its unfinished predecessor, apart from the use of a common character, Jerry Chambers.

Norway finished his collaboration with Burney in spring 1940. He now had to think of what to do next, as he did not consider writing novels a worthwhile principal occupation during wartime. He was after all from a public school background in which serving your country in times of conflict was something you did without question. In addition, he was becoming increasingly worried about the safety of his family. Although the so-called 'Phoney War' still existed as far as many on mainland Britain were concerned, the Battle of Britain and the Blitz were not far away, and by July 1940 Portsmouth and surrounding areas would become targets for enemy bombers. Their current home at Langstone Tower could therefore no longer be considered a safe haven.

By mid-year he had solved both problems. On 21 June he joined the Royal Naval Volunteer Reserve (RNVR) as what he later called 'an elderly yachtsman', and on 26 June his wife and daughters left Liverpool on board *The Duchess of Atholl* bound for Montreal. Norway assumed that now he was in the RNVR he would be spending long periods at sea and that his family would be safer in Canada. The government had just begun a second phase of evacuation of children, this time focusing on the South and East Coast. The process was still not compulsory, but by making their own arrangements the Norways avoided any possibility of mother and daughters being separated. It is not clear why Canada was chosen as a destination as neither Nevil nor Frances had any family connections with Montreal, although Nevil had visited the city on the R.100. Interestingly, joining the RNVR and sending his family to Canada is a replica of the action that the Shute character Peter Corbett had taken in *What Happened to the Corbetts*.

Within two days of joining the RNVR, not even long enough to have ordered his uniform, Temporary Sub-Lieutenant Norway found himself being called from his training at HMS *King Alfred* in Hove to attend a meeting with Commander Charles Goodeve from the Admiralty. The Royal Navy had now investigated his previous experience a little more fully and realised that he would be far more use to the war effort working on weapon development than by seagoing duties. By 25 June, Norway was part of the Royal Navy's recently formed Inspectorate of Anti-Aircraft Weapons and Devices (IAAWD), which had been set up with a remit to develop weapons to defend merchant ships and small craft. Britain was at a low point in the war, with the evacuation of Dunkirk having occurred only a few weeks beforehand. Norway's dream of a life at sea was over; he would spend the rest of the war developing a range of ingenious and in some cases extraordinary weapons, in many ways a prefect role for an experienced engineer with a novelist's imagination.

Furious at this change in direction, there was little he could do; he was no longer his own boss and had to obey orders. Since he would now be working for the Admiralty from a shore-based facility, HMS *President* in London, he moved from living at Langstone Tower to the Oxford and Cambridge University Club in Pall Mall. With his family now the other side of the Atlantic, solitary evenings in Langstone Tower were no longer an attractive proposition. He therefore reverted to a previous life, working at the IAAWD during the day and writing for relaxation during the evenings. He spent many weekends writing at Langstone Tower and visiting Flora Twort, who still lived nearby.

In November 1940, *Landfall: A Channel Story,* the first of Nevil Shute's war novels, was published. Set in Britain six months after the start of the war, the novel tells of a romance between a flying officer based at an aerodrome near Portsmouth and a barmaid. The pilot, while working for coastal command, sinks a submarine which the navy believes to have been British. A court of inquiry finds him guilty and officially reprimands him. Convinced he is innocent, the pilot requests a transfer away from the town and people he knows, particularly the barmaid. Looking for escape, he volunteers to act as a test pilot for the development of a new secret weapon. The weapon is being developed by a university professor, who had many of the characteristics of Barnes Wallis, and believes that everything is being done in too much of a hurry. The work is very dangerous, and the pilot is eventually seriously injured while flying a test mission. The barmaid, who he has become very fond of, successfully fights to prove his innocence. In a happy conclusion, the pilot is exonerated, receives an AFC for bravery, the couple marry, and the book ends with them on a ship bound for Canada.

On the face of it, the novel is a straightforward girl meets boy from a different background, boy has problems, girl saves boy, wartime romance. However, it is packed with well-observed, authentic detail which had already become a trademark of Shute's writing and was well received on both sides of the Atlantic. Ralph Straus in *The Sunday Times* selected it as a Novel of the Week, describing it as a story which was 'extraordinarily interesting and delightfully told'. It was equally well received by *The Times Literary Supplement*, which nominated it as its First Choice Novel of the Week. Shute's novel also caught the eye of the literary critic, essayist, journalist and novelist George Orwell. Although his classics *Nineteen Eighty-Four* and *Animal Farm* were still a few years away, he had already established a reputation as one of the leading novelists of his generation, and like Shute his novels often contained elements based on personal experience and observation. Orwell thought that 'The present war, owing to its peculiar character, has not yet produced literature of its own, but Mr. Shute's *Landfall* is a beginning. It is a straightforward, convincing story, and I shall keep an eye open for Mr. Shute's books in the future'. He also thought that the novel was 'a good, simple story, pleasantly free from cleverness, and at times genuinely moving'. He was not always as positive, describing the other book he was reviewing in the same article as 'one of the most pretentious novels I have read for a long time'. The British public obviously agreed with Orwell's views, as *Landfall: A Channel Story* was reprinted less than a month after publication.

Equally positively received in America, United Artists paid $25,000 (equivalent to $425,000 in 2016) for the film rights before the book was even published, a significant supplement to the salary of a naval officer! Production of the film was delayed, and it was not released in Britain until 1949, a period when, as the first post-war election had shown, most people were wanting to look forward rather than backwards.

Norway was again spending his days in a stressful environment, working to develop fully operational weapons against tight deadlines, and often fighting the government bureaucracy that he had always so disliked. Finally, it caught up with him, and early in 1941 he had what was in all probability a second minor heart attack. He told Flora Twort that it was indigestion, and the Admiralty doctor came to much the same conclusion. However, it was another warning that his health was not all it should be, and something he needed to take care of.

By the summer of 1941 it had been decided that Frances and the children could return from Canada. The trip had been a mixed success. While Frances had managed to find work as a doctor in Ontario, there had been problems in accessing the money that her husband had deposited in an account there during his visit to Canada in 1939. It was also now clear that he would not be spending the war at sea, and so there did not really seem any point in the family continuing to be separated. There was however the need to find somewhere new to live.

In August 1941, Norway bought Pond Head House on Hayling Island. At that time the island was a popular destination for British holidaymakers because of its temperate climate and closeness to London. Pond Head House was a large detached property set in 5 acres of grounds. No doubt it would have been idyllic as far as Norway was concerned. Close to the beach, a few miles from Portsmouth Aerodrome, a private jetty at the bottom of the garden and a separate building to house a study and workshop – all of his needs would be catered for once the war was over. It was certainly an impressive house, and it was an indication that the Norways were now a wealthy family. Somewhat surprisingly, Frances and the children did not actually see the house until they arrived back in England at the end of September – by then, Norway had already bought it. They did not know it at the time, but this was to be their last house in England.

While the Norways now had a house, because of the difficulty of travelling during wartime, Nevil usually stayed at his club in Pall Mall during the week, returning to Hayling Island at the weekend. Frances

Peace and War

continued to manage the house, garden and domestic staff, while their daughters attended a day school on the island. Life was as normal as it could be at that time.

In 1941 the IAAWD expanded both its remit and size, being renamed the Department of Miscellaneous Weapons Development (DMWD), to become known colloquially as the Wheezers and Dodgers. It was now clear that its work was relevant to an increasingly wide range of naval activities. The beauty of the DMWD was that it was an eclectic mix of individuals, encouraged to think outside of the box, with a small number of regular naval staff at the top to interface with the military bureaucracy.

Now with an acting rank of acting temporary lieutenant commander, Norway, as head of the engineering section, took responsibility for investigating a host of ideas for new weapons. Of course, many never got past the early prototype stage and some were considered crackpot inventions, but anything which could help protect the troops and bring a quicker close to the war was welcome. Examples of the many developments that Norway was involved with included the Pig Trough, a device capable of firing up to fourteen rockets vertically from the deck of a ship, and the Rocket Grapnel, which could be used for cliff face assaults. Perhaps the most famous example of an invention which got part the way there but ultimately failed was the Great Panjandrum. This was a one-ton explosive charge supported by two giant wheels which were turned by rockets attached to the edge of each wheel. The intention was that the weapon could be remotely controlled and be capable of overcoming most obstacles as it was steered towards the enemy during a beach landing. Unfortunately, the weapon proved anything but controllable and is now best remembered when a variation of it was used in a 1972 episode of the television comedy *Dad's Army*. During this period he also made use of the experience he had gained establishing the Airspeed College by setting up a training school in rocket weapons at Portland.

The paths of Norway and Barnes Wallis also crossed again. Early in 1942 Wallis proposed the development of a pilotless glider that could be launched from a ship and be used to lay smoke over beaches during an invasion. The resulting Swallow Glider was developed by a team led by Norway, but in the end it was never used operationally. The history of the IAAWD and DMWD is described in detail in the book *The Secret War* (which includes a foreword written by Nevil Shute), while Norway's particular role in this venture is covered in detail in the book *Parallel Motion*.

Though he was very busy with the DMWD, whenever possible, Nevil Shute continued to write. His second war novel *Pied Piper* had all the hallmarks of success well before it was published. At the beginning of September 1941, Twentieth Century Fox bought the film rights. This was already the fourth of Shute's eight novels for which film rights had been sold. Quite an achievement for an author not yet fully established. A new experience this time was a ten-part serialisation of the novel in the American weekly magazine *Collier's*. In many ways, although great advance publicity for the novel, it is surprising that Shute agreed to an abridged version being published, as he was always so reluctant to allow a manuscript to be altered in any way once he had submitted it to the publishers. It can only be assumed that Shute himself produced the abridged version.

Possibly in response to the good-natured criticism from Flora Twort that since *Marazan* he always seemed to have written about men or women in their mid twenties and to 'for goodness sake write about a different age group', this story revolves around an old man and a group of young children. The book's central character is a 70-year-old retired solicitor, John Howard, who takes a fishing holiday in France in early 1940. As the war in Europe intensifies he decides to return to England and is persuaded to reluctantly take the two young children of an Englishman back with him to stay with their aunt in Oxford. He picks up a number of refugee children along his increasingly difficult journey through what is now occupied France and eventually arrives back in Plymouth with seven in his care. Although renowned as a quick writer, *Pied Piper* seems to have been exceptional. Commander Charles Goodeve said that Shute had thought up the outline of the story on an overnight train journey and been given three days' leave so that he could dictate the outline to a former secretary. In later years Goodeve called *Pied Piper* one of the most successful by-products of the DMWD.

When *Pied Piper* was published at the beginning of 1942, it was reasonably well received on both sides of the Atlantic. As with many of Shute's novels, the praise was often double-edged. Typical was the reviewer in *Time* magazine, who wrote that 'Pied Piper reads like a semi-final draft for one of the best sentimental novels to come out of World War II. The telling is not all it might be, but the materials of the tale are surefire'. *The Saturday Review of Literature* called the novel 'a most improbable tale in a quite probable setting' and concluded 'It is, to be sure, the sort of book which you can take or leave alone. But, if taken, it will certainly please'. As far as Britain was concerned, the public certainly did decide to take it, as Heinemann reprinted the book three times in 1942 and three more times again in 1943. It was also chosen as the monthly selection by the Reprint Society Book Club. This was the first time a British book club had chosen a Shute book for its members. A. Dwye Evans, from William Heinemann, was a member of the Club's inaugural editorial board and would become a lifelong friend of the Norway family. Nevil Shute was becoming a household name in both Britain and America.

At the end of the year the film *Pied Piper* was released in London. It had already been showing in America for two months and was proving to be very popular, eventually being chosen as one of *The Film Daily's* ten best films of the year. Starring Monty Woolley, Anne Baxter and a 14-year-old Roddy McDowall, it also gave the future film director and producer Otto Preminger his first part in a feature film. The film was nominated for three Academy Awards in 1943 but was unsuccessful. It was a year in which the film *Mrs Minever* dominated the Awards ceremony, taking most of the major honours. Shute, though, was becoming popular in both books and films.

The year 1942 was a very productive year for Shute as by the autumn he had completed a manuscript called *The Other Side* which was eventually retitled *Most Secret*. Now he was in the RNVR he had to submit everything he wrote to the Admiralty censor for clearance. This time they refused publication as the story about a secret wartime mission had elements similar to some work being undertaken at the DMWD. Norway was furious, and, never a man afraid of speaking his mind, he let his superiors know this. At one stage he threatened to resign from the RNVR However, no matter how much he blustered, there was little he could do but put the book aside and wait for the war to end. Although Norway had a hatred of bureaucracy, and at times found the military requirement to obey without question difficult, he did not impose such restrictions on the men who worked under him. His general approach was to give people a free hand with project development once the objective had been defined, providing help only when needed. As far as getting around the paperwork, he became famous for doing something and then worrying about justifying it to his superiors afterwards. This process became known as 'Doing a Norway'.

At the beginning of 1943 the planning for Operation Overlord, the codename for the Allied invasion of France, began. With a target date of mid-1944, the DMWD was working flat out to complete projects that might assist the invasion. Nevil Norway was kept extremely busy over this period, and so Nevil Shute rested for the first few months of that year.

Although writing had temporarily stopped, he continued to make progress with the day job, being permanently promoted to the rank of acting temporary lieutenant commander in March. In a report supporting his promotion, the director of DMWD Captain G. O. C. (Jock) Davies noted that Norway 'has been outstanding in the performance of his duties'. He rated his professional ability, personal qualities and intellectual ability highly, but, perhaps not surprisingly given Norway's distaste for bureaucracy, he was less impressed with his administrative ability.

Shute started writing again in the evenings in the spring of 1943 and by early autumn had completed the manuscript of his next novel *Pastoral*. Over the next nine months he then wrote a series of six articles called 'Second Front', and two others called 'Beach Assault' and 'Tank Landing Craft'. All were about aspects of the preparation for the D-Day landings, with some containing dramatic pen and ink illustrations by his friend and colleague from DMWD Ian Hassall. Most of these articles have a postscript indicating that they might be suitable for magazines such as *Collier's* or the *Saturday Evening Post*, but they were never published.

On Monday 5 June 1944, a turning point in the Second World War was reached with the beginning of the Allied invasion of France. Around 7,000 ships left ports in Britain to arrive off the coast at Normandy early the following morning; the long-awaited invasion of Western Europe had begun. Four days before, Lieutenant Commander Norway had been watching tests of a new weapon, when he received a message to report to the Admiralty. The next day he found himself with a group of war correspondents and photographers. They were to be part of a follow-up force, with a goal of observing and reporting on the Normandy landings. In Norway's case, his orders were simply to report on whatever he saw fit. Travelling on a landing ship across the Channel, Norway arrived at the Juno Beach sector off the coast of Normandy on the afternoon of D-Day. After a delay in landing because of bad weather, he then spent thirty hours ashore on the beach, sleeping in a foxhole at night and observing the conflict at first hand. Arriving back in England on 10 June, he had safely completed his first assignment as a war correspondent. The result was a 40-page manuscript *Journey in to Normandy*, which combined a novelist's flair with an engineer's eye for detail to give a well-constructed personal account of the Normandy landings. It was never published, but copies remain in government archives. He also kept a detailed diary of his nine days away, and along with many other of his manuscripts, this is stored in the National Library of Australia, Canberra.

Shute's final war novel was published in autumn 1944. He later wrote that *Pastoral* was written 'at a period of the war when it seemed to be going on for ever, and it looked as though all joy and fun had gone out of the world; the purpose of that book was to show that it wasn't'. When it was finished though, he was rather dismissive of the outcome, describing it as 'rather a trivial little book' that was 'written in a hurry'. Many of the reading public were to disagree, as ten years later it was still selling around 10,000 copies a year in Britain alone.

Set on an air base in Oxfordshire, the novel tells the story of a romance between a flight officer, Peter Marshall, and a young WAAF officer, Gervase Robertson. Peter flies Wellington bombers over Germany on risky missions with high losses. The romance starts slowly, but as the relationship develops, his need to finish his second term of flying operations safely starts to play on both their minds.

Reviews were generally positive but hesitant about its literary merit. For instance, *The Times Literary Supplement* chose it as their 'First Choice' in fiction, noting that the novel was 'as live, charming and touching a piece of storytelling as this engagingly modest writer has given us', while the reviewer in *The New York Times* observed that it was 'a good workmanlike job of novel writing' but that 'six months after you had laid it down it would be astonishing indeed if you could remember a single thing about it, save that it was a love story laid at a British bomber base'. John Betjeman, like Norway, previously a student at Oxford Preparatory School, and destined to become one of the best-loved English poets of his generation, also reviewed the book. He commented, perhaps somewhat surprisingly for a Nevil Shute novel, that after reading novels on distressing subjects it was a 'relief to read a first-class love story'. The public in America also loved *Pastoral*, where it sold 430,000 copies in less than a month after publication. It was serialised in both *The Australian Women's Weekly* and *The Ladies' Home Journal*. It was chosen as the September Book of the Month Club Selection, and the film rights were bought by Metro-Goldwyn-Mayer. It seems that, in spite of the reservations of some literary critics, Nevil Shute now had quite a following.

Following the Normandy landings, the workload at the DMWD began to decline. Norway's appointment was terminated and he was transferred to the Naval Reserve in December 1944. He left the RNVR as an acting temporary lieutenant commander, a rank he had first achieved in an acting capacity in March 1941. Although a number of his colleagues promoted at the same time had received further promotion, Norway stayed where he was. Maybe his passion for speaking his mind and the disagreement over withholding the publication of *Most Secret* had left its mark on some of his superiors.

Norway had initially been very sceptical about spending his war years in the IAAWD and DMWD, a move he believed would make no meaningful contribution to help winning the war. He was later to admit that with hindsight this observation had been 'very, very wrong'.

8

Home and Abroad
January 1945–August 1948

Although no longer part of the Department of Miscellaneous Weapons Development (DMWD), Lieutenant Commander Norway's contribution to the war effort was not yet over. He had in fact being given indefinite leave from the Royal Naval Voluntary Reserve in order to take up work for the Ministry of Information. In spite of the apparent lack of interest in the articles he had written for the Ministry during the Normandy landings, he was now to be employed as a correspondent to report on another theatre of the war, the Far East.

The civilian life that Nevil Norway was beginning to return to in January 1945 was certainly not a rosy one. The weather in Britain was dominated by periods of intense frost and considerable snow. In many ways the bleak weather matched the mood on the streets. The prime minister, in a cautiously optimistic New Year's Eve speech had said that 'today we are entering upon a year that should bring us victory in Europe'. However, he warned that 'until that end there can be no return to our normal habits'.

With increasingly encouraging news from the Western and Russian fronts, the Allies were now winning the war in Europe, however it was clear that the enemy was not going to give up easily. The Normandy landings were now six months in the past, yet people in mainland Britain were still under threat. Since June 1944, Germany had been attacking Britain with a new secret weapon, the V1 flying bomb (known colloquially as 'Buzz Bombs' or 'Doodlebugs'). This devastating weapon had a 1,870 lb high-explosive warhead and a speed of around 400 mph. While London was the principal target of this weapon, they were also aimed at cities such as Manchester, Portsmouth and Southampton. V1 attacks were joined in September 1944 by the more advanced and much harder to stop V2 rocket. With a devastating one-ton warhead and a speed of around 3,600 mph, this was the world's first ballistic missile and could reach London five minutes after being fired from mobile launchers in the occupied Low Countries. By the time the last V2 struck Orpington, Kent in March 1945, these two pilotless weapons had killed more than 8,000 Londoners, seriously injuring at least 25,000 more and destroying thousands of houses and factories.

Apart from ongoing safety concerns in some of the major cities, after over six years of conflict, the civilian population in general was becoming war weary. There seemed to be a shortage of nearly everything, whether it was rationed or not. In fact, restriction of some goods, such as clothes, was being tightened even further. Austerity would be something Britain would have to live with for years to come. While most believed (or wanted to believe) Churchill's prediction that the war in Europe was coming to an end, it did not seem that the good times would be returning anytime soon.

The Ministry of Information (MOI) which Norway was about to be seconded to, had a bit of a chequered history. It had originally been established by the British government at the beginning of the Second World War to manage propaganda and publicity both at home and overseas in Allied and neutral counties. During its early years the Ministry experienced many teething troubles, changes in structure and conflicts with the press over censorship and its inability to function smoothly. With over 10,000 reporters in London alone, the MOI initially found itself quite incapable of dealing with press requests. Four different ministers headed the MOI during this turbulent period, before stability was reached under the leadership of Brendan Bracken in July 1941, and the Ministry was finally in a position to function as a counter to Nazi propaganda.

By November 1944, with victory in Europe on the horizon, the MOI turned its focus increasingly to the Far East. Winston Churchill was becoming concerned that the morale and well-being of forces in this area needed improving, and that 'the people at home and the men serving abroad, or liable to be sent abroad, should be fully informed on all aspects of the war in the Far East'. As part of this strategy, the MOI were directed to develop plans to increase publicity about the Far Eastern campaign. Using skilled writers like Nevil Norway to report on Allied successes was part of a new strategy intended to keep morale high and also remind people at home that the defeat of Germany did not mean the end of the war.

It was originally planned that Norway would leave for the Far East sometime in February and spend the next three months reporting stories of British successes. Unfortunately, because of communication problems between the Ministry of Information and the Treasury, his trip was delayed. No longer part of the DMWD, he found himself with time on his hands. Nevil Shute therefore re-emerged and turned his attention to a new written form: film scripts.

At the end of the previous year it had being widely reported that *Pastoral* would be part of the MGM schedule for 1945. MGM's British production chief, Sir Alexander Korda, had even got as far as naming Carol Reed as the producer and director. What was not being reported was that Shute himself would be writing the screenplay. It is not clear whether the initiative to write the screenplay came from Shute or Korda, but the precision with which such pieces had to be crafted would have appealed to the engineer in Norway.

Korda had taken the precaution of using an experienced screenwriter, film director and producer Ian Dalrymple to advise Shute during the process. By the end of January 1945, a script had been produced which Dalrymple had reviewed and found generally acceptable. However, for unknown reasons, the project never got any further and the film was never made. It was quite common at that time for a studio to have many scripts ready to go at any one time and in the end only actually take one or two of them forward to filming.

In the case of *Pastoral*, it may be that Korda and MGM believed that both American and British audiences were beginning to lose their appetite for war movies. The box office hit of the previous year had after all been the musical comedy *Going My Way*, while the top-grossing films in 1945 would turn out to be dominated by stars such as Bing Crosby,

July Garland and Ginger Rogers. Although Nevil Shute's career as a screenwriter seemed over before it had really begun, it was a form he had not quite finished with yet.

Still unable to leave for the Far East, Shute returned to a topic he had first partially explored in *An Old Captivity*: the probable discovery of North America by the Icelandic explorer Leif Erikson. He started work on *Vinland the Good*, which is now considered by many to be the least successful book he ever wrote. In addition to working on *Vinland the Good*, he also launched one of his regular broadsides at government bureaucracy. This time he wrote to *The Times* complaining at length about a recent statement by the Secretary of State for Air that in Transport Command it was the responsibility of the pilot to decide whether or not a flight should start. Norway fundamentally disagreed with this, and in his usual forthright manner he explained why such a policy was wrong. It seems that when something upset him, rather than just shrug his shoulders and let things pass, he had to direct his anger at someone. His younger daughter Shirley remembers that her father had a 'fearsome temper' and 'was quite frequently enraged'. Interestingly, he gave his address as the Oxford and Cambridge University Club, which seems to indicate he was still living in London at least for part of the week.

Arrangements for his trip to the Far East were finally sorted out, and by mid-April Norway was finally a MOI correspondent in Calcutta (now Kolkata). Locally he was attached to the RAF Public Relations section, but all his written work while overseas was controlled and approved by G. Grafton Greene, a features editor at the MOI in London.

Within two weeks, Norway had been moved from the safety of Calcutta to the forward area in Burma (now Myanmar). Japanese resistance was crumbling in central Burma, with the Allied forces now making significant progress along the Irrawaddy valley, moving towards their goal of recapturing the capital Rangoon (now Yangon) and effectively ending the conflict in the country. The first article he sent to Greene on 30 April was based on a mixture of conversations with military personnel in Calcutta and observations of what he had seen as he was flown nearer to the front-line action in Burma. A letter accompanying his manuscript expressed the doubts Norway had regarding the suitability of his submission. He was aware that what he had written 'was not properly a war article at all, but a record of Calcutta gossip'. He was convinced that the war in the region would soon be over, and that he would not be able to produce any war articles. He asked for guidance. It seemed that he and Greene had not discussed in much detail, if at all, exactly what he was to report on during his time in the Far East.

A month later Norway was in Rangoon and beginning to get more than a little frustrated. He had just completed his fifth article and yet still not received any response or feedback from Greene. Finally, on 29 May, he received a short telegram informing him that the first article was disappointing because it was objective, the second was out of date and the third was closer to what was required. Greene wanted 'stories of definite British achievement with plenty of detail'. Norway's reply a day later told Greene rather bluntly that he 'must face up to the fact that there is no, repeat NO, British achievement going on in this theatre of war at present, and that there will be none during the period of my stay out here'. He ended the letter by reminding Greene that if the MOI and Treasury had not taken so long in finalising his trip then he could have been in post by February and produced 'a fine sequence of articles leading to the fall of Rangoon'. This was a typical Norway response in such a situation. When he was unhappy about something, diplomacy did not feature high on the agenda.

Norway and Greene tried to agree on what to do next. This was complicated by the time it took communications to travel between the two of them, and the rapidly changing situation in the region. In the end, little was agreed or approved, and on 24 June, Norway sent his sixth and final article, an account on the difficulties of operating aircraft in tropical conditions during wartime. In the covering letter, he advised he would be returning to England as soon as he could get a flight, and that he would meet Greene as soon as he arrived in London. None of Norway's six articles were ever published, and his short, rather unsuccessful career as a war correspondent was over. It might have seemed that Norway's trip to the Far East had been unsuccessful, however much of what he had seen would provide characters and elements of storylines in future novels.

Norway returned to England at the end of June. He had been away just over two months, and during that time a lot had happened. On 30

April Hitler had committed suicide in Berlin, and on 7 May Germany had officially surrendered at Rheims. The war in Europe was over, and even though the prime minister expected the coalition government to remain in place until the Japanese had been defeated, two weeks after the celebrations of VE Day the Labour Party withdrew its support from the government and a general election was called.

It soon became apparent that even though the nation was grateful to Churchill for the part he had played as a wartime leader, many were now looking for change. The Labour Party under Clement Attlee offered a promise of huge social reform: a National Health Service, social security for all, a minimum school-leaving age of 16 and state ownership of key industries, while Churchill's Conservatives offered to 'Finish the Job' which was taken to mean more of the same. This past-versus-future argument was starkly reinforced when Churchill unwisely suggested in an election radio broadcast that a 'Socialist Government conducting the entire life and industry of the country' could not allow public expressions of discontent and 'would have to fall back on some kind of Gestapo' in such circumstances.

The people voted on Thursday 5 July, but results were not released for three weeks because of the number of votes from the armed forces still serving overseas that had to be collected and counted. The result was an overwhelming victory for the Labour Party; they were elected with a majority of 146 seats. Churchill and the Conservatives had been routed. This was bad news for Norway, who would certainly not have been in favour of more state control and did not believe in the principal of one person one vote. For the first time he probably began to question whether Britain was now the right place for him and his family.

Like many others in Britain, Norway read in his morning newspaper on 7 August 1945 that the world's 'First atomic bomb hits Japan'. At approximately 8.10 am the previous day, the America B-29 aircraft *Enola Gay* had dropped a uranium bomb on the Japanese city of Hiroshima. Approximately 70,000 people were killed almost instantaneously, with at least another 70,000 dying over the coming weeks from radiation poisoning. Three days later a plutonium bomb was dropped on the city of Nagasaki with equally devastating results. Within days, the Japanese had surrendered and World War Two was at an end.

Much of the home newspapers' comment at that stage was about the 'technical genius' of the achievement and the part that Britain had played in the development of this awesome new weapon, rather than the huge numbers of civilians that had been slaughtered. However, it would soon become apparent that the atomic bomb was more than just another weapon, and unless handled with care it could lead to mankind's ultimate destruction. This is something which would occupy Shute's mind over the coming years, and just over ten years later it would result in one of his most powerful and controversial novels – *On the Beach*.

With his brief association with the MOI at an end, and the war now over, Norway could return to life as a full-time novelist. Compared with what had come before, mid-1945 to mid-1947 was a period of relative stability. For the first time since buying the property, he and his family were able to settle down to life together at Pond Head on Hayling Island.

Life for Norway was of necessity based on routine. His day was usually split up into three distinct parts separated by breakfast at 8.15 am, lunch at 1.00 pm and dinner at 7.30 pm. The rigid meal times may well have been due to the fact that the family still employed domestic staff to run the house and garden, even after the war. The first part of the day from 9.00 am until 1.00 pm would be spent in his office, and be set aside for writing. The afternoon session was used for recreational hobbies such as sailing or oil painting. Finally, during the evening he would return to writing for another few hours or spend time in his workshop making engineering models. He liked to do things with his hands for some part of every day.

While a novel was in preparation, this routine was followed seven days a week, with one Sunday a month off to attend church. His day was one during which he happily spent a great many hours alone, and one in which his wife and daughters did not participate. He was a Victorian/Edwardian in attitude, with clear views about the responsibilities of a husband. His role was to provide, and it was that of his wife to manage the household and bring up the children. As far as his children were concerned, he must have often seemed a somewhat distant, authoritarian figure. The younger daughter found him 'a quite harsh unloving father', but also admitted that he 'gave her a sense of honour and of what was right and wrong'.

He employed Gladys Bessant as a secretary from late 1947. She would come in three times a week to deal with correspondence and to type final drafts of his manuscripts. When he was writing, Shute typed his manuscripts out directly rather than writing them by hand first. After he had planned a story he could generally write around 1,000 words a sitting, with a novel taking typically nine months to complete. Once a draft manuscript was finished, the first chapter would then be rewritten, often a number of times. Using such a strict routine, he averaged a novel a year for the rest of his life.

Although he now had the manuscripts of *Most Secret* and *Vinland the Good* in the pipeline to keep his publishers happy, never one to stand still for long, Shute was soon moving on to his next novel. He started work on *The Chequer Board* (originally provisionally titled *The Guided Feet*) in the later part of 1945. This time, combining observations from the Far East with a recent interest in the treatment of African-American soldiers in Europe, he planned to explore the post-war experiences of soldiers from different countries and social backgrounds.

Detailed work on this had to be put briefly on hold, as in mid-August the wartime embargo on *Most Secret* was finally lifted. Written in late 1942, publication during the war had been refused, as it was considered that some aspects of the novel were a bit too close to projects Norway had been connected with at DMWD *Most Secret* tells the story of an odd mixture of four British Army and Navy officers from a civilian background, all of who for one reason or another have an abiding hatred of Germans and wish to do something to boost the morale of the civilians in occupied France in the early 1940s. They develop a plan to use a French fishing boat armed with a massive flamethrower to attack and destroy enemy ships along the coast of Brittany. This was a novel about the extremes ordinary people will go to in war when driven by hatred. Shute later wrote that he had written the book 'to perpetuate the mood of bitterness and hate which involved England in the latter stages of the war'. He also considered it to be one of the 'best formed books' that he ever wrote.

As was often the case, the literary critics did not always agree. While choosing it as one of its Novels of the Week, *The Times Literary Supplement* considered the construction of the novel to be 'partly laboured and fragmentary'. However, in a more positive conclusion the reviewer noted that 'Mr Shute always has good things to offer, and, in spite of some weaknesses, "Most Secret" retains much of his power to convey the springs of heroic conduct in the lightest and least assuming of tones'. In the *Evening Standard* the novelist Graham Greene reviewed the book. He was not particularly generous to his fellow Heinemann author. While admitting Shute had the gift of readability, he also noted, 'Mr. Shute is too confident that his gift of readability will allow him to get away with anything. There is a sense of laziness about his talent'.

Two months later the book was published on the other side of the Atlantic. Again reviews were mixed, but many now at least acknowledged that whatever the artistic merits of his work, Shute was a natural storyteller with an eye for authentic detail. Typical of this begrudging attitude was *The New York Times,* which concluded that 'as a work of fiction it is smooth and interesting, but undistinguished. But as a graphic account of a fantastic and horrible method of waging war it is gruesomely effective'. Although Shute's reason for writing *Most Secret* was now a thing of the past, it seems that the public were still interested in wartime exploits as the book was in *The New York Times* Best Sellers list for eight weeks, and reprinted nine times in England alone over the next decade.

Shute finished *The Chequer Board* in early 1946 and immediately began firming up ideas for his next novel. Not everything he wrote always ended in a novel, and *The Seafarers* was typical of this. Like *The Chequer Board*, the novella is concerned with post-war themes. The story concerns a naval lieutenant and Wren (a member of the Women's Royal Naval Service) who meet for the first time at the end of the Second World War, and it explores their developing relationship and the difficulty both have in adjusting to life as civilians once they have been demobilised. Having completed this short story, it was initially shelved but later published as a three-part serial in the short-lived Australian magazine *Home* in 1948. He then rewrote and extended the story before seeming to lose interest in it. He was to return to the theme of war and post-war experiences again, but the two manuscripts of *The Seafarers* were found among his papers after his death. Just over forty years later, in 2002, the second of these was revisited, and after some minor editing, it was finally published.

By mid-1946, the optimism that many in Britain had felt a year earlier with the ending of the war in Europe and the election of a new Labour government had almost completely dissipated. The harsh reality was that the country was destitute and many of its people exhausted by years of austerity. The unexpectedly abrupt ending of America's Lend-Lease scheme, and its replacement by a tough new loan, meant that in spite of progress being made in areas such as the nationalisation of the iron and steel industries and the introduction of a National Health Service, everyday life for many was still tough. Rationing of some commodities had been further tightened, and as a result of crop failures, bread and flour rationing was introduced at the end of July, something which had not even occurred during the war. Industrial action by dockers had caused problems with the flow of goods, and there were also already warnings that the country had insufficient coal stocks to get through the coming winter. Not surprisingly, the number of families looking to migrate to countries such as Australia, Canada and South Africa in search of a better life was rapidly increasing. The Norways were to some extent insulated from many of the everyday problems faced by large sections of the population. Compared to many they were wealthy, they owned a large comfortable house which was run with the help of domestic staff, and Nevil Norway had complete control over his working day.

As was the case in the Great War, the Second World War had bought a huge advance in aircraft technology in a very short period. All metal aircraft were now common, and of course they were flying faster and further. The design of the world's first passenger jet airliner was already being considered at de Havilland, and in less than three years the first prototype of the de Havilland Comet would make its maiden flight. Of course, such rapid development also bought its own problems. There was still not a full understanding of the behaviour of many materials when subjected to long periods of stress in harsh environmental conditions. Norway had known Professor Alfred Pugsley since the days of the Imperial Airship Scheme, and through their later conversations he was aware of this problem and of the work that had been going on at the Royal Aircraft Establishment in recent years on metal fatigue. By the autumn he had started work on his next novel. Tentatively titled *The Mental Flight*, but to become *No Highway*, Nevil Shute returned to the subject of aviation. However, this time his interest was passenger aviation in the post-war years and the increased potential for catastrophic air disasters to occur.

With his thoughts focused on his latest project, he now had to briefly return to a previous one, as *Vinland the Good* was published in both Britain and America in October 1946. This book revisited a subject Shute had first partially explored in *An Old Captivity* six years earlier: the theory that North America had first been discovered by the Icelandic explorer Leif Erikson at the beginning of the ninth century. He thought Erikson's trip was 'one of the most fascinating adventures in history' as it concerned 'a journey by the common man, a farmer, seeking to get a load of lumber to build cow houses and discovering America on the side'. Since writing *An Old Captivity* he had read more about the Norse sagas on which the Erikson theory was based. He had made contacts with scholars in the field, including Edward Gray (a well-known but somewhat controversial researcher of Norse mythology), and aware that he had only touched on the subject in his earlier novel was keen to write more. As he showed many times during his writing career, Shute took the factual background of his novels very seriously and was not afraid to consult experts in specialist areas in order to get things right. This time, not wishing to produce a second novel on this topic, and perhaps still intrigued by techniques he had used in his screenwriting project for *Pastoral* the previous year, he decided to tell the story in the form of a play. The book was laid out in a conventional stage play format, complete with instructions to the actors on delivery and the director on scene layout.

Set in an English public school at the end of the Second World War, a young inexperienced teacher, Major Callender, is returning to the school after six years away and is given as his first duty the task of introducing the history of the United States to the Lower Fifth. The majority of the book is concerned with the subsequent lesson that Callender gives the boys, telling the story of Eric the Red, Leif Erikson and their adventures. Although many of the class are inspired by Callender's unconventional lesson, the headmaster is not, and the play ends with him suggesting that the young teacher should take up an earlier job offer he had been made selling electric razors in Paris. Shute endeavoured to base the book on the history of Leif Erikson as was known at that time, believing it to be 'as true a representation of what happened as any novelist can be expected to produce'. He only resorted to true fiction near the end when he incorporated the story of the two Scottish slaves Haki and Haekia that he had first described in *An Old Captivity*.

A new novel by Shute was becoming a big event for William Heinemann and William Morrow. When *Vinland the Good* was published it was announced with banner headlines and extensive advertising. Unfortunately, this time the book was ignored by most mainstream reviewers, and those that did bother were less than enthusiastic. While Shute had been excited by the story, it seems that the public were not. Maybe the play format was a step too far for readers bought up on Shute's previous novels and style. The book was a commercial failure, and the only one of Shute's books Heinemann did not reprint after its initial release. In a complete collection of his work that Heron Books published in the 1960s, *Vinland the Good* was also omitted. Whether it was because of its commercial failure, or whether he had just lost interest in the technique, the play format was a form Shute would never to return to.

The early months of 1947 were marked by the publication of *The Chequer Board*. Following completion of his duties with the Ministry of Information and now fully demobilised from the RNVR, this was the first novel he had produced on his return to post-war life as a full-time author. It had been written in an intense period of activity between September 1945 and February 1946, and it tackled an issue which he genuinely expected would adversely affect his sales in America, that of racial prejudice. Norway had come across the book *A Rising Wind* sometime soon after its publication in 1945. It examines the treatment of African-American soldiers in Britain during the Second World War, and one case highlighted in the book was that of a soldier unjustly accused of the rape of a British girl in Portsmouth. Such was his interest in this case, he wrote to the author, Walter White, for further information. Walter White was a prominent American civil rights campaigner and secretary of The National Association of Advancement for Coloured People, and a correspondence developed between the two.

White's fight for racial equality interested Norway, and combining this with his own observations of American troops in Britain, and of attitudes towards different races and cultures during his time in the Far East, he developed *The Chequer Board*. This novel was one in which Shute told a story with a purpose rather than purely to entertain his readers. It was also another of his novels in which a very ordinary person is put in circumstances which make them do unexpected things.

Set in post-war Britain, the story is centred around John Turner, who has a comfortable if somewhat uneventful life as a salesman for a flour company, with a small house in the London suburbs and an unsatisfactory childless marriage. This life is changed forever when he learns that a serious head wound he received in the war has deteriorated and that he only has months to live. In 1943 he had been a captain in the Royal Army Service Corps when he was caught running a black market operation selling army stores. The aeroplane returning him to Britain to face a court martial was shot down, and seriously wounded he found himself under guard in a civilian hospital sharing a ward with three other men: an African-American soldier serving in Britain who had tried to kill himself when facing trial unjustly accused of rape; a British paratrooper who was charged with killing a man in a brawl in a London pub; and the second pilot of the aircraft which had been flying Turner back to face trial and whose recent marriage was already falling apart. Turner decides to find out what has happened to these people in the three years since he last seen them. The subsequent journey takes him to locations as far apart as Cornwall and Burma and allowed Shute to explore topics such as racial equality and mixed marriages.

In covering what were then such controversial topics in a popular novel, Shute was bound to open himself up to criticism, and so it proved. *Time* considered the plot to be 'embarrassingly slight' and 'a heavyweight plea in a lightweight novel', while the *The Times Literary Supplement* concluded *The Chequer Board* to be 'a rather disjointed novel, lighter and more perfunctory in tone than the sum of its parts warrants'. *The Saturday Review of Literature*, however, gave far more credit to Shute for tackling a big topic, but perhaps slightly exaggeratedly declared that 'despite our vaunted liberalism, our strident soap-box screams for tolerance, no American could have written The Chequer Board'. Not for the first time, the opinions of many of the literary critics proved to be at odds with those of the buying public.

The book was chosen as the April selection by the Literary Guild of America, and after its publication it spent fifteen weeks in *The New York Times* Best Sellers list, reaching number six. Shute's foreboding about sales in America had turned out to be ill-founded. In Britain the book proved equally popular and was chosen as the June selection of The Book Society, the first of Shute's books to receive this honour.

While Norway's professional life was a success, it seems that his private life was not. On 5 March 1947, Flora Twort noted in her diary that a strained Frances Norway had visited with the shocking news that Nevil had left her. Frances had married Nevil because he liked travelling, could fly, and therefore she thought they would have an exciting life together, but it was clearly not turning out that way.

Frances and Nevil had been married for almost exactly sixteen years, and like many other couples they had spent a great deal of time apart during the war. Whatever the reasons for the breakdown in their relationship, Nevil was serious about a separation and visited his solicitor, who advised him not to be a fool. After a few days, things between the Norways improved, and it was agreed that Nevil would continue living at home until their eldest daughter was 18.

In early May, an apparently reconciled Nevil and Frances Norway left for a seven-week tour of America, proposing to fill the trip with a mixture of business and pleasure. This time, rather than travel by ship, they flew using BOAC's (British Overseas Airways Corporation) transatlantic service. There was a small problem on arrival in Boston when the aircraft's undercarriage failed, although fortunately no one was injured. Always on the lookout for interesting new material, the incident stuck in Nevil's mind and found its way into the novel he was working on at the time.

The business side of the trip was concerned with the promotion of *The Chequer Board*, which had been published six weeks previously, and so any personal appearances by the author could only help sales. Still wary about the reaction in the country to the book, Norway had written to Walter White:

> 'There is, as you have pointed out, bound to be adverse criticism from the diehards, and in view of the unexpected distribution, there may be quite a lot of it. In view of this, I have decided to come over to your country at the beginning of May and stand up to be shot at, which should be great fun.'

In the end, he need not have worried, the tour was a great success. He was becoming a literary celebrity and treated as such with meet and greet events being held in venues such as the Crystal Room of the Ritz-Carlton

Hotel in New York. One journalist reported Shute 'standing amid a bevy of young women, beaming and shaking hands'. Away from the formal part of their tour, the Norways hired a car and travelled throughout the Midwest and some of the southern states. Wherever possible, the novelist did his best to experience small-town America. Perhaps in the back of the mind he was considering the country as a future home.

Back from America at the end of June, the country and what he thought of as its supportive view of Britain had clearly left a very positive impression on him. Almost immediately, he wrote to the *New Statesman and Nation* questioning whether, for its part, the British press was really being fair to America. He noted that 'In the bad temper bred of weariness and shortages and rationing it is easy for us to pick on aspects of their policy which we do not like, and highlight them. It is a pity if, in dealing with these controversial matters, we neglect to emphasise the intense good that exists in America towards this country'. It seemed he was beginning to get frustrated with aspects of life in Britain and was perhaps beginning to think of whether there was a better alternative elsewhere.

In comparison to the vibrant life he and his wife had experienced in America, everyday life in Britain after the war seemed to be certainly getting worse rather than better. The beginning of 1947 bought record amounts of snow, with the already low supplies of coal in the country forcing the closure of some power stations and making the problems even worse. Large parts of the country ground to a standstill and unemployment shot up as thousands were laid off work. The government introduced a range of draconian measures to try and cope with the shortages, such as limiting both industrial and domestic use of electricity, suspending television services and shortening radio broadcasts. The severe cold weather and the record-breaking floods and gales, which almost inevitably followed, also had a dramatic effect on food production. Potato and cereal crops were either frozen or rotted in the ground, and large numbers of animals were lost. The government had little choice but to tighten food rationing; in some cases it was now worse than it had been during the war. Although the government was continuing to press ahead with many of its promised social reforms, financially the country was struggling. In August, the prime minister Clement Attlee told the nation, 'I have no easy words for the nation. I cannot say when we will emerge into easier times'. He was preparing his colleagues and the country for further austerity, including more cuts to rations, a ban on holidays abroad and the abolishment of the basic petrol ration to stop motoring for pleasure. On 12 November the Chancellor of the Exchequer presented an emergency Budget, which among other things drastically increased the purchase tax on items such as cosmetics, radios and heaters. People were now being dissuaded from even buying modest luxury items to brighten their everyday lives.

Norway and his family were cushioned from the austerity that many were facing by his rapidly increasing income from book sales and film rights. A few days earlier, he had written to the author and poet John Pudney, taking great exception to an article in which he had written 'I know of no writer in Britain today who lives by books alone'. In his usual forthright manner, Norway was keen to put him right. He now strongly believed that he was both successful and adding to the wealth of the country, and he was even prepared to invite Pudney to dinner and show him his financial accounts should he need any more proof! In a passing shot at some of the literary fraternity, he also added that 'An unsuccessful author is not much good to his country in this time of crisis; a successful one can earn large sums for the country in foreign exchange'. Norway was certainly of use to his country, but whether his country could continue to meet his needs was an altogether different matter.

By the autumn of 1947, with *No Highway* well underway, Shute began to face a problem that had troubled many novelists before him: where to get ideas for future books. *No Highway* when it was published would be his thirteenth book in just over twenty years. However, for the majority of that period, writing had been his second job with lots of opportunity to find new material from his everyday work experiences. Now that he was a full-time author, he had to look elsewhere for inspiration. To him the contents of a book were of prime importance, far more so than style. He believed that novelists could usually get a few good books from their life experience, and that in his case the war had provided material for another four. Now, if he was to continue to write books which would be of interest to the public, he had to look elsewhere. In this case, 'elsewhere' was to consider a journey back to the East, taking in the Persian Gulf, India and Burma.

At first he had considered driving most of the way, shipping his vehicle between countries. But the journey gradually grew in his mind, and it soon seemed only a small jump to Australia. As he later wrote, after studying a map of northern Queensland: 'I found a large white space several square inches in area, with nothing printed on the paper at all except one little black dot labelled hut'. He was sure that if he were to travel to this hut, he would come back with something new to say. A short trip to gather new material quickly grew into a six-month expedition to fly his own aircraft to Australia and back, a trip which would define the future for both him and his family.

Having decided on the flight to Australia, planning for this trip took more and more of his time during the first months of 1948. He did, though, continue to write, and by early March he had completed just over a hundred pages of *Blind Understanding*. The novel is another that deals with the aftermath of the Second World War and is set in England in 1949. Using a flashback technique, it tells of the experiences of a Wren both during and after the war. However, for whatever reason, Shute did not continue with the novel. Either he was losing interest in the topic or else the planning for his flight to Australia was starting to take over more of his working day. Much of this aborted manuscript would, though, appear in his novel *Requiem for a Wren* seven years later.

As 1948 progressed, and Britain prepared to host the Olympic Games, Norway continued preparations for his flight to Australia. Like his novels, he was planning things in great detail. The trip would be done in easy stages, only flying during the day and wherever possible at low altitude. The trip was expected to take six months: two months to fly to Australia, two months in Australia, and two months getting back, servicing the aeroplane himself along the way. By the spring he had already bought an aircraft, a new Percival Proctor Mk V. A single-engine, four-seater monoplane, the British-made Proctor was popular among post-war private pilots, and once it had been modified for longer journeys to include long-range fuel tanks, a VHF radio, improved compass and air thermometer, it seemed ideal for the trip. Although he had held a private pilot's licence since 1924, Norway had only accrued about 180 hours of solo flying experience in the intervening years. By the time he left for Australia, he had added around another 50 hours in the Proctor. Even so, he was planning to fly to Australia with only 230 hours solo flying experience and never having flown for longer than 2 hours at a time before.

Norway decided he needed a co-pilot for the trip. He first approached the author Alan Moorehead, who was interested but declined for the time being, and so on 28 March he wrote to another author, James 'Jimmie' Riddell. Giving very brief details of his planned trip, Norway asked, almost as an aside, if Riddell would be interested in joining him. They had met the previous autumn when Norway had first talked in general terms about collecting material for new books. Ten years younger than Norway, Riddell had been a champion skier for Britain in the 1920s and 30s and had been seconded to the Australian 9th Army in the Middle East during the Second World War. As a chief instructor at the 1st Australian Corps Ski School, he had taught advanced skiing and winter survival techniques to thousands of soldiers. After the war he resumed his career as a children's author. He had studied languages at Cambridge, was an accomplished photographer, widely travelled and seemed an ideal companion. Though not a licensed pilot, Norway still felt Riddell was capable of keeping the Proctor on a steady course in the air while he dozed. Riddell accepted without any hesitation; the key things needed for the trip now seemed to be in place.

No Highway was published in America at the end of August. In this novel Shute returned to an aviation theme, this time with a focus on the growing passenger aircraft industry and the potential risks that too rapid development could bring. The central character of the novel, Theodore Honey, is a middle-aged, rather unprepossessing widower, who works as a research scientist at the Royal Aircraft Establishment in Farnborough. Totally absorbed in his work, he struggles to bring up his young daughter, not always devoting enough attention to her, and involves her in his investigations into controversial historical theories such as the Great Pyramid and the ten lost tribes of Israel. Honey is currently investigating metal fatigue in aircraft structures, and in particular the tailplane of the Rutland Reindeer, a new airliner in service on transatlantic routes. He is convinced that metal fatigue will cause the tailplane of the Reindeer to fail when the aircraft reaches 1,440 flying hours, and having predicted this theoretically, he is part way through a test to prove it experimentally.

When a Reindeer crashes in Labrador, Newfoundland, Honey is sent to examine the debris of the crash. Somewhat ironically, the aircraft taking him to Canada is also a Rutland Reindeer, which he is alarmed to find has twice the number of flying hours than any other of its type in service, and it is near to the 1,440 he believes will bring disaster. Convinced that the passengers are in danger, and unable to persuade the captain to stop the flight, he deliberately sabotages the aircraft on a stopover at Gander by lowering the aircraft's undercarriage to make it inoperable. He is aware that this action has almost certainly finished his career. Two passengers on the flight, an air stewardess and a middle-aged Hollywood actress, take an interest in this rather strange man and in different ways try to help him and his daughter. Displaying a sentimental streak, in a book immersed in the often unsentimental world of aeronautical engineering, Shute ensures the novel ends happily both for Theodore Honey, his daughter and his professional reputation.

Norway rarely consulted his family about his novels, except for checking with Frances on medical matters, however on this occasion he asked Heather about Theodore Honey's teenage daughter. Always keen to make things as accurate as possible, he wanted a young woman's view on whether he had got it right.

The engineer in Norway was intrigued by metal fatigue in aircraft, and he was sure that this would be of great topical interest as even five months earlier he had been urging his literary agent to speed up publication. A British South American Airways aircraft had disappeared without trace over the Atlantic Ocean at the beginning of the year, and he was convinced that metal fatigue would turn out to be a factor. As he somewhat testily wrote to Watt, 'The characterisation of my writing has always been that I have taken a chance dealing with somewhat difficult topical subjects. My writing on these lines has paid everybody very well. I am now showing the red light about this book. I want it published damn quick'.

Reviews in America again covered the full spectrum, some thinking that it lacked the old magic while others thought it was as good as his best. However, it proved to be not as popular in America as his previous novel, and it was only in *The New York Times* Best Sellers list for two weeks. The story certainly appealed to Hollywood, as Twentieth Century Fox quickly snapped up the film rights for £20,000 (equivalent to £700,000 in 2016), at a time when many studios were complaining about the lack of suitable material for films.

This time, though, there was more than the reaction of the literary reviewers to worry about. While the Rutland Reindeer aircraft that Shute had used in *No Highway* was purely fictitious, the airline company he described as operating it was not. The state-owned British Overseas Airways Corporation was not happy to find its name being used without permission in the book and being associated with aircraft disasters. As soon as the book reviews with references to BOAC started appearing in America, the company was in touch with William Heinemann asserting that *No Highway* constituted serious libel on the company and its chairman. This was a threat which neither William Morrow nor William Heinemann could ignore, with urgent action being required. Such was the seriousness of the situation, that on 21 September, the day before Norway was due to leave for Australia, he found himself part of a top-level meeting in London with the chairman of BOAC, Sir Miles Thomas, the chairman of William Heinemann Ltd, Alexander Frere, and legal representatives from both sides. At this meeting it was agreed that all references to BOAC be deleted from *No Highway* and that the airline company referred to in the book be called the Central Air Transport Organisation (CATO). Norway also agreed to change the name of the British South American Airways Corporation and delete the second and third paragraph of his author's note at the end of his book. BOAC also insisted that they have direct contact with Twentieth Century Fox to ensure that the content of the film should be appropriate. Although Norway had often been resistant to making changes to his books, this time the consequences could have been a costly legal battle without any certainty of a positive outcome and perhaps the need to delay his long-planned trip to Australia.

The threat of legal action had delayed the publication of *No Highway* in Britain, and the revised version was eventually published on 13 December. Reviews were positive and in some cases almost affectionate. For instance, the literary reviewer in *The Observer* wondered 'if any novelist writing in this country today is so liked by so many as is Mr Nevil Shute', while the novelist J. B. Priestley considered that 'this is perhaps his finest performance so far, containing the essence of what is both excellent and original in his fiction'. Priestley also assumed that the book would be ignored by the more 'highbrow reviewers', believing that 'it is one of the cultural weaknesses of our time that only highly introverted work is regarded as having any definite literary significance'. Priestley was highlighting something that Shute would face throughout his career. No matter how popular he became, some mainstream reviewers would continue to treat his novels with disdain. The Book Society selected *No Highway* as its monthly selection, the second year in a row it had chosen a Nevil Shute novel, while another renowned novelist Daphne du Maurier nominated the book as one of the best novels of 1949 (even though it had been published in 1948). After a shaky start, all was turning out well.

Norway was unaware of how his latest novel was being received in Britain, as on 13 December 1948 he was already on the other side of the world. To be precise he was in Cairns, northern Queensland, preparing his small private aeroplane for a flight into outback Australia. He was part way through a trip which had been intended to provide material for future novels but which ultimately would do more than that – it would change his life.

9

Australia and Back
September 1948–March 1949

The 23 September 1948 was not a big news day in Britain. Although on the world front, events which would have major long-term consequences such as the blockade of Berlin where taking place, little had happened the previous day to interest most readers at home. Clement Attlee's Labour government still had a huge majority in the House of Commons, and while post-war life in the country could not by any means be described as easy, there was little prospect of another general election until 1950. The lack of news meant that some national newspapers had to resort to filling their front page with headlines more usually found in local newspapers, such as 'Marjorie of Ealing Dances With Star' and more bizarrely 'Mrs. Dobson Sings 3 Notes for £5 5s'. No newspaper seemed to have picked up that early on the afternoon of the previous day a Percival Proctor G-AKIW had taken off from Portsmouth Aerodrome bound for Tours in the centre of France with two authors on board.

The single-engine aeroplane, which was known affectionately as Item Willie, after the military phonetic alphabet's words for the last two letters of its registration, was being piloted by Nevil Norway. Alongside him was his navigator and companion for the trip, James (Jimmie) Riddell. Their destination that day was just over five hours away, but the ultimate objective was Australia. The trip had been over a year in the planning, and the aeroplane was crammed full of everything they expected to need for such a venture, from engine spare parts to a rubber dinghy. The plan

146

was to fly in short hops, by daylight only, staying each night at a local hotel, and reach Darwin around 20 December. Their route, with stops in Basra, Karachi, Rangoon and Bali, would expose them to a wide range of climates and cultures. They then intended to explore Australia and leave for home around the end of January, arriving in Britain towards the end of March. While the trip was being undertaken at a relaxed pace, it was still a very ambitious undertaking for a pilot with so little flying experience, no experience of flying outside mainland Europe, and with an inexperienced navigator.

The aeroplane Norway had chosen for the flight was a single-engine, low-wing monoplane, the Percival Proctor Mk V. The first Percival Proctor had flown in 1939, but up until 1945 it had been made solely for military applications and used mainly for short-range communication duties or as a radio trainer. At the end of the war, a model intended for the civilian market, the Percival Proctor Mk V, was finally released. Although reliable, it soon developed a reputation for being difficult to handle at low speeds, in bumpy conditions or in crosswinds. Like many other wooden aeroplanes its construction could also become suspect when used over a long period in tropical conditions.

In view of the nature of the trip and the minor celebrity status of the travellers, it may have seemed surprising that their departure was so low-key, not even attracting the interest of the local press. This, however, was deliberate. Norway had written some material on the trip for his publishers, but he instructed Heinemann not to release it until he was confident that the venture was achieving something. By half past six that evening, after stops at Eastleigh to clear customs, and Dinard, they had landed safely in Tours and were heading towards the Hotel D'Univers where they would be spending their first night. At last a journey which would have a significant effect on the life of Nevil Norway and the literary output of Nevil Shute was underway.

The global wars in Europe and the Far East were now over, but there were still plenty of regional conflicts in progress. On the outward route they were taking, these included the Greek Civil War, the dispute between India and Pakistan over Kashmir, an internal conflict in Burma (now Myanmar) and the Indonesian National Revolution. Countries such as India and

Burma were part of an ever growing list that had gained independence from the British Empire, but as is so often the case separation had brought new problems. They would certainly not always be flying through regions that could be considered stable. For most of the time they would be on their own, with no ground support team and relying on prearranged local contacts at each stop to help with servicing, refuelling and accommodation. As far as navigation was concerned, apart from what Riddell considered lousy maps, the only thing they had to help them find their way was a VHF radio transmitter and receiver with a range of about forty miles.

While Norway described Riddell as a stimulating companion and good friend, he was not a pilot or mechanic and at best only an amateur if enthusiastic navigator. The responsibility for flying and maintaining the aeroplane would fall squarely on Norway's shoulders; quite a weight for someone approaching fifty who had already had two minor heart attacks. This trip would be by no means a walk in the park.

Both Norway and Riddell kept a record of the trip, each reflecting the different personalities and objectives of the two men. Norway's contained a very detailed entry for every day of the trip, noting what had been done and people they had met. Exactly what you would expect from an author collecting new material for future novels. Riddell's, on the other hand, was far more unusual, the sort of diary someone going on holiday might keep, with observations about climate, culture and, more unusually, long descriptions of dreams he was having – sometimes it was difficult to differentiate between his dreams and actual events. He also did not write an entry every day if he did not think there was anything worth saying.

While there was no such thing as a typical day during their outward trip, the time spent in Baghdad gives an example of the challenges that were faced during the course of the journey. They arrived just before midday on 3 October, having left Beirut at 7.30 am. They had used tarmacadam roads and oil pipelines to assist their navigation across the Syrian Desert. As was the case for much of the flight to Australia, they flew into the sun the whole time, so that even short flights were tiring in the tight confines of the Proctor's cockpit. However, Riddell was in a positive mood, and noted in his diary that 'the trip is now really getting somewhere'. On landing, the first thing that hit them was the heat, so after lunch at the local Sinbad Hotel they slept under a punkah until tea. In the evening they dined in the hotel garden which overlooked the Tigris, it was still 85°F inside the hotel. Following meetings with the local de Havilland representative and a local Iraqi Airways captain, they finished the day drinking at the Airways Club with aircrews.

The following day, Norway was at the aerodrome early to start work on the 30-hour engine service which was due on Item Willie. He hit unexpected trouble almost immediately, finding that one of the engine's cylinders had a blown gasket. Working all morning, Norway concluded that the damage to the engine was such that it needed a new cylinder barrel – a spare they did not carry. The necessary spare part was tracked down to Habbaniyah Aerodrome fifty miles away, and so the following day a local BOAC captain flew Norway and Tull, the de Havilland representative, to Habbaniyah in an old and rather dilapidated Auster monoplane. The pilot had extensive experience of flying large airliners like Liberators and Vikings, but the single-engine Auster was something new. After what can only be described as a hair-raising flight, in which each take-off and landing was an adventure in itself, a relieved Norway, now with a new engine cylinder barrel, arrived back in Baghdad. He later wrote in his diary that 'quite seriously, I have never flown with such a bad pilot in all my life, yet he is first class on his Viking'.

Norway worked on refitting the engine the rest of that day and in the heat of the following morning, finally testing that everything was working and ready to go at sunset. During the days Norway had been working on Item Willie, Riddell, not able to be of much help, occupied himself by visiting local museums and catching up on letters and telegrams. Their stay in Baghdad ended with a beach party given by a local Iraqi road contractor, and despite a late night, they were up at 6.30 am the following day, ready to leave for Basra at 9.00 am. They had been in Baghdad nearly four days – and so the trip continued.

By 10 October they had reached Karachi. Somewhat poignantly they used the airship hanger that had been built for, but never occupied by, the ill-fated R.101 as a landmark to help locate the civilian airport. Norway was now confident they were 'getting somewhere', and so he wrote to Dwye Evans at William Heinemann, asking him to release the publicity material he had written about the trip. The wider world could now be made aware of their adventure.

In Rangoon, a part of the world that Norway knew well, they visited U. Prajnananda, a 70-year-old Buddhist priest who lived in an ashram on the outskirts of the city. In Norway's case he was remaking an acquaintance, having first met the priest when he was in Burma in 1945. U. Prajnananda was no ordinary Buddhist priest. He had been born Frederick Charles Fletcher and studied theology at Oxford University, intent on becoming a Methodist minister. During the First World War he had risen to the rank of major in the Royal Engineers, seeing action at the battles of Ypres and the Somme. Travelling to the then closed country of Tibet in 1924, he entered the monastery at Shigatse as a novice. Fleeing the region following local riots, he travelled with nothing but his robes and a begging bowl across the mountains to Calcutta (now Kolkata) before moving to Bombay (now Mumbai) and then on to Ceylon (now Sri Lanka). Although there is now some doubt as to the accuracy of all of the account given by U. Prajnananda to a reporter of *The Age* in 1941, when Norway and Riddell met him he was definitely living the life of a monk. This was the type of story that fascinated Norway, and not surprisingly, a character based on U. Prajnananda later appeared in his novel *Round the Bend*.

On 23 November, sixty-three days after they had left Portsmouth, Norway and Riddell were finally flying over the Timor Sea towards Australia. Both were hot and nervous, as they were flying above a layer of cloud and so far it was the longest time that they had flown over sea without any sign of land in sight. Riddell was especially anxious, and wrote: 'Dismal feeling sitting here inactive – just waiting for minutes to pass … such miles of nothing – and this little Perspex bubble is such a speck in the blue'. So, it was with some relief that three hours after leaving Koepang (now Kupang) Riddell spotted a small patch of land through the clouds, which he identified as Eclipse Island. Just over eighty minutes later they landed on the dusty airstrip at Wyndham Aerodrome – they had reached Australia.

If Norway had wanted to experience something different during his time in Australia, then he had found it straight away with the first stop. It was certainly a low-key reception, a lone Australian stripped to the waist in the midday heat. They were driven to their accommodation at the Six Mile Hotel in a truck that was too hot to touch. Memories of that first afternoon were the unforgiving heat, red dust, the hotel creaking under its corrugated roof, flies everywhere, sweat pouring from all parts of the body, and constantly drinking anything they could lay their hands on. In spite of the challenging climate, dinner was still a large plate of meat and vegetables! This was certainly different from life at Pond Head.

Wyndham is the oldest and northernmost town in the Kimberley region of Western Australia. It had originally been a thriving gold rush town, but by 1888 that was over and since then it had fallen into decline. When Norway and Riddell visited, Wyndham was little more than an isolated township serving the local pastoralists who had settled in the area. The permanent population had dropped to around 30, with an influx of 600–800 cattle slaughtermen for four months each year to work at the local meat works. With little to keep them in Wyndham, and in spite of suffering from an upset stomach and diarrhoea, the following day Norway flew on to the Northern Territory and its capital Darwin.

In Darwin, they had their first meeting with the press in Australia. While Norway did not naturally seek publicity, and was often uncomfortable in the public arena, he was pragmatic enough to realise that it was a necessary evil needed to promote his books. Like many of the regional newspapers, Darwin's *Northern Standard* reported the arrival of two authors from London in a small aeroplane and devoted quite a few column inches to their trip and the hunt for new material. However, after this initial interest, press coverage dropped away and as the trip progressed was mostly limited to short items in local newspapers, noting arrival at a new location and the occasional brief local radio broadcast. It is probable that Norway preferred it this way. There are no recordings of any of the radio broadcasts Norway made during the trip, as in the 1940s radio was generally a live medium which was not recorded.

As Norway and Riddell travelled from Darwin across the top end of Australia, they experienced the beginning of the wet season. With its two-season tropical climate, from November until April, northern Australia is very hot and humid with regular heavy storms – a period known colloquially as 'the wet'. Norway struggled in the debilitating climate, but even so it seems he was enjoying every minute of the trip. This was just the new experience he had been looking for, and so he was keen to see and do as much as he could. Townsville impressed him very much as 'a beautiful little town' where 'one might have a very happy life', and he thought 'the coast between Cooktown and Townsville the loveliest I have ever seen'. He was also intrigued by Cooktown, a gold rush town which had once had a population of 30,000 but had now declined to around 300. There were no road or rail connections, but the town still survived because it was situated in first-class farming country with a typical property covering 30,000 acres. Children from these who attended the only school in the region could take four days to get home for their holidays, travelling by air, jeep and packhorse. Norway felt he was really beginning to see the real Australia.

For Riddell, it was a different matter. He was suffering physically, and, maybe because of this, did not have the same curiosity for his surroundings as Norway. By the time they reached Townsville he was facing some sort of crisis. In his diary he noted that 'the name Townsville is almost enough for me. I know what is wrong but find it difficult to put it right' ... 'Nevil is more sensible than I. He is thoroughly enjoying it. He has even bought himself a new straw hat and is now more Townsville than Townsville! He is getting a lot more out of the place than I can at the moment. I expect, and hope, that I shall recover soon'.

Norway was keen to see the Gulf Country, the large area south of the Gulf of Carpentaria he had seen long ago on the map marked as just white space. This was not something that attracted Riddell, and so it was decided that he would fly down to Sydney and meet Norway there at the end of December. Norway was worried that this might be the end of their trip together, noting, 'He still professes himself very keen to fly home in Item Willie, and I hope this is genuine'.

So, on 14 December, Norway and Riddell parted company. Riddell headed for the comfort of Sydney, where he was going to catch up with friends over the Christmas period, while Norway had arranged to tour the Gulf Country. His passengers for the trip were Reg McAuliffe, a local insurance agent who was a frequent traveller in the area and knew many people there well, and Dr Marcus Clarke, who was currently a locum in Cairns and accompanying Reg to certify a number of prospective life insurance customers.

The 'Gulf Country' is the name given to a remote region of 71,000 square miles in north-western Queensland. Covered by large areas of woodland and savanna grassland, this often inhospitable country is well off the tourist track, populated by many small townships which are connected by roads that are frequently impassable during the wet season. When Norway first visited the Gulf, the main industries were beef farming, built around the region's huge cattle stations, and copper, zinc, lead and silver mining centred around the industrial city of Mount Isa. It was the beef farming that interested Norway, and so during the next week he flew to as many of the region's small towns and cattle stations as he could. Neither Norway nor his immediate family had any history in farming, so it is not clear what prompted this sudden interest in cattle. The nearest he had so far come to practical farming was keeping a few pigs and chickens at Pond Head.

Typical of the small towns he visited was Burketown, which again had once been a prosperous town serving the gold rush boom but whose local population had now dwindled to fifty permanent residents. The town of corrugated roofed houses had a hotel, one general store, school, police station and not much else. It served the local farming industry. It was a place where station managers could come to stock up on provisions and stockmen could come to drink. The town offered minimal entertainment, no newspapers, no local radio and a visiting cinema every few weeks. A town with very few women, it was typical of those in the Gulf Country. Lacking in facilities, and dominated by a beer-drinking culture, it was not surprising that most women brought up there moved to the cities as soon as they could. Norway though was fascinated by Burketown and its inhabitants, and it eventually became a model for the fictional community of Willstown in his best-selling novel *A Town Like Alice*.

In Normanton, another of these small townships, Norway first met Herbert James Edwards. Known locally as 'Ringer' Edwards, he had been born in Fremantle, Western Australia, and spent most of his life so far involved with cattle in some way or another. Now in his mid thirties he was recently married and manager of the Glenore Cattle Station. Glenore was typical, with an area of 1,500 square miles, a single homestead situated up to a hundred miles from the furthest station boundary, and run by the manager and ten or so stock men (known as ringers), who were mainly Aborigines.

Edwards was a great source for Norway in his search for information on life in the Gulf Country, but he had another interesting aspect to his life. During the Second World War he had enlisted in the Australian Army and had been initially posted to Singapore. Captured by the Japanese, he was one of the many forced to work on the infamous Thailand to Burma Railway. Caught killing cattle to provide food for themselves and fellow prisoners, Edwards and two accomplices were effectively crucified by being hung by their wrists from a tree. When Edwards managed to free one hand from the wire binding, he was further punished by having the wire driven though his hand. He survived this ordeal, but the others did not. Elements of this story, and the personality of 'Ringer' Edwards himself, were later transformed by Nevil Shute into Joe Harman, one of the main characters in *A Town Like Alice*.

On 21 December Norway found himself in the local press in an unexpected way under the headline 'Author Makes Mercy Flight'. The previous day, while at a stopover in Cooktown, he had been contacted by the ambulance service at Cairns. The local air ambulance was undergoing an annual overhaul and they urgently needed someone to fly to Georgetown to attend a seriously ill six-day-old baby and take the infant and mother back to Cairns if necessary. Even though it was the middle of the day, and a flight in such hot conditions in the Proctor would be bumpy over difficult country, Norway readily agreed, taking Marcus Clarke with him. The flight went without incident, and mother and baby were flown to Cairns, where the baby made a full recovery. Norway refused to accept any payment for his service, and a month later he received a letter of appreciation from a grateful Cairns Ambulance Committee. The flight also highlighted the problem of not having a doctor on call, and resulted in the appointment of a permanent doctor to travel with the Cairns aerial ambulance to outback centres. So, in a small way, Norway had already made a change to a region that so fascinated him.

A combination of fatigue and the trying weather conditions were now beginning to take their toll. Norway was also increasingly suffering from prickly heat (miliaria rubra) and was keen to take things easy in Cairns before flying down to Sydney on Boxing Day. He therefore spent the Christmas period as quietly as possible, but he could not avoid what he called 'a colossally merry lunch which most of the Cairns elite attended' on Christmas Day itself.

Shortly after flying out of Cairns bound for Sydney, Norway was in the local press again. This time it was 'British Author-Pilot Helps Search for Surf Victims'. On leaving Rockhampton after refuelling, he had been asked by a local airline pilot to search the beach near Coolum during his flight for the bodies of two surfers, presumed drowned. Surfing anywhere along the beach at Coolum was considered dangerous because of the strong rip tides that were present. Despite deviating from his trip to search the beach, he found nothing. He was again exposed to a side of life in Australia very different from that in England.

When he arrived in Sydney, Jimmie Riddell was there to meet him, but Nevil Norway was not in a good mood. On landing at Bankstown Aerodrome he was told that unless he took off and flew immediately to Mascot Aerodrome (now Sydney International Airport) to clear customs, police action would be taken. As a result he had to fly from Bankstown to Mascot, complete the formalities, and then fly back to Bankstown. Finding and then landing at Mascot was no easy task, as there was poor visibility and the small Proctor was surrounded by airliners taking off and landing at the airport. Mascot was normally out of bounds to light aircraft, being reserved for use by commercial airliners. As was often his habit when frustrated by bureaucracy, Norway let off steam by writing to someone. This time it was the director general of Civil Aviation. What he saw as 'absurd customs regulations' was something that continued to frustrate him during the trip.

Whether it was the difficulties he experienced on arrival or the sudden change between regional and suburban Australia, Norway's first impression of Sydney was not good. He described it as 'an ugly, cheap city, full of drunks'.

By the end of the 1940s the population of Sydney had grown to over one and a half million and it was facing similar problems to other growing cities around the world. There had been an increasing drift of people from the regional areas of the state to its capital city, and the infrastructure was struggling to keep up. There was a tendency for industry and business to be concentrated in a few central areas while living areas were being pushed further and further out of the city.

Though spending so much time in London had made him very familiar with the problems that a quickly growing city faces, Norway could not seem to generate much enthusiasm for Sydney. He even suggested that the famous harbour 'was spoilt by the meanness of the city'. The heavy and consistent rain they were experiencing of course did not help, but when he was taken on day trips away from the city by friends his mood improved.

As 1948 ended, Norway and Riddell spent the evening dining at the Union, University & Schools Club. Norway had obtained an introduction to this most English of institutions from the Oxford and Cambridge Club in London, of which he was a long-time member. He did not stay up to see the New Year in, but Riddell decided to join the wet but happy crowds celebrating in the King's Cross district. The revellers, most of whom were looking forward to a return to normal weather for the main holiday period in Australia, were in a good mood, the atmosphere being described by Riddell as 'large number of drunks, with lots of noise and confusion'. Across the world in London's Trafalgar Square, people were also celebrating the start of the New Year in the rain, but in this case they faced a difficult journey home as the capital's bus and tram workers were about to go out on strike.

A few days later, Norway and Riddell were interviewed by a staff reporter from *The Australian Women's Weekly* who was preparing a feature article on the authors and their trip to Australia. Not normally one to volunteer to be interviewed, this was one Norway could not really turn down. The magazine, which had been launched in 1933, still remains one of the most popular magazines in the history of Australian publishing. By 1948 it had a weekly circulation of over 700,000, quite an achievement for a country with a population then of around 8 million. The weekly was a big supporter of Nevil Shute, having already serialised three of his novels, significantly adding to his popularity in the country. Unusually for Norway, the resulting article ventured into his private life. He talked about the trip that he and Frances had made to America in 1947 and revealed that they had been thinking seriously about moving there to live. However, they had concluded that their daughters 'could have equal opportunities and just as full a life at home'. He also believed 'that in England you still receive the same amount of benefit from hard work as you do anywhere else'. If this was really what he was thinking at the time, it was an opinion which would begin to change quite fundamentally in the coming months.

Despite his dislike of the place, Norway spent much longer in Sydney than he had expected. The maintenance required by Item Willie was more complicated than first thought, and the holiday period also added to the delay in finishing the work. They finally took off from Mascot with some relief on 15 January 1949, after what the usually mild-mannered Riddell called 'another unbelievable example of Sydney Customs. Obstructionism and rudeness'.

Following their departure from Sydney, they spent short periods in Melbourne and Adelaide before heading north again to Alice Springs. Although they had both found Melbourne and Adelaide an improvement on Sydney, on leaving for Alice Springs, Norway still wrote, 'I am delighted to be back in the out-back and away from the rather dreary towns'.

On 29 January, Item Willie left Darwin heading for Dili, the capital of Portuguese Timor (now East Timor). Norway and Riddell had been in Australia for nearly ten weeks. During that time they had seen and experienced a great deal, but now it was time to head home.

By mid-February they had made their way through Bali and Java and reached Palembang on Sumatra. Struggling to find accommodation for the night, they finally received an invitation to stay with Mr Geysel-Vonck, one of the heads of the Shell organisation in the region. During the war, both Geysel-Vonck and his wife, along with the other Dutch nationals living on Sumatra, had been taken prisoner by the Japanese. Geysel-Vonck was placed in an internment camp, while his wife and their six-month-old baby were moved around Sumatra with a group of other women and children, as the local Japanese commander did not want to take responsibility for them. In two and a half years they were continually moved from village to village and ultimately forced to walk over 1,200 miles. Many of the women and children did not live through this experience, but Mrs Geysel-Vonck survived. She became the model for Jean Paget, the other major character in *A Town Like Alice*, and her story became a key part of the book. There is now some doubt as to whether Norway misunderstood what Geysel-Vonck and his wife told him that night, and it may be that the women and children were transported from camp to camp rather than being forced to walk. Whatever the truth, Mrs Geysel-Vonck's experience became the catalyst for one of Nevil Shute's most famous and popular novels.

A little over a month later, after a steady but at times frustrating journey through countries experiencing fundamental change, such as Burma, they finally reached the relative safety of Europe. Early on 14 March they took off from Athens on route to Brindisi; London was now just a few days away. At Brindisi, Norway ran into trouble. He was unable to talk directly to the local air traffic control so took his directions from the airport's weather vane, landing on the long runway in a crosswind. He managed to land Item Willie successfully, but the strong crosswind blew the aeroplane off the runway and out of control. The left-hand side of the undercarriage was severely damaged and the main front spar cracked. It was immediately obvious that their journey was over.

Riddell's first reaction was 'one of immense sadness for Nevil'. As far as he was concerned this had been Nevil's 'journey – his plan and his whole undertaking. He has had all the responsibility, and it is only through his own meticulous efficiency that we have travelled this immense distance'. Norway was a little more sanguine, recording that it was 'very sad that the journey should end like this, but Item Willie has served us well: we shall get home on time and free to start work'. He may not have remembered it at the time, but Norway had predicted the journey may end like this. Five months earlier, he had suggested, perhaps somewhat lightheartedly, to Dwye Evans, 'I'll probably prang it soon because all the strips are one way and a Proctor's not so funny in a cross wind landing'. As it turned out he was right.

Norway and Riddell arrived back in London on 17 March 1949. It was not the triumphant return aboard Item Willie they had imagined, but instead they were in the rather more luxurious surroundings of a KLM Convair airliner.

In spite of the rather low-key ending, a great deal of which they could be proud had been achieved. The Proctor had flown over 30,000 miles in six months. Not bad for a pilot with less than 250 hours flying experience who had never flown more than 2 hours at any one time before. Both men had kept detailed diaries during the trip. Riddell's would be published as the book *Flight of Fancy* the following year, for which Nevil Shute wrote a foreword. Norway's flight log was never intended for publication but remained among his papers until his death.

On his return to Britain, Riddell focused on writing books about travel and skiing. He married a former ski racer Jeannette Kessler in 1959 and eventually became president of the Ski Club of Great Britain. He died in Hampshire, England in 2000, but as far as is known never visited Australia again.

For Norway, the outcome of the adventure was very different. He had collected enough material for at least two novels, which he was eager to start work on. More importantly though, he had seen the land which would very soon become his home.

10

Exasperation
March 1949–July 1950

When Nevil Norway returned to Pond Head House in March 1949, he had been away from England for six months. Communication with his wife and daughters during that time had been limited to airmail letters, with telegrams reserved for anything urgent. He arrived back with his head and a flight logbook full of potential material for future novels, but before he could think about any of this he had a backlog of correspondence to deal with.

Like other popular novelists, his mail increased as his books became more widely known. There were the usual letters commenting on his books and asking for autographs, along with those from more regular correspondents such as friends he had made when collecting information for previous work. All needed answering, but his secretary and a newly acquired Dictaphone helped ensure that this did not take up too much of his working day.

Among his mail was a reminder that part of him was still an engineer. As a diversion from his writing, he now spent many evenings in his workshop working with his hands. When he had been a full-time engineer he had used writing in the evenings to help him relax and forget about the day job, now it seems he was using engineering to help him unwind from his job as an author. However, like his writing, this was an activity which isolated him from his family. He was a keen model engineer and a supportive member of a number of the local engineering societies. The previous year Norway had invited a reporter from the magazine *The Model Engineer* to visit him at Pond Head House to see his facilities and the latest model he had just completed. Aware of the interest there would be in an article about a famous author who was also an enthusiastic model maker, the invitation was readily accepted. His workshop was a converted boathouse at the bottom of the garden, which now contained nearly everything a model engineer could need, from a forge to a wide range of metalworking machines and tools. His visitor was clearly impressed with both the facilities and the quality of Norway's latest model, a 1/8 hp horizontal petrol engine. The result was a three-page article on the model-making author, with photographs of both model maker and models taken by Frances Norway.

While there had been a large amount of correspondence to deal with, only ten days after arriving back in England, Norway started work on a new book. He was confident that the material he had collected during his trip to Australia would provide the background for at least two novels. The first he had in mind was what he termed an entertainment book, while the second would have a more serious message and purpose.

Perhaps aware that it had been well over a year since his last novel had been published, he started work on the book intended for entertainment and profit first. Using the unconnected experiences of Jimmy 'Ringer' Edwards and Mrs Geysel-Vonck, he started to write a simple love story set against a background of the Far East during the Second World War and outback Australia after it. With the experience of these regions still so fresh in his mind, he wrote very quickly. The novel he was writing would turn out to be one of his most popular, *A Town Like Alice*.

Naturally, Australia and the time he had spent there was much in his thoughts while working on this novel, but there was still no indication that he was yet considering it as a place to live. A month after his return, writing to someone he had met in Townsville, he complained how cold and bleak England seemed in comparison, and although he realised England was his home, he often wished he was back in northern Queensland.

In the middle of May, Norway took time off from writing to, somewhat belatedly, complete the final part of his Australian trip. Item Willie had now been repaired and was awaiting collection in Brindisi. He travelled out to Italy and flew Item Willie back to the Percival factory at Luton so that the aeroplane could receive a new Certificate of Airworthiness.

Back in England, he continued to write at pace, and by the first week of July had completed a 205-page manuscript. The novel had taken only three months to write. His working notes show that there were few changes to the draft manuscript. Following his usual practice, and reflecting his continued interest in poetry, he had selected quotations of poems to be included at the beginning of the book. His original options were from poems by Rudyard Kipling and Horace, but on publication a stanza from the much loved poem *When You are Old* by W. B. Yeats was used.

He had finished *A Town Like Alice* well ahead of schedule, with Heinemann not planning its publication until mid-1950. For this novel he received an advance of £3,000 (equivalent to £98,000 in 2016) and a royalty of 20 per cent of the 8s 6d (£0 42½p) purchase price for all copies sold. The publisher was intending to produce an initial print run of 100,000, which was soon shown to be quite an underestimate. Nevil Shute had come a long way since the days of *Marazan* and its advance of £30 (£30 in 1926 equivalent to £1,500 in 2016).

He took a break from writing for a few months over the summer, but by early October he was at work again on what would become his fifteenth published book. Again using material he had gathered during his trip to Australia, he began *Round the Bend*. The book begins in a very familiar environment for Nevil Shute – aviation in Britain between the wars – but by its conclusion it has moved on to very new territory: the Middle and Far East, religious cults, and the relationship between the spiritual and practical aspects of everyday life. The roots of the book lay in the conversations Norway had with the Buddhist priest U. Prajnananda during two trips to Burma and the experience of maintaining his own aeroplane with the help of Asian labour during his trip through the Far East to Australia in 1948. His most ambitious book to date, this was definitely one of his novels with a message, although what the message was may not have always been that clear to reviewers when it was published. Norway, though, thought highly of it, and when reflecting on his books towards the end of his life, he believed that this would be the only one that would be read in fifty years' time.

With the publication of *A Town Like Alice* still some months off, the Shute name was kept before the public when the film version of *Landfall* was finally released in Britain in November. Despite the fact that the film rights had been bought even before the novel was published in 1940, it had taken over nine years to reach the big screen. Directed by Ken Annakin, who went on to make big-budget war films like *The Longest Day* and *The Battle of the Bulge*, this was a modest, straightforward adaptation of Shute's wartime novel. The film joined a growing list of those which went straight out on general release without receiving a premiere in the West End. Not surprisingly, at a time when the public appetite for war films was waning, it was only a moderate success, eventually grossing just over £140,000 at the box office. For reasons which were far from clear, the film's release in America was delayed even longer, not being seen by the public there until 1953.

For many in Britain, 1950 began with a sense of optimism. Piccadilly Circus was lit up for the first time on a New Year's Eve since 1939. There were at least 250,000 revellers in the streets between St Paul's Cathedral and Piccadilly Circus, with 10,000 people packed around the Christmas tree in Trafalgar Square, all waiting to see in the New Year and new decade. Nineteen Fifty was not just the start of a new decade, but it would also be what many newspapers were calling a year of decision. Clement Attlee's Labour government had been in power since 1945, and with the maximum permitted span of a parliament being five years, it meant that a general election had to be held by July at the latest.

Since the end of the war, life in Britain had changed a great deal, the Labour government having fulfilled many of their key election pledges. They had nationalised the coal industry, the railways, the gas and electricity industries, road haulage, the inland waterways, the Bank of England, and most recently had introduced plans to nationalise the iron and steel industries. The welfare state was now in operation with a National Health Service, a social security system, and free education for all those under the age of 15. Unemployment was at a post-war low of around 1.5 per cent, and the trade deficit between the United Kingdom and the rest of the world had been reduced from £630 million in 1947 to £110 million in 1949. Although the British Empire was rapidly diminishing, Britain was now looking to lead the world in other ways, most notably manufacturing. By 1950 the United Kingdom was responsible for a quarter of world trade in the manufacturing industries, showing the way in ship production, coal, steel, cars and textiles. The government's mantra was one of more state control, growth, and low unemployment.

Below the surface, however, life was not that always that easy. While it is true that many had a job (well the men at least), most people were employed in a manual capacity. A scarcity of building materials and skilled labour meant that the repair or replacement of buildings damaged during the war had been slow. There was a serious urban housing problem with nearly half the population living in often substandard private rented accommodation. Air pollution in the bigger cities was getting worse as the emissions from factories, power stations, steam trains, road transport and the number of households burning coal fires increased. Smog was a common problem, and it eventually became so bad that in five days in December 1952 the Great Smog would kill an estimated 12,000 people in London. The Clean Air Act 1956, which among other things banned the emission of smoke in any region designated a smokeless zone, was a direct response to this disaster. Life in rural areas was often not any better, with poorly paid workers living in tied cottages. The accommodation commonly had no electricity or sanitation, and the tenants would of course be homeless if their employment ceased.

The basic rate of income tax was 45 per cent for those with incomes of up to £2,000 per year (which was the majority of the population), and so most people did not have much spare money to spend. Even if they did, there was little to spend it on. Everyday commodities such as meat, sugar, butter, soap and petrol were still rationed, and there was a general shortage of many consumer products. Although the war had been over for four years, it seemed that austerity had not gone away.

Like many, Nevil Norway was probably reflecting on his life and future as the new decade started. While his rapidly increasing wealth of course helped insulate him from the everyday problems faced by many, rationing and the income tax system were two that he could not avoid. In fact, rationing would be the trigger which would ultimately make him start considering his future in Britain altogether.

Given that all petrol used in Britain at the time had to be imported, it is not surprising that at the outbreak of the Second World War it was one of the first commodities to be rationed. By 1942 the sale of petrol to the general public for private use was stopped completely, from then on only being obtainable for essential work by special permit.

In June 1945, petrol was again available for private use but it was rationed. Administration of the system turned out to be difficult and misuse was widespread with the black market flourishing. Petrol consumption again needed to be reduced, and so at a Cabinet meeting on 22 March 1948 it was agreed that from 1 June, every person owning a private vehicle would be entitled to a standard allowance sufficient to allow ninety miles of motoring a month. Petrol intended for commercial use would be dyed red and there would be severe penalties for those selling this commercial petrol to private users, or those found with red petrol in their car's tank.

On 10 January 1950, Clement Attlee called a general election for 23 February. The Labour Party manifesto 'Let Us Win Through Together' promised to extend the policy of nationalisation, while the Conservative Party, still led by an increasingly frail Churchill, who had suffered a stroke the previous year, promised to promote free enterprise but not repeal the Act under which so many of the country's major industries had been nationalised. Opinion polls predicted that although the Labour government's majority would be reduced, they would retain power.

With the prospect of more state control on the horizon, Nevil Norway was therefore probably not in the best of moods when on 17 January he wrote a letter to the Ministry of Fuel and Power requesting an increase in his supplementary petrol allowance. In a detailed letter, he requested that the allowance he received for his Austin car be increased from 20 to 40 gallons a month. He reasoned that as a full-time author he needed to travel widely around Britain for literary research and business purposes, and that the invisible export he generated for the country because of his book and film rights sales to America more than justified an increase in his allowance. The response would have not gone down well. It was a very brief 'Dear Sir/Madam' pro-forma letter with sentences that did not apply struck though, rejecting his request.

Not to be put off, Norway tried again on 27 January, but this time he suggested that he was willing to accept a reduction in the petrol allowance he received for his aeroplane in return for an increase in his car allowance.

He also, more importantly, first raised the issue of perhaps moving from Britain, referring to 'the continual thoughts of residence in the United States which your restraints induce'. This time he at least received a personal response from the regional petroleum officer, but still the answer was no. The response also suggested that the fact that Norway might have to use public transport was just unfortunate and that 'the inconvenience and delay which may be caused by the use of public transport is to be regretted, but it is common to all those who are obliged to make use of this form of transport daily'.

This response clearly lit a fuse in Norway, and he exploded. On 13 February he responded with a five-page rant, in which, after again reminding the Ministry of the amount of foreign exchange he made for the country, he complained of being 'bound by arbitrary rules which bear no relation whatsoever to the requirements of my work' and 'in consequence I doubt if I shall write of England again, except critically. In the circumstances, it seems better to get out of it and start again in the United States, where I am known and popular'. He also threatened not to go quietly, suggesting that in order to meet his business needs he would obtain additional fuel by 'a variety of unconventional ways' and then challenge the government to take him to court. He also intended to post copies of his correspondence on this issue to every Member of the House of Commons and, when he had left the country, to every senator and congressman in the United States.

After Norway had cooled down, his solicitor suggested that he be allowed a final attempt to resolve the matter. Ten days later, Attlee's Labour Party was returned to government with a much reduced majority of only five seats. It seems that for Norway this was the last straw.

Only six weeks after Norway's last forthright letter to the Ministry of Fuel and Power, he made good on his threat to leave the country, only the destination was not to be the United States but Australia. This was a very surprising decision to say the least. Neither Frances nor their daughters had ever been to Australia, and it is doubtful if any of them had been consulted over the decision. It is not clear why he changed his mind about the United States as a destination, but one possibility is that as an ardent monarchist he wanted to stay within the bounds of the British Commonwealth.

It is not difficult to guess how the rest of the family felt about this decision. Both of Frances' parents were still alive but becoming old and frail. Heather was 18 and being privately tutored for the entrance examinations to Oxford University, while 15-year-old Shirley had finally found a school she was happy with. In 1950, communicating with somebody across on the other side of the world was a lot more cumbersome than it is today. For many, moving from Britain to Australia was a move for good. Communication with the home country was usually limited to flimsy airmail letters, and trips back home were very few and far between – if at all. It is therefore not surprising that, apart from Nevil, none of the family were exactly overjoyed about the move.

In 1950, migrating to Australia was relatively straightforward. In fact, if you were British it was positively welcomed. The government of the time believed that with a population of just over 8 million Australia did not have enough people to build the strong industrial base that would be needed for the future. As a result, in 1947 the country embarked upon a period of sustained mass immigration, but it was made clear right from the start that in order to protect the then British character of Australian society, the overwhelming majority of new migrants would have to be British. In fact, in 1946, the Minister for Immigration Arthur Calwell had stated that 'for every foreign migrant there will be ten people from the United Kingdom'. In order to attract migrants from Britain, the Assisted Passage Scheme was developed. Under the scheme, ex-service personnel would be able to travel to Australia for free, while others meeting the selection criteria would pay £10 per person for each adult and £5 for each child between the age of 14 and 18 towards their passage (those under 14 travelled for free). In return they would be expected to stay in Australia for a minimum period of two years. In order to be accepted for the Assisted Passage Scheme, applicants needed to be healthy, have no criminal record, and be 'predominantly European in appearance, descent, and culture', i.e. white. Although controversial, the 'White Australia' policy remained in operation until the early 1970s.

While he was not eligible for the Assisted Passage Scheme because of his wealth, Norway and his family still needed to meet the same criteria in order to receive permission to settle in Australia. Over the next weeks they needed to undergo medical examinations (most importantly, X-rays to check for tuberculosis), provide evidence of having no criminal record, and attend an interview at Australia House, London in order to confirm that they were white. By mid-April they had successfully completed all of these tasks. Norway booked passages for himself and family on board the SS *Strathnaver*, leaving 20 July, and put Pond Head House up for sale. By that time, through the intensive efforts of his solicitor, he had finally persuaded the Ministry of Fuel and Power to increase his petrol allowance to the 40 gallons originally requested, but the experience he had endured, had, in his mind, made the decision to leave Britain irrevocable.

Although family and close friends such as Flora Twort had been told of the Norway family's decision to emigrate soon after it had been made, by mid-April the news was beginning to spread further afield. By then their destination had become clearer, now being somewhere near Melbourne. On 21 April in a letter to Dwye Evans at Heinemann, he explained that there were many social and tax reasons for the move, but that factors included Australia's closeness to Southeast Asia, and the prosperity that the new immigration policy was likely to bring the country.

On 29 April, *The Australian Women's Weekly* ran a full-page article promoting the fact that they would be serialising Nevil Shute's forthcoming novel *A Town Like Alice* later in the year. In addition, under the banner headline 'Best-seller Nevil Shute to live in Australia', they printed an interview with the author talking about his reasons for emigrating. He also revealed that although they would take a small suburban house in Melbourne, that he 'rather fancied the country up Cairn's way'. This must have been a further shock to the rest of the family, who were still no doubt having difficulty coming to terms with a move to what they assumed would be metropolitan Australia, let alone the Gulf Country.

In the middle of May, Norway delivered the manuscript of *Round the Bend* to his publishers, and at the beginning of the following month *A Town Like Alice* was published in the UK (in America it was released under the title of *The Legacy*). Nevil Shute's fourteenth published book made use of environments and people he had come across during his recent trip to Australia. As he later said, 'I found part of *A Town Like Alice* in Kuala Selangor, another part of it at Kota Bharu and a great hunk of it at Palembang in Sumatra. Most of the rest of it was found in Normanton in the Gulf Country'. Using these locations as a backdrop, he added the real experiences of Jimmy 'Ringer' Edwards and Mrs Geysel-Vonck to construct an intriguing love story. It tells of how Jean Paget, a young English woman, and Joe Harman, a sergeant in the Australian Army, first meet as prisoners of the Japanese in the Second World War. Jean is one of a group of women and children being marched from village to village across Malaya, while Joe is being used as a driver by his captors. Joe is caught stealing food to help the group, and as a result he is tortured and then crucified. Jean and her fellow prisoners are marched on to the next village, believing Joe is dead. Three years after the end of the war, Jean is left a large inheritance which she decides to use to help one of the villages she was in during her time in Malaya. There, she learns that Joe survived and so sets off to Australia to find him. Criticised by some as being two separate stories, Shute reasonably argued that he described the wartime and post-war experiences of a man and woman, and that as such it was two parts of a single story.

Initial reviews in Britain were generally lukewarm. C. P. Snow in *The Sunday Times* thought the book readable but not well constructed and not as ingenious as *No Highway*, but he admitted that Shute's fascination with detail 'pushes one from page to page'. In his review, John Betjeman was not the first to compare Shute to John Buchan, but he believed that Shute 'lacked Buchan's elegance of style and sense of the mysterious'. Again the reviewers seemed at odds with the public, as by November Dwye Evans was writing to Norway that 'there is no doubt that 'Alice' has proved by far the most immediately popular of your novels'. At that stage it had already sold 165,000 copies, and by the end of the year Heinemann had needed to reprint it four times. As so often happened with a Shute novel, film rights were quickly acquired, this time by the Rank Organisation, and non-other than Clement Attlee had chosen it as one of his Books of the Year in *The Sunday Times*. Under the title of *The Legacy,* the novel proved to be equally popular with the public in America, spending a total of eighteen weeks in *The New York Times*' Best Sellers list, and getting as high as number four.

Perhaps with an eye to future connections, Norway had sent a pre-publication copy of *The Legacy* to Robert Menzies, who was then leader of the opposition Liberal Party in Australia but by the end of the year would become the country's prime minister. Menzies had provided some introductions for his trip to Australia the previous year, and Norway described him as 'a fan'.

There was one country, however, where *A Town Like Alice* did not go down well. At a meeting of the Republic of Ireland's Censorship of Publication Board on 6 October 1950, the book was banned for being deemed indecent! Although no reason for the Board's decision, needed to be, or, in fact, was given, it may be that the crucifixion scene caused offence in the deeply Catholic country. Perhaps fortunately, Norway was already on the other side of the world by this time and so did not get involved in any argument over this decision. William Heinemann appealed the decision, and seven weeks later the ban was overturned.

As far as the move to Australia was concerned, there was a lot to do in a very short time. Pond Head House and *Runagate* had to be sold, and all possessions either shipped or disposed of. Nevertheless, in mid-July, a still clearly indignant Nevil Norway had a final passing shot at the British government. Over dinner with a *Sunday Times* journalist, he retold the story of his battle with the Ministry of Fuel and Power and the petty restrictions he believed had hampered his work and set him on the road to emigration – knowing very well that this would all be published.

Finally, at 16.43 on 20 July 1950, the SS *Strathnaver* left its mooring at Stage 16, Tilbury. Nevil and Frances Norway and their daughter Shirley were on board. It had been agreed that the elder daughter Heather would stay in England until the outcome of her application to Oxford University was known. Also on board was Norway's secretary Gladys Bessant. Now divorced, after a short unsuccessful marriage, she had probably decided that it was worth a gamble to join her employer in Australia in search of a new life. Norway also generously guaranteed to provide her with a first-class return ticket should things not work out. Six months ago the Norway family had been seemingly settled on Hayling Island; now they were heading for the other side of the world.

Somewhat ironically, petrol rationing, something which had caused Nevil Norway so much grief, had come to an end in Britain in May 1950, and a year later, following another general election, the Labour government itself would be gone.

Part 3

July 1950–April 1960

The Great Southern Land

11

A New World
July 1950–December 1951

The SS *Strathnaver* was not a new passenger liner, but to many on board that July day it may have felt both new and luxurious. Originally launched in 1931, at the time she was the largest and fastest ship in the P & O fleet. Following service as a troopship during the war, it had been refurbished and resumed service on the England to Australia route on 5 January 1950.

With accommodation for 573 first-class and 496 tourist-class passengers, the ship now had a dual purpose: to take fare-paying passengers to en route destinations such as India and Ceylon (now Sri Lanka), and would-be migrants to Australia. This was not a holiday cruise, the intention being to get those on board to their destination as quickly and comfortably as possible. Airlines were beginning to offer serious competition to ocean liners and so journey time was becoming an increasingly important factor. The ship's route reflected this, with just five ports of call on the voyage between London and Fremantle.

For first-class passengers like the Norways, the accommodation was indeed luxurious and comparable to a top quality hotel. Spread over the upper five decks, they had facilities to ensure that their journey would be as enjoyable as possible. Whether it was the cabins, lounges, reading rooms, a nursery for the children or swimming pool, luxury was the focus. The décor, with its wood panelling, decorative plasterwork and soft furnishings, further reinforced an atmosphere of opulence and refined living.

For those travelling in tourist class things were not so grand. Accommodated in the lower two decks of the ship with a separate dining area, passengers were given access to the sports deck but not to the first-class decks. Although those in tourist class were placed in shared cabins, with four or six to a cabin, and segregation between the sexes, they received the same meals and waiter service as those in first class. For most in tourist class, though, it was the trip of a lifetime. As one passenger described:

> 'We led a most privileged existence. We were, after all, being treated to a world cruise on a well-equipped liner, complete with servants, who cleaned and tidied our rooms, cooked and served our meals, and in every other way tended to our needs, and all for the princely sum of ten pounds a head!'

For those from a working-class background and used to life in austerity Britain, it must have seemed like a dream.

Whether you were travelling first class or tourist class, life on board was dominated by food. With multi-course lunches and dinners, and waiter service for all, eating took up a big part of each day. The crew organised a range of events to keep the passengers entertained and to try and alleviate boredom during the many days at sea. Of course, no matter how luxurious the surroundings for either class, nothing could compensate for the weather. At 22,270 tons, the SS *Strathnaver* was not a large ship by today's standards. On its maiden voyage from England to Australia, following the refit earlier in the year, the master of the ship had described the voyage as the worst trip he had ever experienced in thirty-nine years at sea. During the 33-day trip, passengers suffered a hurricane in the Bay of Biscay, a sand storm in Aden, a tropical cyclone off the Western Australian coast, and gales off of Adelaide and Melbourne. Fortunately for the Norway family, their trip turned out to be far less eventful. On 15 August 1950, twenty-six days after leaving Tilbury, and with seven consecutive days at sea since leaving Colombo, the port of Fremantle in Western Australia finally came into view.

When a liner from England docked at Fremantle in the 1950s, there were always reporters around eager to get quotes from any interesting people bound for Australia. Having just published *A Town Like Alice*, Nevil Shute certainly fell into this category, but there was the added bonus that he and his family had come to live in the country. Naturally, reporters were interested in his motives for migrating. He now suggested that it was not about tax but the fact that he wanted to be nearer Southeast Asia and that he also wanted to give his daughters the opportunity to finish their education in Australia. The latter may have been a surprise to them, one of whom was studying for her Oxford University entrance examinations and the other who had recently found a school she really enjoyed in England. It may of course well be that this was just another example of 'doing a Norway': making a decision then thinking of reasons to justify it afterwards.

For most on board, the SS *Strathnaver's* arrival at the port of Fremantle was the beginning of a new chapter in their lives. Certainly, those on the Assisted Passage Scheme were hoping that they were moving from a land of austerity to a land of opportunity. Although Nevil Norway did not know it at the time, his family's arrival in Australia coincided with the beginning of a long and sustained period of economic growth, low unemployment and rising standards of living. This was the start of what later became known as the Menzies era.

In December of the previous year, Robert Menzies had been sworn in as the prime minister of Australia for the second time, and he would remain in office for just over sixteen years. As leader of the relatively new Liberal Party, which in spite of its name had much more in common with the Conservative Party in the United Kingdom than the Liberals, he promoted a philosophy based on the freedom of the individual, the importance of the family, the role of private enterprise and the justice of rewarding individual endeavour – all of which would have been music to Nevil Norway's ears. While in many ways Menzies was lucky to gain office just as the previous Labor government's policies were beginning to show a return, he effectively built on these to produce the 'long boom'. Policies such as a protective tariff on imported industrial products, which encouraged overseas companies to set up manufacturing plants in Australia, and the sustained level of migration all helped to keep the boom going for decades.

Internationally, although Menzies was keen to develop Australia's relationship with the United States, he was first and foremost a committed Anglophile and champion of the Commonwealth. Australia had recently taken a step forward in defining its own identity with the Australian Citizenship Act 1948. This had introduced the notion of Australian citizenship for the first time, before that all Australians having been by definition British subjects. Nonetheless, in the view of Menzies and most of the population, Britain and Australia were still inexorably bound together. However, while Menzies might have been 'British to his bootstraps', like Nevil Norway he was opinionated and not afraid to criticise. He famously once said: 'You've got to be firm with the English. If you allow yourself to be used as a doormat they will trample all over you'.

In many ways the Australia of Menzies in the 1950s suited Nevil Norway perfectly; it had many of the conservative British characteristics and morals that he liked but without the state control and overpowering government bureaucracy which had so irritated him. Finally, there was the question of money. Australia's income tax system was by no means perfect, but it did in Norway's view encourage someone to succeed. Under what he saw as England's punitive tax regime, he had estimated that he would have been able to keep about £3,000 of the £18,000 he had expected to earn from his current novel. In Australia this would increase to over £6,000. For Norway, it would seem that Australia was the place to be. In fact, he would very soon be declaring that this was a country where 'everybody was making money and everybody had a smile on his face'.

After calling at Adelaide, the SS *Strathnaver* finally reached the Norway family's destination of Melbourne at mid-afternoon on Sunday 20 August 1950. They were arriving at the end of autumn and so the weather that greeted them was cool and cloudy, with isolated showers – not quite the blue skies that they might have associated with Australia. It was also Sunday, and so everything was closed and the city relatively empty.

Even so, the Melbourne press were waiting and eager to both photograph and speak to some of the city's more newsworthy new residents. Nevil again talked of England being a depressed and frustrated country where 'everyone and nearly everything is controlled, and no one seems to know what will happen next', but this time the reporters also wanted to talk to his wife. Frances made her own headlines with

'Novelist's Wife Reads No Novels – Except His!' Behind the attention-grabbing headline she revealed that she preferred travel and current affairs books to novels. In a wide-ranging interview she also talked about her love of travel, photography and sailing, and the prospect of looking for a home in the Dandenong Ranges so that she could be near both the mountains and the sea.

Like the rest of Australia, the state of Victoria was highly urbanised. In 1950, over 50 per cent of the state's 2.2 million inhabitants lived in Melbourne. Second only in size to Sydney, the city was once described as 'a Victorian community overseas' because of its Britishness and architecture. However, while that may have been attractive to Norway, who would have seen it as the good parts of a Britain of the past, it was nevertheless still a city. As Australia had moved away from the primary industries of agriculture and mining as its principle sources of income towards manufacturing, then Melbourne had quickly become the most industrialised city in Australia. This growth, which was seen as a good thing by many of the city's political and business leaders, was fuelled by a large increase in immigrants from Britain and acceptable countries in Europe. While it had better weather, Melbourne was really no different to many other cities in Western Europe that were growing their manufacturing base and as a consequence expanding their population. Nevil Norway though was looking for a different way of life to that which inner city Melbourne could provide, and so he and his family began to explore further afield.

The Mornington Peninsula lies to the south-east of Melbourne. With an area of 72,300 hectares, it is bordered by Port Phillip to the west, Western Port to the east and Bass Strait to the south. The good soil in the region attracted dairy and fruit farmers, while with the ease of access to Melbourne and secluded beaches, small towns along the coast road soon became popular seaside destinations. The unspoiled coastal vistas tempted the more wealthy to build imposing holiday homes on the cliff tops overlooking Port Phillip Bay. Some had even gone so far as to describe the area as being comparable to the Bay of Naples.

In 1922 a block of land just outside the small coastal village of Mount Eliza was bought by a timber merchant, John Taylor, as the site for a seaside garden suburb he was intending to develop. He employed the renowned architect Walter Burley Griffin (who had been responsible for the design of the national capital Canberra) along with his wife Marion Griffin and the surveyor Saxil Tuxen to plan what would become the Ranelagh Estate. Intended as a seaside resort and country club for the wealthy, it was designed to be an exclusive location where successful people could build their holiday homes among a planned landscaped area which also contained a country club, recreational parks and leisure facilities for private use. The Ranelagh Club soon developed a busy social programme offering such things as sailing regattas, tennis tournaments and dances. Prominent members of Melbourne society became associated with the club, including such notables as Robert Menzies. The Norways rented *Harfield*, a house on Rendlesham Avenue on this estate, soon after arriving in Melbourne. With its rural setting and sea views, it must have reminded Nevil very much of Hayling Island and would certainly have provided the tranquillity he needed to write. However, the rest of the family might have seen things differently. It was twenty-six miles from Melbourne and remote from much in the way of the lifestyle that they had left behind in England. The nearest village, Mount Eliza, had a population of just over 900 and consisted of little more than two shops and a petrol station. To reach Melbourne by public transport required a walk to the estate's main entrance, followed by a three-mile bus journey to Frankston, and an hour on the train to the city. A car would have been an essential to both Nevil and Frances, and even to their daughters as soon as they were old enough to drive.

On top of the somewhat remote location of their new home, there was also the weather. While it had been cloudy on their arrival, things would soon warm up. During the summer months of December to February they could expect many hot, dry days, with relentless sunshine and temperatures frequently over 80°F and sometimes over 100°F. Again, very different to what they had been used to at Pond Head.

With somewhere to write, Norway soon surrounded himself with other familiar activities that had been so much part of his days at Pond Head. A long-time member of the Oxford and Cambridge Club in London, he was soon admitted as a member to the very exclusive Melbourne Club on Collins Street. He enjoyed being part of formal, old-fashioned, male-only institutions and before long would be going there once a week to meet up with new friends. He also bought a new sailing dinghy *'Nicolette'* and joined the nearby Davey's Bay Yacht Club. Finally, his much loved Percival Proctor had been shipped to Australia, and by November it was reregistered and housed at Moorabbin Airport, with Norway himself by then already a member of the Royal Victorian Aero Club.

Not one to waste time once he had made his mind up, within three months of arriving in Australia, Norway had also bought a small farm at Langwarrin, about eight miles inland of where they were living at Mount Eliza. The 30-acre property consisted of 20 acres of pasture and 10 acres of uncleared woodland. Soon afterwards he had also bought the 22-acre property next door. His plan was to join the two together, build a new house in the middle and start raising a herd of beef cattle. In time, the amount of land Norway farmed would grow to a few hundred acres.

Now that plans for a farm were in place, he needed somebody to run it. Rather than choose somebody locally, Norway decided on one of his old employees, Charlie Wilson. Charlie had been the gardener at Pond Head since around 1947, and his wife Connie had also worked for the family. So in October, Norway invited Wilson, his wife and son to join them in Australia, and by 16 November they were on a ship bound for Melbourne.

With the manuscript of *Round the Bend* with his publishers and not due for release until 1951, Nevil Shute could afford to take a break from regular writing while he settled into life in Australia. Nonetheless he took every opportunity to look for new background information, and so for a week at the beginning of December he visited the Snowy Mountains Hydro-Electric Scheme. Situated in the mountain ranges on the border of Victoria and New South Wales, this huge engineering project had been started in 1949 with the aim of providing water to the inland farming industries of New South Wales and Victoria, and cheap electricity to a large part of the country's most populated states. When it was finally completed in 1974, the system consisted of 16 dams, 7 power stations and 225 kilometres of tunnels, pipelines and aqueducts covering an area of 5,124 square kilometres. Much of the manpower needed to sustain such a venture would come from migrants, both from Central and Eastern Europe, who were coming to the country on the post-war Displaced

Persons Scheme, and those now arriving on the Assisted Passage Scheme. The vast engineering challenges of the project fascinated the engineer in Norway, while the wide mix of nationalities working on it would have been of interest to Shute the novelist. The Displaced Persons Scheme would be an important theme in his next novel, which was already beginning to form in his mind.

What had certainly been a year of great change for the Norway family ended with the news that they would all soon be reunited. Heather had been unsuccessful in her attempt to gain a place to study law at Oxford University, and so four days before Christmas she too was on a ship bound for Melbourne.

Whenever possible, Norway liked to visit a location before he wrote about it; he was always keen to ensure that the background detail in his novels was as accurate as possible. The planning for his next novel *The Far Country* was no exception, and so early in 1951 he spent a few weeks visiting Victoria's alpine region, known locally as the 'High Country'. For ten days of this, he stayed at the Merrijig Hotel (now the Hunt Club Hotel) exploring the area between Mount Buller and Mansfield and writing notes.

At the end of February, Nevil Shute's fifteenth novel, and the last to be written in England, was published in America. *Round the Bend* was certainly ambitious, and it was a book he did not really expect to be successful. While none other than the chairman of Heinemann had been very positive about it, Shute himself was less sure, although he did acknowledge that 'whenever I throw commercial interests overboard, and set out to write the best book that I can, somehow that all seems to make more money than any of the others, which is very odd'.

Round the Bend begins in the familiar Shute territory of aviation, but it soon moves into a very new realm for him, that of religion. Beginning in the 1930s, the story is narrated by Tom Cutter, a boy from a working-class background who is determined to get into aviation, and he begins this journey by joining Alan Cobham's 'National Aviation Day', first as an odd-job boy and then as an apprentice. While there, he first meets the other main character in the book, Connie Shaklin. British by birth, but with a Chinese father and Russian mother, Shaklin soon shows that he has a keen interest in religions of all types. Cutter completes his apprenticeship, learns to fly, and after an unsuccessful marriage starts a small charter freight transport business in Bahrein (now Bahrain). Here he meets up again with Shaklin, who by now is a fully qualified ground engineer, and so Tom employs him as the chief ground engineer in his rapidly expanding business. Cutter keeps costs down by only employing Asian labour, and he soon discovers that Shaklin has started a cult among the ground staff which emphasises the connection between a strong religious belief and high-quality work. Shaklin's reputation as a religious teacher starts to spread across the region, and after being expelled from Bahrein by the British, who are worried about the growing influence he is having, he settles in Bali still working for Cutter. The link between the two men develops further when Cutter meets Shaklin's sister and a romance develops. Meanwhile, on learning that he has leukaemia, Shaklin decides to travel across Asia, meeting many of those he has influenced, before returning to the village in Cambodia, where his teaching had started, to die. Cutter resolves to honour Shaklin's legacy by using his philosophy to guide the future development of his business.

While recognising that this was Shute's most ambitious work to date, few reviewers thought that he had been particularly successful, considering any message in the book lightweight. Typical was the view that while '*Round the Bend* carries little conviction, it still remains moderately entertaining'. Although it did not sell as well as his previous novel in America, *The Legacy*, it was nonetheless far from the commercial failure Shute had envisaged. Chosen by the Book of the Month Club as its March selection, and spending ten weeks in *The New York Times* Best Sellers list, it seemed that the public were still happy to try something new.

With *Round the Bend* now released, at least in America, and the design for a new farmhouse for his property at Langwarrin underway, Shute could finally sit down to concentrate on his next book. So at the beginning of March he began *The Far Country*. He intended this novel to show a very different part of Australia to that he had described in *A Town Like Alice*. As his first book to be written in Australia, he was keen to show potential migrants in England what the southern areas of Australia were like. He was obviously more than happy with the move he had made and wanted to encourage others to follow in his footsteps.

Living close to Norway in Dromona was an old colleague from his days in the Department of Miscellaneous Weapons Development, the artist Ian Hassall. He had reported to Norway during the war and illustrated some of his later articles for the Ministry of Information. Hassall had arrived in Australia in 1949, and since then, in addition to earning a living from teaching art, he had been developing a growing reputation as a local artist. Invited to open an exhibition of Hassall's work at the Melbourne Book Club Gallery on 30 April, Norway described him as being someone who paints to please other people rather than himself. He therefore not only enjoyed his work, but he also saw a strong affinity between what Hassall was trying to achieve as an artist and what he was trying to achieve as a writer. In reality of course, Shute did both, writing books such as *A Town Like Alice* to please others and *Round the Bend* to please himself.

Although Norway had left what he often considered the petty bureaucracy of British officialdom behind, he was still not afraid to start a crusade if he encountered something he thought needed changing. The middle of 1951 bought two such events. Firstly he believed that Australian authors were being paid unreasonably low rates for their work. He wrote to the Society of Authors in London, setting out the problem in detail and suggesting that they think about opening a branch of their Society in this quickly developing country. He used as an example the fact that he had been paid only £150 by *Australian Women's Weekly* for the serial rights to *A Town Like Alice*. He was confident that he was now capable of looking after himself, but he believed that young Australian authors needed somewhere to go for advice to ensure they were fairly paid for their work. The second issue was nearer to home. Heinemann had opened an office in Melbourne and were now beginning to publish Australian editions of their books, rather than publish and ship them from Britain. Shute believed that they were making unauthorised corrections to what would be the Australian edition of *Round the Bend* and became very irate. He was not afraid to tell Heinemann that he thought that 'their affairs in Melbourne appear to be in complete chaos' and also of course how the problem should be solved!

In the middle of June, *Round the Bend* was published in Britain. The reviews were somewhat mixed, as they had been in America. For instance, *The Observer* believed that Shute was wrong in trying to tell two stories simultaneously, and that the matter of fact level in which he had approached the core themes of materialism and mysticism produced an uneasy amalgam. In his review, John Betjeman thought that Shute was probably the most successful English novelist of his time, and he was keen to try and understand why. He believed that it was not the quality of his prose, but his ability to tell a story and choice of subject. He came to the conclusion that Shute 'does not sound priggish or false, because he is obviously sincere. He is not a self-styled plain man with loud, dull opinions. He is humbler than that. He writes because he wants to give us hope. He does not write literature, but I think he succeeds in his mission'.

The buying public agreed with Betjeman. It was chosen as the monthly selection by The Book Society, and Heinemann were soon reporting that they had achieved record pre-publication sales of 100,000 across the Commonwealth. While Shute did not have any issues with his publishers over the title this time, after publication it was found that a book entitled *Round the Bend* had previously been published by Temple Press Ltd. Later copies of Shute's novel contained a note acknowledging this. Meanwhile, on the other side of the world, Shute continued to work hard on his new novel, and by the end of July he had finished a first draft of *The Far Country*.

At the beginning of August an irate Norway was in the news again. This time he had taken huge exception to an article in *The Australian Women's Weekly* in which an Englishman, Captain Mitchison, who was visiting Australia to prepare for a forthcoming royal visit, described the country as being in the Victorian era and how backwards he thought things were, especially in the major cities. Norway was soon on the phone and, in what the magazine described as 'a roar of rage', rushing to the defence of his new home. In a wide-ranging blast at all those visitors who dare criticise Australia, he also used Charlie Wilson's son as an example of the opportunity the country offered, having been promoted to the position of foreman only three months after starting work in Victoria.

Just as Norway was beginning to feel quite settled and optimistic about his move to Australia, a cloud appeared on the horizon; during the late summer he suffered another heart attack. This time he was driving along the coastal road on the Mornington Peninsula when he experienced a chest pain that was so severe he had to stop. Unlike the previous incidents, this time the pain did not go away after a short while. Although numerous tests failed to find the source of the problem, he was confined to bed for three weeks and he began to think about what might have happened if he had been flying his Percival Proctor at the time. While the doctors had not discovered the reason for the attack, he was fully aware just how incapacitated he had been when it had occurred, and he knew he would now have to seriously start thinking about giving up one of his lifelong passions. He was still only 52, but his health was of increasing concern, and already beginning to affect his lifestyle.

The film version of *No Highway* was released in Britain in the autumn. Starring James Stewart, Marlene Dietrich and Glynis Johns, it was an accurate adaptation of the novel, and warmly reviewed. One reviewer noted that '*No Highway*, on the whole, is a splendid film, and fully deserves the round of applause it got'. Although Norway could not be present at the film's premiere in London, a message from him was projected onto the screen before the start of the film. While of course the big stars in the film took the headlines, the cast also included a number of uncredited actors who would become very familiar faces to British cinema audiences over the coming years. These included Kenneth More, Dora Bryan and Wilfred Hyde-White.

What had been another eventful year ended on a mixture of highs and lows. Norway received planning permission to start building a 3,289 square foot brick house, which he had estimated would cost about £16,000, on his land at Langwarrin; his family could soon have their own home again. More worryingly though, Frances was admitted to hospital at the beginning of December to remove what fortunately turned out to be a benign internal growth. At Christmas Frances decided that the Norway family would try what was a common practice for many in Australia and have their celebration meal at the beach. This was not a great success, perhaps a step too far for the rather conservative Nevil. The following year normal English tradition was resumed with turkey, Christmas cakes and mince pies at home, although in recognition of the climate the turkey was eaten cold with salad.

Professionally, Nevil Shute had enjoyed another good year, in which his reputation as a novelist people wanted to read had been further enhanced. He was now starting on a novel which, in his country of birth at least, would test that reputation to the full.

12

Flying a Different Flag
January 1952–December 1953

Thousands of people packed the city of Melbourne to welcome in the New Year at the end of 1951. The traditional venues of the Elizabeth Street Post Office, the bank of the River Yarra and the seaside suburb of St Kilda were far busier than usual because there were many extra interstate and overseas visitors in town. Australia were playing a Test Match against the West Indies at the Melbourne Cricket Ground, and Flemington Racecourse, the home of the Melbourne Cup, was hosting a New Year's Day race meeting. Fine weather was predicted to continue, which all added to the high spirits of the revellers, holidaymakers and sporting crowds.

Over on the Mornington Peninsula the Norway family also had a lot to celebrate. Nevil's manuscript for *The Far Country* was with the publishers; Frances was out of hospital, following a successful operation and was recovering steadily; Heather was in her second year as a law student at the University of Melbourne; and Shirley had passed her School Leaving Certificate and was staying on at Toorak College, where she would be both a prefect and captain of her house. The family had now been in Australia well over a year, and as far as Nevil was concerned there was no doubt about it, the move had been a great success. A few weeks later he wrote to a friend: 'I really think this is about the happiest country in the Commonwealth, if not the world'. Neither Frances nor her daughters had Nevil's enthusiasm for their new country, but they were also well aware that there would now be no going back to Britain at least in the foreseeable future.

For the country as a whole though, things were not quite as rosy as seen through Nevil's glasses; there were a few clouds on the horizon. Over recent years, Australia's economy, which had been supported by the highly profitable primary industries of wool and wheat, had been the envy of many other countries in the world. Although this seemed likely to continue, by the beginning of 1952 things were becoming less straightforward. Like those before them, the Menzies government's main tool for economic management was the balance of payments, the principal objective being to maximise the difference between export earnings and import costs in order in order to generate foreign capital. The balance of payments surplus had more than tripled from £77 million in 1950 to £242 million in 1951. Wool was still the overwhelming contributor to the country's exports, and Britain still the main customer. The sharp rise in world wool prices since the beginning of the Korean War had only enhanced the influence of this commodity on the economy. While the high price for wool was not expected to continue, most economists believed that for the foreseeable future the exporting of primary products would continue to pay for essential imports.

As far as imports were concerned, the bulk of these were still fuel and raw materials, the prices of which were also increasing. At this time Australia was still producing coal in many pits at pre-war levels and had no profitable oil wells. Both coal and fuel oil had to be imported. As a result of instability in the region, the government had also been overseeing a large rearmament effort since the middle of 1950. This was continuing, and defence spending was predicted to nearly double in the coming year.

At home, wages had been rising rapidly, but manufacturing output had not. The government had for a long time levied taxes on imported goods in order to protect local manufacturers from global competition and to try and stimulate industrialisation. Some believed that, far from encouraging growth in these areas, it was leading to poor quality goods with little incentive to improve, and that the country could not continue 'to ride on the sheep's back'. In its New Year leader for 1952, *The Argus* went as far as to warn that 'Fantastic prices for exports will not always subsidise a way of life in which industry is slovenly or complacent, and labor seeks only to diminish its own function'.

Internationally, Australia was still involved in the Korean War. The previous year there had been genuine concern among the world powers that the conflict could escalate into another World War and that this time Australia would be right in the middle. In a letter to Dwye Evans at Heinemann, Norway had in fact written that 'The news today is terribly bad and I am afraid it looks very much as if we are in for a full scale war again'. In 1950, Australia had been one of the first countries to commit troops and join the United States to fight against the North Korean invasion of the South, partly because of their concern for security in the region and partly because of a desire to build a military relationship with the United States. This relationship had been further strengthened when in September 1951 Australia had joined New Zealand in signing the ANZUS Treaty with the United States. While Australia and New Zealand were members of the British Commonwealth of Nations, there was a growing recognition that the United States would be of more immediate help than the mother country should a regional conflict erupt. Australia was no longer a part of the world which need not worry too much about global tensions.

Early in January, Norway received Heinemann's first response to his manuscript of *The Far Country*. This was the first novel he had written since arriving in Australia, and he wanted to use it to give the rest of the world a picture of what life was like in the country for the average person, a complete contrast to the outback he had described in *A Town Like Alice*. It was being written to encourage people to follow in his footsteps and come and live in Australia. In an interview with *Australian Women's Weekly*, he was quite clear about his objective for the book, saying 'I want British people to realise that there are many parts of this country where they can live in an environment similar to their own at home, but under much happier circumstances'. Heinemann were delighted with the manuscript and were giving it first priority for typesetting, aiming for publication in the autumn. Layout and preparation for publicity were already well under way. For the back of the book jacket, the perhaps rather over-imaginative publicity office in London were keen to use a photograph of the author on his estate, possibly with sheep! Norway rejected this idea, rightly saying that since he was only farming about 100 acres with 20 cattle at that stage, and certainly not an experienced farmer, he would then have to spend most of his time 'apologising to pastoralists for a somewhat phoney piece of advertising'. In the end Heinemann settled for a more traditional photograph of the author at his desk.

At 9.50 pm on 6 February, the prime minster Robert Menzies officially announced to a packed and silent House of Representatives the shock news that George VI was dead; he was only 56. Australia did not have a television service until the mid fifties, and so the full impact of this news would not fully hit the country until the release of the following morning's newspapers. Melbourne's *Argus* then described how the previous evening, as rumours had begun to circulate in the city, the crowds at the main railway station had stopped 'as if they had run into an invisible barrier', and that after hearing the news from taxi radios 'many still stood as if dazed around the chief city streets, discussing the news' with 'many seen crying'. Theatre shows and films were stopped midway through their performances, and restaurants were soon empty. Though it was the other side of the world, it was clear that Australia was still heavily bound emotionally to Britain.

Less than a week before, the King had been at London Airport to see Princess Elizabeth and Prince Philip off on their trip to Australia and New Zealand. Nevil Norway had written an article on the character of the Australian people to be included in a special supplement on Australia which *The Times* was preparing to mark the royal tour. Now the tour was being cancelled and the Princess recalled to London, where she would soon be proclaimed Elizabeth II. Later, on 7 February, the Governor General of Australia, Sir William McKell, issued a proclamation that Elizabeth was now 'Queen of this realm, and of all Her other Realms and Territories, Head of the Commonwealth, Defender of the Faith, Supreme Liege Lady in and over the Commonwealth of Australia'; the country now had a new Queen. This new Queen would be an important character in the controversial new novel that was now beginning to take shape in Nevil Shute's study at Mount Eliza.

In February, the atomic bomb, another topic that would soon always be associated with Nevil Shute, made the news in Britain and Australia.

Britain had first started research into the feasibility of such a weapon in 1942 under a programme ambiguously codenamed Tube Alloys. This work was later subsumed into the American-led Manhattan Project, which had resulted in the world's first atomic bomb. However, in 1946 America had decided to restrict the access of other countries to their nuclear technology, and so Britain recommenced an independent programme to develop an atomic weapon.

On 11 February 1952, Churchill informed his Cabinet that a British atomic bomb was to be detonated in Australia, probably during the summer. Churchill and Menzies had been holding secret talks for some time about the use of Australian land as a test site, and the announcement therefore came as a surprise to most of their Cabinet colleagues. Given that rumours of an atomic test were now beginning to appear in the press, it was decided that a formal announcement would need to be made simultaneously in Britain and Australia as soon as possible. In the event, the announcement was made, perhaps deliberately, at a time when the newspapers in both countries were preoccupied with the funeral of George VI. In *The Times*, a piece of news which would have significant consequences for both countries was limited to a couple of paragraphs and hidden away on page four.

With his reputation as a well-known popular novelist, it was not surprising that Nevil Shute was someone who many clubs and societies around Melbourne wanted to associate with as soon as they heard he had moved to the area. Of course, he was well aware that some public appearances were essential when a new novel was published in order to encourage sales. These were arranged by his publisher and usually carefully controlled. He was, though, by nature a private person who did not normally seek publicity, and certainly he was always very wary about giving interviews to the press. His initial reaction to unsolicited requests for an interview was usually no.

As far as the local community were concerned he was more open. Having decided to settle in the Mornington Peninsula he was keen to become part of the community and so right from the beginning accepted invitations to speak at local meetings such as those organised by the Rotary Club. Initially his talks were connected to safe topics he knew well, such as writing or his life as an author. It was indeed the business of writing which was the theme of a lecture he gave to Toorak College on 21 March. No doubt the fact that his daughter was a student at the College helped persuade him to agree to the talk in the first place.

A few months later, one of Norway's previous employers made the news headlines. On 2 May, a de Havilland Comet 1 took off from London bound for Johannesburg. This was the first flight of a jet airliner with fare-paying passengers, and what many thought of as the start of the commercial jet age. Norway did not know it at the time, but a year later the airliner would be in the news again, in circumstances which bore an uneasy parallel to the issues he had explored in *No Highway*. This time, though, the topic of metal fatigue would be for real.

As expected, as the international price of wool dropped and domestic inflation increased, the Australian economy began to run into trouble as 1952 progressed. Although this would turn out to be only a short-term problem, nonetheless the government had to impose more comprehensive import controls on all foreign purchases in order to try and keep the balance of payments in check. One commodity which seriously felt the effect of this change was books. While this did not affect Nevil Shute directly, since his novels were now being printed and published locally, he was sufficiently concerned about the effect such import restrictions would have on the academic sector to write to *The Sydney Morning Herald*. As he had done in Britain, he was not afraid to put his head above the parapet on national issues, if he felt strongly enough about them.

Norway had finished the first draft of *In the Wet* by the end of May, but he still had plenty to keep him occupied at home. The construction of the new family home was nearing completion, and although he was employing a foreman, at this stage of the build there were many details about which Norway needed to be consulted on an almost daily basis. In addition, activity on the farmland around the house was increasing, with land being cleared and stock added. Nonetheless he was off on his travels again. This time he was planning to visit the Northern Territory and northern Queensland, but on this occasion he would be travelling with another author, Alan Moorehead. Norway had first met Moorehead briefly during the war, and early in 1948 he had invited him to join the proposed trip to Australia and back before asking Riddell. Moorehead had begun his career as a newspaper journalist in Melbourne, but he moved to Europe during the Second World War where he made his name as a war correspondent for the *Daily Express*. Now he was developing a growing reputation as an author of historical fiction and non-fiction and was paying a return visit to his home country in order to gather material for a series of newspaper and magazine articles and maybe a book on his impressions of Australia. Norway and Moorehead's lives had taken them in opposite directions, with Norway now living close to where Moorehead had spent his childhood and Moorehead resident in London.

They had arranged to meet in Alice Springs. By then, Moorehead had been in Australia a week, which he had spent touring in the south. His car had then been put on a rail transporter for the 825-mile journey to Alice Springs, where he met up with his fellow author. Norway was more than ten years older than Moorehead, conservative both politically and in nature, and still apprehensive about his reputation as a writer, yet over the next month 'they got along splendidly'.

The previous year Norway had read an intriguing piece in his local Melbourne newspaper about a young Aboriginal and his wife who were part of a team droving a thousand or so cattle from the Northern Territory to Queensland. The article focused on the wife's refusal to leave her husband even though she was expecting a child in less than three months. What fascinated Nevil however was the name of the couple – Mr and Mrs Walter Norway. Once in Alice Springs, Norway began to make enquiries about his namesake, eventually tracking him down to Dajarra, a small township south of Mount Isa. In his early twenties, Walter was of mixed heritage with an Aboriginal mother and European father, although he had never known who his father was. His wife Grace was an Aborigine, and while he was hard-working and ambitious, Walter was beginning to find that the kinship customs of the extended family were making it difficult for him and his wife to establish their own life together. Unable to cope, he had taken to drinking, and it seemed that the future for him looked bleak.

As he was to demonstrate many times during his life, Nevil Norway would frequently help others, not for any personal gain or recognition but for no other reason than because it was something he could do. In this case, he arranged to move Walter, his wife and child down to Alice

Springs, found him a job and lent him money to build a house. Nevil's kind deed paid off as, in 2010, a now 83-year-old Walter was settled and still living with his family in Dajarra.

While Nevil Norway was not to know it, Walter was not really a Norway. His father had indeed been a white European, a postmaster at Barrow Creek, and his mother a full-blood Aboriginal. As was common practice for mixed-race children at the time, he was taken from his mother and educated at an institution called the Bungalow in Alice Springs. It was here that Walter was given the surname Norway, presumably to protect the identity of his real father.

As far as their tour was concerned, after a brief stop in 'The Alice', Norway and Moorehead drove to Darwin then back across the Northern Territory through the rolling plains of the Barkly Tableland to the massive Brunette Downs Cattle Station, where they experienced the famous outback race meeting. They then drove on to Camooweal and Mount Isa, where they left the car before flying on to Townsville. Here they parted company and Norway returned to Langwarrin. Norway's purpose for the trip was mainly to look around and not to do research for any particular new novel. Some of what he saw did eventually appear in the final manuscript of *In the Wet*, including the Aboriginal wife of a European drover giving birth on a cattle drive. At the end of his visit Moorehead wrote a long article on what he had seen for *The New Yorker*, and the following year he published *Rum Jungle*. This evocative, exotic account of life in the more remote parts of Australia received very good reviews.

Norway arrived back home towards the end of June. Home was still Mount Eliza, although their new eight-roomed bungalow at Langwarrin was nearing completion. They now had a visitor, as Frances' sister Phoebe had come to stay with them for a year. A teacher of the blind in Somerset, England, she was recently widowed, and her sister probably thought that a holiday in the relaxing environment of the Mornington Peninsula would do her good.

There had also been a change in the farm manager. Charlie Wilson had hurt his back and so Norway invited Wilson's daughter and son-in-law, Ruth and Fred Greenwood, to also move from England to join them. Fred would remain Norway's farm manager for the rest of his life.

The weather in southern Victoria during the first half of the year had been particularly eventful. A few months earlier, residents on the Mornington Peninsula had been warned about the prospect of water shortages, and yet by mid-July the region was suffering some of the most sustained downpours for sixty years, with hundreds of suburban homes in Melbourne being flooded.

The variable weather did not hold up building work though, and by August the house at Langwarrin was finished and ready for occupation. The new Norway residence was large and impressive. Built in a single-storey ranch style, with brick construction, a tiled roof and wide verandas, every aspect had been carefully thought out to cater for the needs of Norway and his family in a climate in which summer temperatures could frequently exceed 40°C. Since the house was not connected to the mains water supply, two large water tanks were used to collect water off the roof before being pumped to an underground storage facility. Internally no expense had been had been spared, with fireplaces made from local stone, polished wooden floors, and luxuries such as handbasins in all the bedrooms. Heather and Shirley had been provided with their own accommodation, a self-contained bungalow joined by a covered walkway to the main house. Always keen to embrace new technologies, the Norways were one of the first families in Australia to own an automatic dishwasher. The engineer in Nevil was particularly fascinated by the feature which allowed the machine to be used as either a dishwasher or a washing machine.

While it had taken just over eighteen months to complete the new house, work on developing the surrounding land had been going on almost since Norway had first acquired it. The farm was really beginning to take shape. Some of the pasture had been planted, scrubland cleared, a small herd of beef cattle were being reared and 22 acres of the property were now being set aside for pigs. This was certainly more than just a hobby farm. While Norway had no background in farming, as always when he took something on, he did so with full commitment.

No matter how elegant the new house was, the move from an estate in Mount Eliza to this isolated property in the small community of Langwarrin must have still been a shock to Frances and her daughters.

Among all this activity, at the beginning of August, *The Far Country* was published simultaneously in Britain and Australia. The novel tells the story of a young English woman, Jennifer Morton, who inherits £400 from an aged aunt who had spent the last years of her life in Ealing in poverty after her pension runs out. Fulfilling a promise she made to her dying aunt to visit relatives in Australia, after some indecision Jennifer reluctantly travels there, where she finds life very different to the dull and austere existence she had left behind in Britain. The family she is visiting are sheep farmers in country Victoria, and are enjoying a period of great prosperity because of the high international wool prices. Jennifer meets, and falls in love with, Carl Zlinter, a migrant from Czechoslovakia. Having arrived on the Displaced Person Programme, he has to work in the lumber industry for two years rather than being allowed to practice his profession as a doctor, something for which under Australian regulations he is not qualified. Just as she begins to think about settling in Australia, Jennifer learns that her mother has died, and feeling she has no other alternative, she returns home to look after her father, an aging overworked general practitioner. Carl finally finds a way of getting to London in order to both go back to medical school and meet up with Jennifer again. They decide that once Carl is re-qualified, they will marry and return to live in Australia, the far country, as soon as they possibly can. Although on the face of it the novel is a straightforward romance, set across two countries, Shute unashamedly used it to compare life in England and Australia at the beginning of the 1950s with a clear message that life in Australia was better.

Perhaps predictably, the response in each country was different. In Britain, the reception among the mainstream reviewers was generally unfavourable, with many believing that he had painted an unnecessarily dark picture of life in Britain. *The Times* thought that Shute was 'too much inclined to drag in information which belongs more properly to brochures for intending migrants', while the author and journalist Marghanita Laski, who clearly did not like it at all, thought the whole book 'propaganda on the level of the worst children's or Communist books'. The reviewer in *The Listener* was similarly unimpressed, believing the novel to be 'the sort of bread and butter letter that courts favour with his new hosts by decrying the country of his birth'. He also thought 'the pictures of modern Britain are farcical'. *Punch*, though, was more positive, concluding that it was 'all the way through, a most satisfying and human book'. Whatever the reviewers may have thought, the book was chosen by the *Evening Standard* as its Book of the Month, it was a Book Society recommendation and ultimately sold well in Britain. Norway later thought 'that the somewhat acid reviews and controversy seem to be helping sales, rather than hindering them'.

Not surprisingly, the response in Australia was far more positive. Unlike Britain, in 1952 Australia did not have any national daily newspapers. It would not be until 1964 that the first national newspaper *The Australian* was published. Up until then, each state relied on its own papers. In Norway's home state, Victoria, *The Age* and *The Argus* were the leading daily newspapers. *The Argus* reviewed the latest Shute novel with the headline 'Nevil Shute is a grand booster for Australia', suggesting that as a benefit to Australia he was worth 'three trade commissioners, a good-will mission, and half a government department'. *The Age* was more restrained but still thought that it was a novel which 'could have a powerful influence on English readers', and just as importantly it should make Australians realise just how lucky they were. *The Mercury* in Hobart was almost unbounded in its enthusiasm, declaring that 'Mr. Nevil Shute is one of the best acquisitions Australia has ever had. Not only can he turn out best-sellers from his home near Melbourne, but in them he makes Australia appear almost irresistible even to those who were born here'. Three days before *The Far Country* was released as a book in Australia, *The Australian Women's Weekly* began an abridged serialisation of the novel. The magazine had become a regular customer for new Shute novels, and with a circulation of 725,000 this ensured massive publicity for both the book and its author. It seemed that Nevil Shute was a bigger hit than ever, but this time in his new homeland.

A month after its release in Britain and Australia, *The Far Country* was published in America. Here it was also well received, and certainly it did not provoke the controversy that it had in Britain. While she was aware that Shute may have had his own reasons for writing the book, one reviewer considered it 'an absorbing tale about convincing and sympathetic people first, and only secondarily a persuasive picture of Mr. Shute's new home – and love'. The book proved popular, spending ten weeks in *The New York Times* Best Sellers list. It never reached higher than tenth position, but was up against very serious competition, with some iconic American authors like Ernest Hemingway, John Steinbeck and Herman Wouk having new novels on the market at the time.

With *The Far Country* now published, the manuscript of *In the Wet* with the publishers, and no new novel yet underway, Norway occupied himself towards the end of the year by working on a chapter for a military history book. Lieutenant Colonel Bernard Callinan, who was living just along the coast at Beaumaris, had written a book on the activities of the 2/2 and 2/4 Australian Independent Companies in Portuguese Timor during the Second World War. As someone with no literary contacts, or previous experience as an author, Callinan contacted Norway for help in getting this book published. Given the letter Norway had written to the Society of Authors the previous year about the urgent need to support local Australian authors, not surprisingly he was generous in his support. In the end he not only wrote a detailed introductory chapter, but supplied his secretary to type the first draft, and no doubt he used his considerable influence with the local Heinemann office in getting the book published.

On 9 October 1952 Nevil finally completed the sale of his much loved Percival Proctor, Item Willie. He had first begun to think about the possibility of stopping flying the previous year, following his latest heart problem. Flying had been an important part of his life since he had first obtained his private pilot's licence in 1924, but now he had finally made the tough decision that it needed to end, and the change of ownership was finalised. Six days earlier, Britain became the world's third nuclear power when they exploded a 25-kilotonne plutonium bomb on the Monte Bello Islands off the coast of Western Australia. This was indeed a sobering few days for both Nevil Norway and the world in general.

By the end of 1952 he had become more ambitious with the topics of his public speeches, and in an address he gave to the Royal Empire Society in October he felt confident enough to move into areas more usually associated with politicians and to make dramatic predictions about the future of England and Australia. He believed that England would ultimately get to a position where it could not feed itself, and that in the near future a million migrants a year would be leaving the country to settle in Australia. He predicted that Australia itself would then begin to suffer from overcrowding but also gain profit, greatness and world stature in return. It was just over two years since he and his family had arrived in Australia. They now had a house, a flourishing farm, Norway was already a well-established member of the community, and it seems that he had also made up his mind that this move was for good. He had summed up his positive view of Australia in a letter to Alan Moorehead a few months earlier, saying, 'I can only tell you that I am delighted with the place still and I do not think that I shall want to live anywhere else'.

Australia approached the beginning of 1953 with a great deal more optimism than had perhaps seemed possible midway through the previous year. The prices in the international wool market were now more favourable, providing a good income without reaching the extraordinary levels of the earlier boom. This growth in export earnings combined with the measures the government had imposed to control imports and inflation were now having the desired effect. The balance of payments had been in surplus during the last months of 1952, and the country's economy was moving in the right direction again.

In addition to the improving economy, it was also clear that 1953 would be a landmark year, since, like Britain, Australia would be getting a new monarch. The date for the coronation had been agreed, and Queen Elizabeth II would be crowned at Westminster Abbey on 2 June. Having had to postpone a trip to Australia in 1952 because of the death of her father, the date for the rescheduled visit had now been set for February 1954, only this time she would be coming not as Princess Elizabeth but as the Queen of Australia.

Norway enjoyed the beginning of the year, and like many Australians during the summer months he spent time sailing and taking short trips to coastal holiday venues such as Woodbridge in Tasmania. Elsewhere in the family, it seemed that after some initial reservations Shirley was beginning to settle into life in Australia. At the end of 1952 she had left Toorak College, having matriculated with a second class honours in French, and was now preparing to enrol at the University of Melbourne to study for a Bachelor of Arts degree.

Even though it was the holiday season, Nevil Shute was still active. By February he wrote to Heinemann to let them know he was making progress on the first draft of his next book, only this one would not be a novel but an autobiography. It is not clear what made Shute decide to write an autobiography at this stage of his life. Maybe it was the heart attack he had suffered in 1951. Whatever the reason, by February he was halfway through what would become *Slide Rule*, with delivery expected to Heinemann by early November.

On 21 March Nevil Norway boarded an aircraft bound for London; this was his first trip back to Britain since leaving the country in 1950. He was planning to spend nearly three months away, during which *In the Wet* was to be published in Britain, Australia and America. The focus was therefore very much around promoting his new novel, although there would also be opportunities to collect or check information he might need for *Slide Rule*. Frances did not join him on this trip.

After a few days' break in both British Columbia and New York on the way over, Norway arrived in Britain at the end of March. As was usual when he stayed in London, Norway based himself at the Oxford and Cambridge University Club in Pall Mall. However, rather than the air of excitement he might have expected to find as the capital prepared for the coronation, he found instead a rather sombre mood. Queen Mary, very much the matriarch of the royal family, had died suddenly on 24 March. The 85-year-old widow of King George V had been widely credited with helping steer the country through a difficult period following the abdication crisis in 1936, and her Victorian resolve for tradition and yet keenness to make the royal family more relevant to a changing country had since won the admiration of many. This was clearly reflected by the 120,000 people that filed past her coffin to pay their respects during two days of lying in state at Westminster Hall. In accordance with the dead Queen's wishes, the funeral on 31 March was held at Windsor Castle, rather than the more usual Westminster Abbey, so that it would not interfere with preparations for the coronation, which were already well underway.

Like others in the country, Norway woke up to the news on 2 May that BOAC Flight 783 had crashed six minutes after take-off from Calcutta (now Kolkata) on its way to Delhi. The de Havilland Comet 1, G-ALYV, had just completed its first year of service, but shortly after taking off in a heavy storm it had appeared to break up and crash, killing all those on board. This of course raised the question of whether the world's first jet airliner was structurally sound. The chairman of BOAC Sir Miles

Thomas was clear in his response when he 'unhesitatingly announced that the Comet services will continue without interruption'. Five years earlier he had threatened to sue Heinemann over the link Nevil Shute had made between his airline and a fictional disintegrating airliner, the Rutland Reindeer, in *No Highway*. Now he was facing such a problem for real, and over the next year fact and fiction would get even closer.

In the Wet was published simultaneously in Britain and Australia on Monday 4 May. This was a somewhat strange choice for Britain since it was the May Day Bank Holiday and people would have been unable to rush out and buy the new book even if they had wanted to. Nevil Shute's sixteenth novel was again set in Australia, only this time much of it takes place thirty years in the future. The story is narrated by Roger Hargreaves, a 63-year-old priest who had been ordained into the Church of England but after an eventful life now finds himself a member of the Bush Brotherhood and parish priest of Landsborough, a small outback town between Cloncurry and Cairns in tropical northern Queensland. Hargreaves is called to attend Stevie, a local drunk who is seriously ill. As it is the wet season, he has to take a perilous journey across waterlogged terrain to the shack which Stevie shares with a local Chinaman on the outskirts of town. Delirious on opium, which he has been given to relieve his pain, the dying man recounts his life story to the priest, who is also suffering a severe attack of malaria and struggling to think clearly himself. Stevie tells how he was once David Anderson, a quadroon of European and Aboriginal parents, who becomes a celebrated pilot in the Royal Australian Air Force and eventually joins the Queen's Flight in 1983. Britain then is firmly in the control of a hard-line socialist government. The country is suffering from severe austerity, and life for the royal family is becoming intolerable, so much so that the Queen's children are refusing to take on the role of monarch once she dies. Following an unsuccessful plot to blow her up, the Queen flees to Australia, leaving a Governor General to run Britain until the country agrees to adopt the multiple vote system that is so successfully being used by Australia. Now that a solution to the crisis appears to be likely, David can leave his position as the Queen's pilot and marry Rosemary, an English girl who also works for the Queen and who he has become increasingly attached to. After finishing his rambling story, Stevie dies. A few months later, when the wet season is over, and by which time Hargreaves has convinced himself that Stevie's story was nothing more than the drug-induced ramblings of a dying man, he is called to a drover's camp to perform a baptism. The child is the new son of a Scotsman and his Aboriginal wife. The drover is called Jock Anderson and they want the child baptised as David.

Shute may have had some inkling that this work might prove controversial as he ended the novel with a detailed author's note describing his reasons for writing it, which concluded by saying that 'Fiction deals with people and their difficulties and, more than that, nobody takes a novelist too seriously. The puppets born of his imagination walk their little stage for our amusement, and if we find that their creator is impertinent his errors of taste do not sway the world'. When the first reviews of the novel came out in Britain it was clear though that many were taking this seriously, did not like it and did think that the author had been impertinent. Robert Andrew in the *Daily Sketch* thought that it was a book 'which is going to make a lot of people very angry. Many will say it should have never been written'. The reviewer in the *The Sunday Times* thought that it was best to say as little as possible about the book, describing it as a 'disgruntled hobbledehoy of a tale'. Another warned that some might find the novel 'unctuous and more than a little vulgar', while *The Listener* thought that no matter what merits the story had, it was 'a work of crude and ill-timed impertinence' and that 'Shute's use of Her Majesty the Queen' was strongly resented. Although Shute believed that it was a reviewer's job to criticise, he was nonetheless dismayed by the initial reaction to the novel. Of course not all reviews were bad. For instance, Betjeman, while concluding that it was 'certainly a most interesting book – controversial, and undisguised propaganda', also admitted that it 'compels me to read to the end'. Interestingly, to illustrate why it may not have been the best time to publish a novel in which the place of the royal family in Britain was being questioned, John Betjeman's review was printed on the same page as a picture of the Queen presenting new colours to Grenadier Guards at Buckingham Palace and an advertisement for a new book *Elizabeth the Queen* by the revered royal commentator Richard Dimbleby.

A few weeks after publication, Heinemann's London office revealed that while they had expected some negative reviews because Shute had included the royal family as a key part of his novel, they certainly 'did not anticipate the kind of attack which has since developed'. On the back of the success that *The Far Country* had achieved, Heinemann had already secured record orders from bookshops and libraries for the new novel, but clearly they were now a little concerned. In the end, though, they need not have worried too much. After the initial furore had died down, sales picked up, but it was not the runaway success that they had become used to with a Shute novel. The response in Australia was more positive, but surprisingly the Melbourne papers were less than impressed with their local author's latest offering, *The Argus* being particularly harsh. Five years later, reflecting on *In the Wet*, Norway believed that a novelist should be able to raise issues considered difficult by politicians or journalists without being accused of bad taste. He was also convinced that he had not been wrong to criticise what he saw as the extreme nature of politics in Britain at the time. He thought the left was obsessed with nationalisation and doctrine, and the right irrationally captivated by the concept of a new Elizabethan Age. However, he admitted that things had turned out better in the end than he had expected.

Following publication of his novel, Norway was kept busy with meetings and book-signing events. Now he was a big name as an author, these were often at high-profile venues such as Harrods. He also found time to attend a reunion dinner of his wartime colleagues and catch up with old friends such as Flora Twort. He finally left Britain for New York on 24 May.

In America he found that reviews for *In the Wet* were also mixed, some very good and some very bad. It seemed that this was a book that would continue to polarise opinion. On 2 June, Norway was able to watch a delayed broadcast of the coronation of Queen Elizabeth II on television in New York. People appeared as excited as if they had been in Britain. Commercial television had not yet begun in Britain, and so he was a little surprised to see the televising of what was, to many, even in America, the event of the year being interrupted by advertisements. However, not all were appreciated, as *The New York Times* reported that even well-respected broadcasters such as CBS had 'permitted a commercial that was in the worst possible taste, a description of a car as the Queen of the Road'. To some in Britain such practices were not only a shock but completely unacceptable, and even led to questions in the House of Lords as to whether the BBC were aware that their broadcast would be used in such a way. Nevil Shute was not the only person upsetting royalists that summer.

After two weeks in New York, during most of which he was suffering from a bad throat infection, Norway left for San Francisco to continue his journey home. During his short stay there, he looked to see if he could find someone who would be willing to stage a play of *Round the Bend*. He found some interest, and following discussions with his agent in America eventually contacted the playwright and novelist R. C. Sherriff, who had written the film script for *No Highway*. Although there was some initial enthusiasm for the idea, the project never came to anything.

Norway arrived back in Australia on 11 June; he had been away for nearly twelve weeks. He had a huge pile of correspondence to deal with but by the beginning of July was making steady progress with his autobiography *Slide Rule*. A month later he was putting his head above the parapet in the press again. This time he was reflecting on some of the differences between life in an almost shutdown Melbourne on a Sunday and those he had recently found in San Francisco on the same day of the week. While not advocating that he or others consider moving to America, he was concerned that too few Australians were taking the opportunity to visit the country to gain new experiences because of exchange controls. Clearly now seeing himself more as an Australian, he proclaimed that 'This situation has gone on long enough. We aren't a pack of Russians, afraid to let our people see what goes on in more prosperous countries than our own'.

By the end of October Shute had finished his manuscript of *Slide Rule*. Heinemann were not that keen on the title, but it seems nobody could come up with a better alternative. There was however the matter of libel. Aware that he had written a great deal in the book about both the R.101 disaster and the difficulties that Airspeed Ltd had endured, Shute was keen that his publishers check the manuscript with their solicitor to ensure that he had not libelled anybody. After the controversy of *In the Wet*, the last thing he would have wanted was the publicity of a court case.

The year ended with another event which would have a big effect on the future economy of Australia: the discovery of oil. On 5 December,

Standard Oil announced that they had discovered oil at Exmouth Gulf, 700 miles north of Perth. Given that at that time Australia was using 100,000 barrels of oil a day, all of which were imported, then the discovery of what appeared to be the first commercial quantities of oil on mainland Australia was really big news. Not surprisingly, share brokers in Perth were being flooded with orders, with many comparing it to the days of the last gold rush in the 1930s. The discovery of oil also provided Shute with the germ of an idea, which would eventually become another novel.

13

The Future and the Past
January 1954–December 1954

The Norway family did not have an easy start to 1954. Nevil Norway often said that one of his reasons for migrating was because he wanted his daughters to finish their education in Australia. At the moment it did not look as if this was being achieved, since neither of his daughters' lives were going in the direction he and Frances had expected. Heather had withdrawn from her studies in law after two years at the University of Melbourne, and now Shirley had lasted only a year on her Bachelor of Arts degree at the same university.

Given Shirley's independent spirit, rather surprisingly she then joined the Women's Royal Australian Naval Service, signing on for a period of four years. It is unclear whether it was the influence of her father or her love of sailing and swimming which led her to do this. After only two weeks she decided she had made a mistake and resigned from the Service. As can be imagined, this did not greatly please her father, and it would not have done much to improve what was often a strained relationship.

For Australia in general though, only one thing seemed to matter at the beginning of 1954, and that was the royal visit. At 10.33 on 3 February the royal barge with Queen Elizabeth II and the Duke of Edinburgh on board landed at Farm Cove, Sydney Harbour, to begin the first tour of Australia by a reigning British monarch. They received what was described as 'the most tumultuous greeting Sydney has ever given any visitor'. It was estimated that over a million people lined every vantage point around the harbour and the surrounding city streets, in what was perfect weather. The next day, the front page of the state's premier newspaper, *The Sydney Morning Herald,* proclaimed 'Sydney Cheers the Queen', and it was not until page eleven that there was any other news than the royal visit. For the next fifty-seven days, there would really only be one news story that most of Australia was interested in.

As an ardent monarchist, Nevil Norway was of course one of those interested in the royal tour, but he also had his livelihood to consider and the year ahead to plan. He strongly believed that a novelist needed to regularly visit new environments in order to generate ideas and help ensure that factual detail in their books was correct. He had always been good at partitioning his time between different activities, and by splitting his year into periods of intense travel and periods of intense writing he was generally able to deliver a novel a year to his publishers for most of his working life. In this respect 1954 was a typical year: he had an autobiography published in the summer, delivered a manuscript to his publishers for a new novel in the autumn, made two tours by road of Australia and spent two weeks visiting the Northwest coast of America.

His first trip of 1954 was a 2,000-mile drive from Melbourne to Brisbane and back. Now that he no longer had his Percival Proctor, driving was his main way of seeing the country, only he liked to do this himself, and as he often travelled off the beaten track, he preferred to camp along the way. In order to make these trips as comfortable as possible, he bought himself a new Ford V8 station wagon which had been specially customised to suit his requirements and provide sleeping accommodation during his trips. This one-off car even made it onto the motoring page of the *Brisbane Telegraph*. However, at £2,600, it was around twice the price of an average imported car, and not one that many could afford.

Back from his road trip to Brisbane, he settled down to his now normal home life of writing and farming. The farm was now becoming well established, and it had grown to 50 head of cattle and 120 pigs. As far as writing was concerned, Shute had started work on his next novel at the end of the previous year, and although this was still at a very embryonic stage, such was his rigid routine, he was confident that he would be able to provide his publishers with a new book for their autumn catalogue. The as yet untitled novel would eventually be released as *Requiem for a Wren*.

The Queen finally reached Melbourne on 24 February. The previous day, *The Argus* had triumphantly proclaimed 'Tomorrow she is all ours!', demonstrating that the enthusiasm for the royal visit had certainly not died down and the parochial nature of the rivalry between the major cities. Every newspaper was publishing special issues, some even exceptionally on a Sunday. Large advertisements were being printed with organisations declaring themselves loyal subjects and saluting 'Our Undoubted Queen'. If there were many republicans in the country at that time, they were keeping a low profile. It was into this excited atmosphere that Nevil Norway once again plunged, voicing opinions that he had first touched in writing *In the Wet*, now suggesting that the Queen should spend thirty-seven days of each year in Australia. While he seemed to be gaining a reputation for his outspokenness on British–Australian relations, this time his opinion seems to have passed most people by.

Slide Rule was published at the end of May in America, as usual by William Morrow & Company Inc. The book begins in 1950s Australia with Norway reflecting on the heart attack he suffered in 1951 and his subsequent difficult decision to give up flying. This health scare may well have been the trigger to write his autobiography, but he also believed that his experiences in the early years of the aviation industry, which at the time he may have considered normal run of the mill events, were in fact unique and deserved being recorded. Subtitled, *The Autobiography of an Engineer*, Nevil Shute tells the story of his life, from his birth in 1899 until 1938 when he left Airspeed to became a full-time novelist. In reality though, it really tells more about the British aviation industry during this period than the author himself.

The majority of the book is concerned with two developments: the R.100/R.101 airship programme and the formation and early years of Airspeed Ltd. In keeping with his lifelong desire to keep his private life just that, there are very few references to his family and little insight into his personality or personal life. Nearly all of the photographs in the book are of aircraft, with only one of Norway himself, and one other group photograph. There is, however, plenty on the R.101 disaster and its aftermath. In a detailed analysis of the airship crash, he is forthright in concluding that not only was this an accident waiting to happen, but also that it was totally avoidable. He is not shy about saying who he thought was responsible. Never a great believer in state intervention, especially in the aviation industry, Norway was convinced that this was a perfect example of why such developments should be left to the commercial sector. Away from the aviation industry, he describes some of his early experiences as a novelist, but this book is essentially the life of Nevil Norway rather than the life of Nevil Shute.

The reviews in America, while certainly not negative, generally concluded that this was a book that would most likely be read by those interested in aviation rather than those interested in literature. The *Saturday Review* wondered whether Shute's followers on their side of the Atlantic would be really that interested in developments in a long since discredited lighter-than-air transport system or the birth of a little-known (at least in America) aircraft company. Book sales were to prove the reviewers correct, as while certainly not a financial disaster, it was the first Nevil Shute book since *Vinland the Good* not to make *The New York Times* Best Sellers list. It seems Nevil Shute's readers preferred fiction rather than fact.

In the late autumn, Australia was gripped by an espionage story that would not have looked out of place in one of Shute's early novels. A federal election had been called for 29 May. The Liberal Party of Australia–Australian Country Party Coalition led by Robert Menzies had by then been in power for five years, but because of declining popularity in many states, there was speculation that they might lose office at national level. The weeks leading up to the election were overshadowed by what became known as the Petrov Affair. In 1954, Vladimir Petrov was officially third secretary at the Soviet Embassy in Canberra. In practice though, his role was to gather intelligence on anti-Soviet groups in Australia and develop an intelligence network. Petrov's wife, Evdokia, was a code clerk, also based at the Embassy. Petrov was not good at his job, and because of poor performance in his role he began to worry about returning to the Soviet Union when he and his wife were recalled to Moscow in March 1954, especially as his KGB superior Beria had been executed the previous year. Finally, on 2 April, Petrov applied to the Australian government for political asylum, which was granted by Robert Menzies two weeks later. It seems, however, that Petrov was not concerned about what happened to his wife, and as soon as the news broke about Petrov's defection, the Soviet authorities sent couriers to Canberra to escort his wife back to Moscow.

On 20 April, newspapers across the world showed pictures of a distraught Evdokia Petrov being apparently forced to board an aircraft at Sydney Airport by Soviet officials, in spite of protests from a large crowd who were trying to stop this. After take-off, a Russian-speaking air stewardess managed to determine that Evdokia did not wish to return to the Soviet Union but instead wanted to apply for political asylum in Australia. As a result, when the aircraft landed at Darwin to refuel, Australian police and intelligence officers boarded and, after some resistance, disarmed Evdokia's minders and led her off the aircraft. Two weeks later, her request for asylum was officially granted and she became a permanent resident in Australia.

Not surprisingly in this climate, the Cold War and the need to protect the country from Soviet espionage became a much discussed topic during the election campaign. As one of the issues Menzies had fought the previous election on was the banning of the Communist Party of Australia, this was all to his advantage. The leader of the opposition even went as far to suggest that Menzies had staged the defections of the Petrovs in order to improve his chances of re-election. Ultimately, Menzies won the election, but with a slightly reduced majority, and would go on to become Australia's longest-serving prime minister, remaining in office until six years after Norway's death. One of his Cabinet ministers, Richard (Dick) Casey, would also become Australia's longest-serving Minister for External Affairs, and an increasingly close friend of Nevil Norway and his family.

Slide Rule was not published in Britain until the end of June. Four months earlier, maybe as part of an advance publicity strategy, the *Sunday Graphic* had published an account by Nevil Shute in which it claimed in typical newspaper attention-grabbing language 'that for the first time he gives a vivid account of the astonishing events that led to the disaster to the airship R.101.'

Even though when it was published in Britain *Slide Rule* could have been accused by some of reviving the controversy of the R.101 disaster and reopening old wounds, it was nonetheless well reviewed. This time, though, in addition to the usual mainstream press, the book was also picked up by some less used to reviewing Shute's work, such as the *Daily Express* and *Flight*, most probably because of the R.101 story or general aviation theme. One reviewer noted that the R.101 disaster was 'a wretched but engrossing story and Mr Shute tells it brilliantly', while another recognised that while Shute had displayed an excess of anti-bureaucratic sentiment, his focus on the airship disaster had been because he still believed, even a quarter of a century later, that there were still lessons to be learnt. What most also agreed on was that this was a book about aviation rather than an autobiography of Nevil Shute Norway. As one reviewer rather dryly noted, 'Either Mr. Shute has had a not-very-exciting private life, or he prefers not to write about it'. Heinemann also persuaded a long-time colleague of Norway, Sir Alan Cobham, to write a review of the book. Cobham's detailed appraisal was enthusiastic and very positive, but when Heinemann tried to place it in the press they found that most mainstream papers already had their own specialist air correspondents and in the end had to resort to using quotes from this review in advertisements.

As had been the case in America, sales did not match those of Shute's recent novels. A non-fiction book with photographs, it was priced at 50 per cent more than a hardback novel and would certainly have appealed more to the restricted aviation history market than Shute's normal novel-buying public.

There were, however, not surprisingly, some in the aviation industry who were less than impressed by the forthright views Shute had expressed about the R.101 disaster. One of these was Sir Peter Masefield. Although he had not been involved in the R.100/R.101 airship programme, during the Second World War he and Norway had re-examined the case for airships to see whether there was any future for them. They had concluded that aircraft technology was now so advanced that airships could not compete. This prompted Masefield to start an in-depth study of the R.101 programme, which would lead, forty years later, to the book *To Ride a Storm*. In this, Masefield wrote that a disagreement had built up between Norway and Vincent Richmond, assistant director of the R.101 programme. As a result he believed that this 'had led Norway to write a distorted and inaccurate account of the airship programme and those concerned with it'. In late 1953, when he was chief executive of British European Airways (BEA), Masefield visited Norway on the way back from a trip to New Zealand. He claimed that Norway had by then softened his views about the failings of the airship programme, but this certainly does not seem to have been reflected in the text of *Slide Rule*, which would have been close to completion at the time.

Someone who had been intimately connected with the airship programme was Barnes Wallis, and Norway sent him a copy of *Slide Rule* when it was released in Britain. In a letter of acknowledgement, Wallis, who was still working for Vickers-Armstrong, wrote that he had read the book with 'a great deal of interest and enjoyment, though I must admit that I started with an unfortunate bias due to my having been shown some extracts from it in the less reputable English Press'. While agreeing with Norway's conclusions on the R.101 enterprise, he wondered whether he had really added anything new to the debate and certainly questioned his wisdom in putting this down in print. He did not believe that Norway was 'sufficiently acquainted with the unwritten history of the whole airship adventure to make a right judgment' and also 'thought it too early for a full and impartial account to be published, since relatives of the principal actors were still living'. Norway replied with a robust defence of his reasons for writing the book and expressing something of the anguish the retelling of the story had caused him.

The other person who would have had more than a passing interest in *Slide Rule* was the co-founder of Airspeed, Hessell Tiltman. Although they had once been close working colleagues, they not been in contact since Norway had left Airspeed in 1938. He sent Tiltman a copy of *Slide Rule*, believing that 'it seemed to be worth putting down a record of our efforts in those days'. It does not appear that Tiltman ever replied, and it is doubtful whether they ever had any further contact during Norway's lifetime.

At one time Norway had planned to write a second volume of autobiography which would focus on his war years, life in Australia and tell more about his development as an author. Provisionally titled *Set Square*, it seems that in the end he had little enthusiasm for this, and at the time of his death the project had not got beyond the title.

Slide Rule had to some extent taken Norway back to a previous life and an industry of which he was no longer part. Having completed what he set out to do by recording his account of that period, he moved back to the present and during the first week of June went on another road trip. This time his destination was Exmouth Gulf in the north-west of Western Australia. He was keen to see the conditions in which those who were developing the country's recent oil discoveries lived and worked.

Originally, Frances had intended to go with him on this trip, but plans had changed and Norway was joined by Ian Syme. Ian was a reporter for the Melbourne newspaper *The Age*, a part of the local sailing community, and the son of the commodore of the Davey's Bay Yacht Club, to which Norway also belonged. The pair drove from Melbourne to Perth via Adelaide and then on to the Exmouth Gulf. Much of the journey from Perth was on dirt roads and through townships normally well off the tourist route, such as Geraldton and Carnarvon. They also spent time at Eucla, once a thriving telegraph station on the border between Western Australia and South Australia. Closed in the 1920s, it was now little more than a stone shell gradually being reclaimed by the sands of the Nullarbor Plain. This building and its desolate location made a big impression on Norway, and it would feature in the novel he was writing at the time of his death.

As it was wet weather, getting bogged down and having to dig the car out became an experience they quickly got used to. They finally reached the oil exploration facility at the Exmouth Gulf, but it was the sociological more than the technical aspects of the operation that fascinated Norway. He was struck by the desolation of the environment in which test drilling was taking place. Writing later to the author Alan Moorehead, he predicted that 'this small settlement of very highly paid Australian and American oil drillers is going to be a little nucleus of civilisation and amenities that will mean a tremendous lot to the whole countryside within a radius of two hundred miles'.

Arriving back in Melbourne on 8 July, they had driven around 5,500 miles in just over four weeks. Norway was very enthusiastic about what he had seen and done, noting in a letter to Dwye Evans that 'as always when I visit the Australian outback I come back with more to write about than I can ever hope to use'. He also believed that if he had covered the journey by horse he would have accumulated even more material. Much of what he had seen on this latest trip would eventually find its way into *Beyond the Black Stump*.

When Norway arrived back at Langwarrin, Frances was already on her way to England. Although they had originally planned to both go to Britain the following year, this had been changed at short notice. Frances' father was now 87 and in very poor health. There was real concern that he may not survive the coming winter, and so it was decided that it would be better for Frances not to wait. She had not seen her parents for four years and was naturally keen to spend some time with them while she could. Since their arrival in Australia, communication had been limited to the blue airmail letters which were the norm at that time. Frances told the reporter who had spotted her at Sydney airport that she was expecting to stay in England for six months; in the end she stayed until the end of November.

Illustrating Norway's ability to keep to self-imposed deadlines whatever the surrounding distractions, a few days after his return from Western Australia he was able to clear the correspondence which had piled high on his desk during his time away and start working on the final revision of his next novel. Although he told Heinemann it did not have a title yet, he confidently expected it to be with them by early September. The untitled manuscript would become his nineteenth book, *Requiem for a Wren*.

Having completed *Requiem for a Wren* by the end of August and posted it off as usual to his literary agent A. P. Watt, Norway was off travelling again. This time his destination was the west coast of America. He and Frances had been invited to visit Oregon, a state renowned for its diverse range of mountains, forests and beaches. They had intended this to be an outdoor holiday, something for which Frances had been learning to ride even though she admitted to being scared of horses. In the end, Frances stayed over in England and Nevil went on his own.

During his stay in Oregon, Norway was the guest of a well-known La Grande resident, Dr Clarence Gilstrap and his wife. They had become regular correspondents and friends after Gilstrap had read one of Shute's novels. It was a friendship that would remain in place until Norway's death and this would be the first of a number of trips he would make to the area. On this visit Norway joined the Gilstrap family for their annual

The Future and the Past

two-week horseback and camping trip into the Minam and Wallowa mountains. During the trip he built up his knowledge of small-town America, which he was already planning to be a key part of *Beyond the Black Stump*. In fact, La Grande would become the inspiration for the town of Hazel in the novel.

The year ended with aviation again making the news in Britain. Unfortunately, the crash of the Comet airliner the previous May had not been a one-off accident. On 10 January a BOAC flight from Rome to London had broken up twenty minutes after take-off, killing all those on board. The airline voluntarily grounded its Comet fleet to allow engineers to make modifications to rectify design flaws they thought responsible for the accident. Seventeen days after Comet flights resumed service on 8 April, a South African Airways flight from Rome to Cairo crashed, again killing all those on board. This time, in order to maintain confidence in an aviation development of national importance, the government acted quickly. The Certificate of Airworthiness for all Comet 1 aircraft was revoked, experimental investigations began at the Royal Aircraft Establishment (RAE) to try and determine the reason for the accidents, and a public inquiry promised.

The public inquiry into the Comet airliner accidents opened on 19 October 1954. Summarising the exhaustive testing that had been undertaken, Sir Lionel Heald, QC for the Crown, described how cyclic pressure testing of a fuselage in a water tank had shown that metal fatigue had almost certainly been the cause of the accidents. The tests revived memories of the cyclic tests that Mr Honey had undertaken of the fictitious Rutland Reindeer in *No Highway*, published six years earlier. Not surprisingly the press were soon talking about Nevil Shute's capacity to write about things before they had happened, and in fact Heald had cited Shute's novel when he opened the proceedings of the inquiry. The final report of the inquiry when it was published the following February would in fact conclude that the accidents had been caused by structural failure bought about by metal fatigue.

Nineteen fifty-four had been a year which to some extent Norway would remember for the publication of *Slide Rule* and his reflection on a previous life in both England and the aviation industry. In writing his autobiography he had also effectively closed the chapter on that part of his life. He and his family had now been in Australia for over five years, the house and farm had become well established, and he was again producing new novels on a regular basis. There is no doubt he was enjoying the kind of lifestyle he had hoped for when he made the decision to emigrate. While the views of his wife and daughters may well have been different, as far as Nevil Norway was concerned, the move from England had been a success and could now be considered permanent.

14

Novelist, Farmer and Racing Driver
January 1955–December 1956

On 1 January 1955, for most of the sports-mad Australian public there was only one place that people wanted to be – the Melbourne Cricket Ground. England was playing Australia at cricket for the much prized Ashes trophy. It was day two of the third Test Match, with the series level at one Test all. England had scored a hard-fought 191 runs on the first day, and now it would be Australia's turn to see what they could do in front of a capacity partisan crowd of over 65,000.

A day later, the less pleasant side of summer in Australia was in evidence as bushfires raged across Victoria. After a day of searing heat in which temperatures had rarely fallen below 100°F, there were at least six fires out of control in the country regions of the state, all being fanned by strong winds. Even holidaymakers became volunteer fire-fighters to help put out many of the hundreds of grass fires that had started around the metropolitan area. In their rural setting the Norways soon learnt about the threat of bushfires, and with a farm in which growing hay was a key part, they needed to be constantly vigilant. On days of searing temperatures with smoke in the air, the tranquil setting of Pond Head must have seemed an age away.

Although now a well-established novelist, apart from contacts with his trusted literary agent and publishers Nevil Shute did not seek to cultivate friendships in the literary world. He preferred the company of those in his local rural community, members of his local yacht club or those he met at his weekly visits to the Melbourne Club. He was, though, an admirer of the writing of the British humourist A. P. Herbert. The feeling was reciprocated, and Sir Alan and Lady Herbert spent an evening with the Norways while on a visit from England in January. Typical of Nevil's desire to be part of his local community without drawing too much attention to himself, during the evening they attended a performance of Herbert's play *Two Gentleman of Soho* not in a prestigious Melbourne theatre but performed by the local theatre group in Frankston.

On 17 February Britain announced its intention to start manufacturing the hydrogen bomb. Like many, Norway was becoming concerned about where the proliferation in nuclear weapons was taking the world, and whether man would ultimately be able to control the power being unleashed. While ideas had been forming in his mind for some time for a novel based around this theme, they were still not advanced enough to start writing. In the meantime, in order to have something ready to send to his publishers in the autumn, he combined experiences of the road trip he had made to the Australian oilfields the previous year with his visit to La Grande on the west coast of America and started writing what would become *Beyond the Black Stump*. For the moment though, it had a number of working titles, starting with *The Dry Hole* followed by the more intriguing *The Kindest Goanna*.

A sign of the growing importance of the Australian market to British publishers was illustrated by a visit of the chairman of William Heinemann Ltd to the country in the spring. This was his first visit to Australia, and Alexander Frere and his wife naturally spent time with Nevil Shute, as he was by far and away Heinemann's most popular 'Australian' author. The Frere's were certainly well connected in the literary world, as Mrs Frere was the daughter of the prolific crime writer Edgar Wallace, and their London apartment was in a building in which other tenants included Graham Greene, Georgette Heyer and J. B. Priestley.

Nevil Shute's nineteenth book *Requiem for a Wren* was published in Britain at the end of April. As with *A Town Like Alice* it explores the wartime and post-war experiences of a young man and woman, only this time the ending is not a happy one. Set in the early 1950s, Alan Duncan, having recently qualified as a lawyer in England, is now returning home to his parents' large prosperous sheep station in country Victoria. He had lost both feet in an aeroplane crash during the war and had gone to England to try to come to terms with his disability and the lonely life he would one day have to face on the family station. On arrival he learns that the house parlour maid, a young woman called Jessie Proctor, had committed suicide earlier that morning. Originally from England, she had been working for the Duncans for just over a year. In an effort to find something out about the dead woman so that any relatives could be informed, Alan searches for her suitcase, which does not appear to be in her room, and finds it hidden in the attic of the house. The case is full of papers and diaries, which reveal that the young woman was not Jessie Proctor, but leading Wren Janet Prentice. She had been engaged to Alan's brother Bill, who had been killed a few days before the D-Day invasion, and since the war Alan had been trying to find her. From reading the diaries in the suitcase Alan learns of Janet's tragic life in which she had to cope with the death of her fiancé, father and dog in rapid succession. The loss of so many things dear to her is compounded by an increasing guilt she feels for earlier shooting down an enemy aeroplane which she later learns may have contained refugees. She begins to believe that the death of those close to her was a punishment for shooting down the aeroplane. After the war she tries to make amends for her actions by helping her own relatives and those of her dead fiancé, and as result she eventually finds herself in Australia and working for his parents. On hearing that Alan is to return home, she realises her past will be uncovered and believes she has no alternative but to take her own life. The story helps Alan reflect on his own life, and as a result he approaches his return home, and the need to take over the running of the station from his aging parents, in a far more positive light.

The reviews in the British press were, as was often the case with Shute's novels, faint in their praise. For instance, the reviewer in *The Illustrated London News*, while almost begrudgingly admitting that Shute was enormously popular for his 'unrivalled journalistic flair for giving interesting, slightly exotic information in the guise of narrative' then asserts that this novel might have been a good story. Another, while praising 'Shute's qualities as an observer of fact', thought the story 'laborious and unconvincing'. Of course, the British buying public had a different view. Heinemann had produced a print run of 100,000 in April. This was becoming the norm for a Shute novel, and in May they had to print another 20,000 in order to satisfy demand.

In Australia the novel had been exclusively serialised in *The Age* prior to publication, with Shute being described as 'an ardent spokesman for his new country' and predicting that the story would be an even greater success than *A Town Like Alice* 'because of its deep feeling and complete sincerity'. Melbourne's other major newspaper *The Argus* was not as enthusiastic, believing that while there was no doubt that Shute's new book would be a success, the fact was that 'from every point of view it is an extraordinarily bad book'.

In America the book was published with the title of *The Breaking Wave*, probably in the belief that the term Wren would not be so familiar to the local audience. There, Waves was the acronym for Women Accepted for Volunteer Emergency Service. Generally well received, the *Daily Boston Globe* summarised that it was 'a very readable and intelligent story'. The reviewer in *Time* was less constrained, noting that 'A skilled storyteller, Shute makes his combat scenes exciting, and his love-in-bloom scenes tender, peppers both with Hitchcocky suspense'. As was again becoming normal for a Shute novel, the book spent a good number of weeks in the Best Sellers List of *The New York Times,* on this occasion thirteen.

With *Requiem for a Wren* now published, Norway was already well advanced with his next novel, keen to have a manuscript finished by the end of the summer. In the meantime, one of his earlier novels, *A Town Like Alice*, was at last being transferred to the big screen. Although The Rank Organisation had bought the film rights for the novel soon after it had been published in 1950, it was only now being made into a film. The up and coming Peter Finch had been chosen to play Joe Harman while the then little-known English actress Virginia McKenna had been cast as Jean Paget. To keep costs down much of the film was being made at Pinewood Studios outside London, with the rest being filmed in Malaya and Australia. In the middle of July the film production unit arrived to spend three weeks on location in Alice Springs and Tennant Creek. Peter Finch and Virginia McKenna were not flown out for this, with locals John Cummings and Sally Brown standing in for the stars during the long shots at the end of the film. This was the first Shute novel with an Australian setting to be filmed in the country. A few years later the Hollywood film industry would be coming to Melbourne in force, to film a second.

By late summer Norway had finished the first draft of *Beyond the Black Stump* and, leaving the running of the farm in the hands of Fred Greenwood, again set off for a trip to Britain and America. As in 1953, Frances did not accompany him but stayed back at Langwarrin. It seems that they were increasingly spending large parts of each year apart.

This time Heather joined him on the trip. Having withdrawn from her law course at the University of Melbourne, she had completed a secretarial course at Stott's College and so could take on the role of her father's secretary during the trip. More importantly though, Norway was becoming increasingly aware that his literary output was developing into quite a significant operation and that nobody else in the family really had any knowledge of this business. In the event of his death, this would present some difficulties. Having decided that of his two daughters, Heather was the most suitable to learn about his business, he thought the quickest way for her to do so would be for her to join him when he visited his literary agent and publishers.

They left Melbourne on 23 August bound for Portland, Oregon. After catching up with Clarence Gilstrap again in La Grande, they intended to travel on to Seattle and New York before heading for London. They were in Britain for the next three months, during which time they met all Norway's key contacts at William Heinemann Ltd and A. P. Watt. They also watched some of the filming of *A Town Like Alice* at Pinewood Studios, which was coming to an end, while Norway also agreed the sale of the film rights of *Requiem for a Wren* to the Rank Organisation. Unfortunately, early in November Nevil suffered another minor heart attack and was admitted to hospital for a few days, but again nothing substantial was found. Nevil and Heather finally arrived back in Sydney on 2 December. They had been away from Australia for just over three months. During that time Heather had learnt much about the publishing world and her father's business, but Nevil had received another reminder about his own frailty.

By his usual standards 1956 was a quiet year for Nevil Norway. On his return from Europe the previous December he had talked of a two-month trip driving along the entire East Coast of Australia towing a boat on a trailer, but this never came to anything. On 17 January 1956 he celebrated his fifty-seventh birthday, and having just experienced his fourth health scare, it seems that age and frequent travelling were beginning to take their toll. Three years earlier he had already confided to a friend in the middle of a twelve-week trip to Europe 'The fact is I'm getting so very tired – seven weeks of talking and travelling are no joke and another five weeks to go before I can get home and rest. One can't do all the trips at 54 that one could at 30'. However, still one for adventure, Norway bought himself a new car. This, though, was no ordinary saloon; he had ordered a Jaguar XK140. With this open-top two-seater, which had a 3½ litre 6-cylinder engine and a typical top speed of 120 mph, the 57-year-old novelist intended to take up a new hobby – off-road motor racing!

The Gala Premiere of the film *A Town Like Alice* was held in London at the Odeon Theatre, Leicester Square on 1 March. The film was chosen to premiere as part of the British Film Academy Awards presentations. Therefore there were even more celebrities than normal out in force that night. Nevil Norway, though, was not there. Still getting over his last health scare, another long flight was probably the last thing he needed. The film, which had been directed by Jack Lee, was not a completely accurate adaptation of Nevil Shute's novel. It only told the first half of the story, depicting in detail the experiences of Jean Paget and Joe Harman in wartime Malaya and only briefly mentioning their reunion and later life in post-war Australia.

Most of the critics present at the first viewing liked the film. Although there was some debate about the ending, the reviews in the newspapers the next day were positive. The film critic in the *Daily Express* defied readers not to cry during the film, and he also urged people not to miss it. Virginia McKenna was singled out for particular praise, and both she and Peter Finch went on to receive BAFTA Awards for their performances.

While one of the most popular film adaptations of a Shute novel, it was not without controversy. Originally entered for the 1956 Cannes International Film Festival, it was later withdrawn by the organisers because they were afraid it would offend the Japanese representatives present. This proved to be an over-reaction as the Japanese government later approved the screening of the film in Japan.

Away from the glitter and politics of the film industry, on the other side of the world Nevil Shute was beginning to start on his next novel. This was to be definitely one of his novels with a message, and the one to which he would become most emotionally attached.

By the spring of 1956, the USSR and the United Kingdom had followed the United States in developing a nuclear weapon capability. The uranium bomb that had been dropped over Hiroshima in August 1945 had already been superseded by hydrogen bombs hundreds of times more powerful. On 1 March 1954 the United States had detonated its first lithium thermonuclear device at the Bikini Atoll in the Marshall Islands. As a result of a design error, the 15-megaton explosion was almost twice that expected, and a 1,000 times more powerful than the Hiroshima bomb. The explosion produced a massive crater with a diameter of 1,984 metres and a depth of 76 metres. Unpredictable weather patterns led to uncontrolled nuclear fallout over an area of over 11,000 square kilometres, exposing local islanders, US personnel and the crew of a Japanese fishing boat to in some cases lethal levels of radiation. The explosion created international anxiety and a diplomatic dispute with Japan. The Castle Bravo Test started to raise real questions about the ability of humans to control the weapons they were now developing. More fundamentally, if the power of nuclear bombs kept increasing as nations tried to outmuscle each other, would the world actually survive a nuclear war if it came? Norway had been thinking about this for some time, but now he started to write about a scenario in which the unthinkable happens and the world ends. He had finally started on what would turn out to be perhaps his best known and certainly most controversial novel, *On the Beach*.

At the end of April, *Beyond the Black Stump* was published in Britain. Although Shute had been persuaded to change the novel's title from *The Kindest Goanna* because it was unlikely to be understood by many readers, to those outside of Australia the new title may have been equally bewildering. The 'Black Stump' is a colloquialism for an imaginary point beyond which the country is considered remote or uncivilised.

Shute's recent novels had all to some extent focused on, and in doing so compared, life in England and Australia. The countries which formed the backdrop to this new novel were Australia and America. The theme of the book probably grew out of conversations Norway had had with Clarence Gilstrap during his trip to La Grande in 1954. Gilstrap had suggested to Norway that the frontier had probably moved, and that the undeveloped white man's country was now to be found in the west of Australia rather than the western states of America.

The novel concerns Stanton Laird, an American geologist working in a remote part of Western Australia. Although living in a hostile region, his employer provides the exploration team with high-quality facilities at the temporary camp from which they work, very different to those experienced by many of the locals living in outback Australia. Stanton becomes friends with a local Australian girl, Mollie Reagan, whose family run a huge sheep station. Mollie's family is unconventional in its lifestyle but not unusual in the frontier country in which they live. A romance develops, and Mollie and Stanton decide to get married. However, before they do so, her mother insists that Mollie first visits Stanton's home town in Oregon to meet his family and understand more about his background and upbringing.

They travel to the small town of Hazel in Oregon, which was once a frontier town but now exhibits the formalities and social norms of more established towns. Initially liking Stanton's family and the new way of life in small-town America, Mollie becomes unsettled when the widow of Stanton's best friend returns to the town to live. As she learns more about Stanton's teenage years, and his attitude towards the death of a friend in a road accident, she becomes increasingly aware that she and Stanton have a completely different attitude to life. She begins to realise she had not been in love with Stanton but more with an image of small-town America which had been fuelled by so many magazines back home. Mollie decides not to settle in Hazel, but to return to the frontier country that is her real home and marry a young Englishman, David Cope, who is in love with her. Cope runs a nearby sheep station, which is large but struggles to get by because of a lack of water. Stanton leaves a final gift for Mollie. Although no oil is discovered, the company finds a vast artesian well which will ensure the Cope's farm can become viable, and that he and Mollie will have something to build their future on.

The reviews of the book in the British press were generally not encouraging, often with the usual double-edged comments. Typical of these was *The Observer*, whose reviewer noted that the book 'was written with Mr. Nevil Shute's customary aplomb' but that 'it is a pity that his style should be of such incredible banality, as this novel has a good theme'.

Peter Green in *The Daily Telegraph* was more positive, considering it to be 'a professionally dovetailed narrative that from first page to last has the air of a cleverly disguised film-script'. He also thought it 'the best novel its author has written for some time'. The reviewer in *The Times Literary Supplement* was certainly not keen, describing the novel as 'a contrived and shallow piece of work' and concluding that 'the insipid, flat writing, with its pedestrian dialogue and trite small talk, leaves a depressing taste in the mouth'. William Heinemann thought differently about the prospects for the book and organised a print run of 120,000, most of which had been sold by the end of the year.

Beyond the Black Stump was published in America at the beginning of August. Reviews were better than they had been in Britain, but they were still not overwhelming in their praise. A review from Oregon, the state described in the book, concluded that 'the ending makes an otherwise dull book worth the reading' but warned that 'some North-westerners won't like Mr. Shute's critical commentary which is applied in the outcome of the story'. More positively, *The New York Herald Tribune* thought it offered readers 'an appealing love story, an interesting account of life on the Australian frontier, and a shrewdly amusing – and challenging – evaluation of two cultures'. In spite of the local theme, the American public were not taken by the novel, and it only spent five weeks at the lower end of *The New York Times* Best Sellers list.

A first print of the film *A Town Like Alice* finally reached Melbourne in mid-June. The manager of the local Odeon, the chain that would show the film in Australia, arranged for Norway and specially invited guests to a private showing on 14 June. This may have been the first time that Norway realised that the film only covered the first half of his novel, but if so it does not seem to have caused him too much distress.

The official Australian premiere of the film took place, appropriately enough, in Alice Springs on 8 August. Nevil Norway and his wife attended, along with Peter Finch and local notables. In true outback fashion the film was shown in the open air Pioneer Theatre beside the banks of the iconic River Todd. Guests were dressed for warmth rather than style, sat in canvas deckchairs, and made full use of blankets to protect themselves from the evening chill.

When it went on general release in Shute's home territory of Melbourne, *A Town Like Alice* was a great success. Even though only a very small part of the film was devoted to Australia, the Odeon was still showing it four times a day a month after it had opened. It was proving equally popular in Britain, and by the end of September the film was already third on the list of post-war top-grossing films on the Odeon's London circuit. Eventually becoming one of the most successful British films of 1956, *A Town Like Alice* is now probably the most fondly remembered of all film adaptations of a Shute novel, or more accurately perhaps half a novel!

Norway had finished the first draft of what had originally been titled *The Last Day* but had now become *On the Beach* at the end of September. Although this was a novel with a message that had been on his mind for a number of years, now it was finished he was genuinely not sure whether anyone would want to read it or whether his publishers would even take it on. However, if the reaction of his daughter Shirley was anything to go by, he would be proved wrong. She later recounted how 'despite having had *On the Beach* for breakfast lunch and dinner for about three years, she sat up in bed reading the manuscript without stopping until four in the morning'.

As with all of his novels Norway went to great lengths to ensure that the background detail to the main story was factually correct. The working notes for this novel show that among other things he researched death rates from radiation, the potential destructive power of cobalt-fusion bombs (which were never built), and made detailed notes when replicating a final car journey that one of the book's main characters takes to Port Phillip Bay. He also asked a friend, Major General Frank Kingsley Norris, who was a physician and director general of Army Medical Services, to check specific aspects of the manuscript. Although this novel was set only six years in the future, the scenario he was predicting was so extreme that in order for readers to believe it, everything had to be plausible, and so the accuracy of background detail was critical.

This was not the only time that Norway explored a disaster scenario with Norris. Shortly before he died he discussed the plot of a novel in which a plague which would destroy all the paper in the world was about to hit the planet. All books, records and archives would disintegrate and there was no known defence against it. This was an idea which never seems to have got past the embryonic stage in Norway's mind, and no development notes for the novel were found among his papers.

With the final manuscript of *On the Beach* delivered safely to his literary agent, Norway took a short break from writing and began his motor sport career. He had taken delivery of his Jaguar XK140 at the beginning of May, and by the beginning of November was confident enough to enter his first off-road competition. Mr N. S. Norway made his first competitive appearance at the Rob Roy Hill Climb competition just outside Melbourne on 6 November 1956. He completed the 760-yard-long course in 32.91 seconds at a time when the club record was 25.77 seconds. However, as he later said, 'he didn't want to be the fastest competitor, just the oldest'.

On 22 November 1956, the eyes of the sporting world were again on Melbourne when Prince Phillip opened the Games of the XVI Olympiad at the Melbourne Cricket Ground in front of a capacity crowd of 103,000. This was the first Olympic Games to be held in the Southern Hemisphere, but the build-up had not been without controversy. There had been arguments between politicians about funding, and then it was discovered that Australia's severe quarantine laws would prevent horses being imported for equestrian events and so a separate equestrian Games was held in Stockholm in June. Finally, what would become the common practice of countries withdrawing for political reasons led to Egypt, Iraq, Lebanon, the Netherlands, Spain, Switzerland and the People's Republic of China not participating in the Melbourne Games.

The sailing events were held in Port Phillip Bay, and so not surprisingly Nevil Norway was a regular spectator. Here he met up with an old friend, Miles Smeeton, whom he had first met during a visit to Vancouver a few years before. Miles and his wife Beryl, and a fellow round-the-world sailor John Guzzwell, had sailed their 46-foot ketch across the Pacific to Melbourne, and after the Games had finished they were planning to sail on to Britain via Cape Horn. Here, in spite of the long-held belief that a small sailing vessel properly handled would endure any conditions, such was the severity of the storm that hit the boat just off Cape Horn that it was holed, dismasted and rudderless and those on board lucky to survive. The Smeeton's experiences provided the inspiration for part of a future Shute novel, *Trustee from the Toolroom*. Shute would write a foreword to

Smeeton's own account of his sailing experiences which was published in 1959.

At the Olympics, Norway also first met Bruce Kirby. Representing Canada in the Finn dinghy class, Kirby would go on to become a successful yacht designer. Years later he still recalled being surprised by Norway's severe stutter, but in spite of that his memory is of a warm, friendly and outgoing individual.

By the end of 1956, Nevil Shute had published nineteen novels, an autobiography and a play. Many of his readers may have been forgiven for thinking that the novelist had reached something of a plateau. He was well settled in Australia, unlikely to now move anywhere else, or for health reasons unlikely to take on any extreme expeditions or adventures in the search for new material. His last two novels, although commercially successful, had been pretty standard fare compared to some of his earlier work. However, the novel by which the name of Nevil Shute is probably now best remembered was still yet to come.

15

Armageddon, Conflict and Decline
January 1957–December 1958

The previous year had promised much as far as an improvement in world peace and stability was concerned. At the beginning of 1956, in a surprise speech at the Twentieth Congress of the Communist Party of the Soviet Union, Nikita Khrushchev had denounced the policies and cult of Joseph Stalin. There was hope that this would mark the start of a new, more positive relationship between the Soviet Union and America. In the event this proved to be a false dawn, and by the beginning of 1957 it seemed that the threat of a nuclear conflict was just as close as ever. If Nevil Shute had wanted his next novel to be one with a message, he had certainly chosen both the right subject and right time in which to deliver it.

In spite of a few economic difficulties the previous year, at the beginning of 1957 Australia was still a good place to live. The economy was growing at 5 per cent and unemployment was close to a post-war record low at 1.5 per cent. Nevil Norway still firmly believed in his adopted country, and he had in fact just persuaded a war colleague Alec Menhinick and his family to join him in Victoria. Like Ian Hassall, Alec had been a member of the Department of Miscellaneous Weapons Development during the war, and among other achievements he had conceived the idea of the Rocket Grapnel, which was successfully used by US forces during the D-Day landings. As well as being a skilled mechanical designer, Alec, like Norway, had a strong entrepreneurial spirit and a love for all things connected with the sea. Rather than settle down to a typical nine-to-five job since the end of the war, he and his family had, among other things, sailed to the Seychelles to establish a shark fishing industry. However, with a growing family and the need of a more stable income, they had returned to Britain, where more recently they had been running a village shop in rural Wiltshire. Norway believed there would be better opportunities for Alec and his family in Australia. He had therefore persuaded them to emigrate, acting as their guarantor for the application.

On the first day of the New Year, like all of the major newspapers, the front page of *The Sydney Morning Herald* was dominated by the fifteen Australian knights that had been created by the Queen in the New Year Honours list. Ties to the mother country were still there, and still important. Everyday life in the city, though, was represented by news of the 120,000 who had welcomed the New Year in at Manley, the weather that could be expected for the public holiday, and of course a list of the sporting fixtures.

The prime minister, in an ambiguous New Year message, believed that 'our economic problems will diminish in 1957, and the true quality of our prosperity will become clear'. The president of the Associated Chambers of Manufacturers of Australia, on the other hand, had no doubt at all where the key to the country's prosperity lay. In the coming year he expected higher wool prices, a larger wool cheque and as a result a noticeable increase in business activity. Although he did not have sheep on his small farm, concentrating on cattle and pigs instead, Nevil Norway would have been happy for the local rural community of which he was now most certainly a part. With *On the Beach* safely delivered to the publishers and in production, unable to do nothing for long, after a brief break he started on his next novel, *The Rainbow and the Rose*. For this he would return to a familiar theme of aviation and also make use of the dream flashback technique that he had previously used in *An Old Captivity* and *In the Wet*.

Although it had been over decade since the Americans had detonated atomic bombs over the cities of Hiroshima and Nagasaki, and in doing so helped end the Second World War, the world was still far from being a peaceful one. Allies in the war had now become foes, and as Winston Churchill famously observed about Europe in 1946, 'from Stettin in the

Baltic to Trieste in the Adriatic an iron curtain had descended across the Continent'. By the beginning of 1957, the 'superpowers' were not just content in having an atomic bomb, they wanted to develop weapons that were even bigger and better than their opponent – the nuclear arms race was well underway.

On 20 January 1957 the Atomic Energy Commission in America reported that they had detected a nuclear test by the Soviet Union. A rocket carrying a nuclear warhead with a yield of 10 kilotonnes had been detonated over western Kazakhstan. This was the first of at least sixteen nuclear tests that the Soviet Union would carry out that year. Four days later, the Atomic Energy Commission announced that it would be commencing its own series of 'low-yield' nuclear tests in Nevada beginning in late spring.

The third nuclear power at that time, the United Kingdom, had been using Australia as a test site since 1952. By the beginning of 1957, nine major nuclear tests and a large number of minor trials had been completed with explosions producing yields of up to 60 kilotonnes. A permanent test site had also now been established at Maralinga in a remote western part of South Australia, and an area of over 3,300 square kilometres declared a prohibited area. Three decades later, the name of Maralinga would come to symbolise many of the negative aspects of the British nuclear tests in Australia.

It is difficult to assess what the public in Australia thought at the time about the atomic tests taking place on their soil, as not that many were even aware of them. From the start there was almost complete government control of the Australian media as far as reporting was concerned. Information provided was limited and designed principally to reassure rather than inform.

It was different in the United Kingdom where, in general, the tests had been much more heavily reported. As far back as the early 1950s there had been sporadic protests against the development of nuclear weapons. However in 1957 these started to coalesce into a mass movement. In April, the annual Defence White Paper published by the then Minister of Defence, Duncan Sandys, signalled the government's strong belief in the continued need for an independent nuclear deterrent, but more alarmingly it made clear that there was 'at present no means of providing adequate protection for the people of this country against the consequences of an attack with nuclear weapons'. Public awareness of the nuclear threat was increased, and the beginnings of an organised protest movement which would ultimately become the Campaign for Nuclear Disarmament (CND) began to evolve. It was into this environment that, in the summer of 1957, *On the Beach* was published.

The novel begins at Christmas 1962 and tells the story of the last months of mankind on planet earth. It originally had a working title of '*The Last Year*' and was the only one of Shute's novels to be set in Melbourne. Apart from the fictitious town of Falmouth, which appears to have been modelled on Frankston, most of the other locations used were real parts of Melbourne and the adjoining Mornington Peninsula with which Shute was so familiar. The nuclear war which would result in the end of man had started only fourteen months before when Albania had used an atomic bomb on Naples. This had developed into a wider Israeli–Arab conflict, into which the superpowers soon became drawn, bringing with them highly destructive cobalt atomic bombs. An intense nuclear war had then spread with bewildering speed, obliterating the whole of the northern hemisphere. Now, what was left of the world's leaders had gathered in Wellington, waiting for the lethal radiation to continue its move southwards, and waiting for the end of the world. As the most southerly major city in the world, Melbourne would be one of the last to succumb. The novel tells the story of the last days of five people in this city as they await their inevitable fate. Peter Holmes, a young lieutenant commander in the Royal Australian Navy is given a posting as a liaison officer on an American atomic submarine which is being sent on a last voyage to investigate two faint hopes for human survival. The other non-American on the voyage is John Osborne, a scientist with a passion for motor racing, much like the person Norway himself had become. Peter's wife Mary refuses to believe that the world is about to end and tries to carry on life as normal, planning the garden, arranging parties and social events. At one of these, Dwight Towers, the commander of the American submarine, meets the fast-living, hard-drinking Moira Davidson. A platonic relationship develops between the two but can become nothing more, as even though Towers knows his wife and children are certainly dead he wants to behave as though they are not. The possibilities for survival that the submarine is sent to investigate both turn out to be dead ends, and it returns to Melbourne with all hope extinguished. Each of the characters then chooses their own way to end their life, and as the quote that Shute used from T. S. Eliot at the beginning of the novel says, 'this is the way the world ends, not with a bang but a whimper'.

Shute's publishers both in America and Britain were really not sure what the public's reaction would be to a novel about the end of the world. The novel was not standard science fiction fare, and to many the understated style that Shute had used just added to the plausibility of the story. An editor at William Morrow said, 'Of course we'd publish almost anything that Nevil Shute wrote. But we had to think twice about readership on this one'. William Heinemann were equally unsure, ordering a first print run of 80,000 rather than the 100,000 which was becoming the usual practice for a Shute novel. There were also some mixed signals in the pre-publication business that Ronald Watt had been negotiating. While the novel had been rejected by all of the major book clubs, an abridged serial called 'The Last Days on Earth' had been published before the novel itself was released in tabloid newspapers and magazines such as the *Sunday Graphic* and *PIX*.

Reviews in the British press were mixed. The mainstream *Times Literary Supplement* gave it the only briefest of reviews, judging the characterisation weak and unrepresentative. Somewhat strangely, the reviewer in *The Sunday Times* almost seemed to miss the whole point of the book completely, believing the theme to be 'scientific work in the Royal Australian Navy'. Others, though, were far more encouraging, with the reviewer in *The Daily Telegraph* regarding the book to be 'quietly and deliberately terrible ... all the more terrible for its characteristic half-muted tones, and subdued colours' and 'by far Mr. Shute's most considerable achievement'. *The Listener* similarly thought the narrative 'skillfully muted and restrained' with the result that the novel was 'both moving and horrifying'.

In America there was a divergence of opinion. The *Chicago Daily Tribune*, with a positive review, concluded that it was 'an austere, grim, moving, important book that could become real'. On the other hand, Orville Prescott in *The New York Times*, who was clearly not an admirer of Shute's work, considered that in spite of the vastness of the theme 'it is still difficult to take Mr Shute's story seriously. The same shortcomings that deface all his work are here as usual: the clumsy structure and awkward writing, the superficial and inadequate characterisation'.

All the concerns as to whether *On the Beach* would be too bleak a novel to be popular proved to be groundless. It sold nearly 90,000 copies pre-publication in Britain and Australia, while in America it was serialised in at least forty newspapers and quickly reached number two in *The New York Times* Best Sellers list, only be kept from the top spot by James Gould Cozzens *By Love Possessed*. By the 1980s *On the Beach* had sold over 4 million copies worldwide, easily becoming the most successful of Nevil Shute's novels.

Shute had wanted it to be a book with a message. His publishers clearly thought the same thing, sending advance copies to a number of politicians, including John F. Kennedy. Then only a junior senator, he would be on the cover of *Time* magazine by the end of the year, and three years after that he would be president of the United States. The book also attracted the attention of some of the old guard. Winston Churchill read the book and intended to send a copy to Nikita Khrushchev, though it seems he did not think it worth sending a copy to Eisenhower. Locally, Norway sent a copy to his friend Dick Casey, Australia's Minister for External Affairs, saying, 'I cannot suppose that you or anybody else will greatly enjoy the story'. Whether people enjoyed the novel can be debated, but what was clear was that its message resonated with many. Professor Paul Brians described it as being 'the most influential work of its kind for the next quarter of a century', while others have gone even further, describing it as 'arguably Australia's most important novel'.

Away from the publicity surrounding the launch of *On the Beach*, Nevil Norway had continued to develop his fledgling career as a racing driver. Competing in an Easter Monday race meeting of the Phillip Island Auto Racing Club, he had come second in an open handicap. Although he had led for much of the race, he was overtaken on the final lap, finishing two seconds behind the winner. A respectable result for a 58-year-old with a heart condition! He continued to race and participate in hill climb events until April 1958, but this second place would be the peak of his short career.

A number of film companies had shown interest in *On the Beach* even before it had been published in America. By 10 September the Australian newspapers were reporting that Stanley Kramer had bought the film rights of the novel. Kramer was by then already a big name in the American film industry, with nineteen films to his credit, including some that would become classics, such as *High Noon* and *The Wild One*. His latest film *The Pride and the Passion* had just been released. Starring Cary Grant, Frank Sinatra and Sophia Loren, he was used to working with Hollywood's biggest stars. A month later, rumours about the new film were rife; the film rights had been bought for $100,000, it would have a production budget of $1.5 million, Cary Grant, William Holden and Deborah Kerr would star in the film, and it would be made in Melbourne. While not all of these turned out to be totally accurate, one thing was clear, Hollywood could be coming to Melbourne.

Over in Britain, public unease about the development of nuclear weapons continued to grow. A fellow William Heinemann author, J. B. Priestley, wrote an article for the *New Statesman* at the end of the year in which he made the case for unilateral nuclear disarmament in Britain. The nuclear arms race between America and the Soviet Union had been moving on at a pace, with one ultimate weapon quickly succeeding another. A new level of tension had been reached on 3 October when the Soviet Union had successfully launched Sputnik 1, the world's first artificial satellite. The satellite weighed 83 kg, but such was the speed at which things were progressing, a day after the publication of Priestley's article, the Soviet Union launched Sputnik 2. This capsule weighed 500 kg and carried a dog, Leika, the first living creature to be sent into space.

In this atmosphere of international competitiveness and ever growing nuclear stockpiles, Priestley's article resonated with a number of politicians, artists and intellectuals. As a result, on 17 February the following year, the Campaign for Nuclear Disarmament was launched at a mass meeting at Central Hall, Westminster. Priestley had written reviews for three of Shute's earlier novels, but it seems he did not write one for *On the Beach*. It would, though, have been surprising if he had not read the novel before writing his article for the *New Statesman*. While Norway wanted his novel to carry a message, he did not want to promote this personally, and he was certainly not a political activist. An invitation to support the Congress for International Cooperation and Disarmament as a sponsor, a few years later, was therefore bluntly refused. He thought that using international conferences to try to influence 'the properly elected government of the country' was 'not a democratic procedure', and something he considered unwise.

Throughout the summer of 1957, despite the distractions being generated by the increasing interest in *On the Beach*, Norway continued to work on his next novel. In mid-July he and Frances took a six-week break in Fiji. This was both a writing and leisure trip. Neither of them had been to the Pacific Islands before, and as always a new environment provided Nevil with potential material for future novels. By the beginning of November he had delivered the manuscript of *The Rainbow and the Rose* to his literary agent, and so he took another break, this time a two-week fishing trip in New Zealand.

As far as writing was concerned, Norway was self-sufficient; he neither had nor particularly wanted much contact with the wider literary world. He was, however, increasingly aware of the difficulties young authors faced in getting established in an isolated country like Australia and the limited opportunities there were for publishing new work. In early December he wrote to the Minister for External Affairs, Dick Casey, suggesting that the government consider subsidising the development of a politics, culture and current affairs magazine along the lines of *The Atlantic* in America or *The Spectator* in Britain. Casey replied that a number of attempts had been made to start a serious review magazine but so far none had been sustainable.

Television had finally been launched in Australia the previous year, and, although initially only available to residents of Sydney and Melbourne, was already beginning to have an impact on people's leisure time.

The year 1958 did not start well for either Nevil or Francis. Nevil had fallen over a bale of hay on their property and broken a rib, while Francis was struggling with arthritis and was bedridden with lumbago. They had planned an extensive overseas trip for later in the year, but for now they were confined to the farm. There was some good news though. The detailed negotiations with the Stanley Kramer Pictures Corporation had been successfully concluded, and on 7 January Kramer signed a contract for the film rights for *On the Beach*.

Having finished *The Rainbow and the Rose* in autumn 1957, Norway did not begin writing his next novel until the end of 1958, an unusually long gap. What had been such a reliable routine was beginning to be interrupted by minor health problems, increasing involvement with Kramer, and maybe even the intrusion of old age. Whatever the reasons, it was certain that no Nevil Shute novel would be published in 1959. He did, though, write something in the spring; on 24 April 1958 he completed his will. He had decided that Heather and The Union Trustee Company of Australia would be the executors of his estate. For someone who had always been so careful in ensuring that the factual detail in his novels was correct, this apparently straightforward six-page document contained enough ambiguities to keep the legal profession well occupied for a number of years after his death.

While Kramer had signed a contract for *On the Beach*, it was still by no means certain that the film would be shot in Australia. Given the size and complexity of the production, there was a significant amount of pressure on him to make the film in America where facilities and skills were far ahead of those in Australia. Undecided, he sent his production manager and production designer to Melbourne in early May to examine the logistics of making the film there. On their arrival, they were 'hijacked' by the Victoria Promotion Committee, and such was the support they were given, by the time the pair left they had been convincingly persuaded that 'nowhere could *On the Beach* be made with such co-operation and efficiency as in Melbourne'. At this stage, Norway was enthusiastic about the film and had taken time to show the visitors the locations around Melbourne that he had used in the novel.

By mid-May, Francis and Nevil were both healthy enough to leave for an extensive four-month trip which would take in America and Britain. Heather was now living away from Langwarrin and working as a shorthand typist in Melbourne. Shirley, showing much of her father's adventurous spirit, had just finished a course at the University of Perugia and was now on her way to London on her newly acquired Lambretta scooter, where she intended to meet up with her parents before moving on to Vienna in October for four months to study German.

Following leisurely breaks in Oregon, Los Angeles, Denver, Washington, and New York, the Norways finally reached London in

June. While there had been business elements to the trip so far, such as a meeting with United Artists to discuss the making of On the Beach and a visit to William Morrow in New York, there had also been a great deal of sightseeing, along with the pleasure of catching up with many old friends.

On 28 July 1958, The Rainbow and the Rose was published in Britain. This was the twenty-second book that Nevil Shute had published since 1926. In that time he had moved from being an unknown author with books selling in their hundreds to a household name with books selling in their hundreds of thousands. A new Shute novel was now a big event for Heinemann, and this time they were marking publication by declaring a Nevil Shute Week. As the author himself was in England, he was available to help with promotion. What neither of course knew, was that this would be the last Nevil Shute novel to be published during his lifetime.

After the bleakness and controversy of On the Beach, Shute returned to his first love, aviation, and writing purely to entertain with The Rainbow and the Rose. Set in Australia in the 1950s, the story concerns an ex-military and commercial pilot called Johnnie Pascoe. Close to retirement, he now runs a small aero club and crop-spraying business in a remote part of Tasmania. He volunteers to fly a mercy mission to collect a child suffering from appendicitis from an isolated property but unfortunately crashes on a mountainous part of the Tasmanian coast. Pascoe is seriously injured in the crash, suffering from a fractured skull. An ex-pupil of his, Ronnie Clarke, agrees to fly a doctor to Pascoe, but unfortunately, because of the extreme weather, is forced to abandon the attempt and return to Pascoe's airfield. Exhausted, he rests in Pascoe's bedroom and while asleep relives episodes of the injured pilot's life. He dreams he is a fighter pilot during the Great War, running a small flying school in England in the interwar years, and finally a civil aviation pilot after the Second World War. Whatever success Pascoe might have had in aviation, his personal life had been far from happy. He had experienced a failed marriage, an affair with a woman who eventually commits suicide, and the birth of a daughter from each relationship both of whom he loses touch with. Clarke is visited by the two daughters, one who wants her father to survive while the other does not. Clarke's second attempt to reach Pascoe is successful, but unfortunately, on arrival, he learns that Pascoe had died during the night.

In *The Rainbow and the Rose*, Shute made extensive use of the dream flashback technique that he had previously used in *An Old Captivity* and *In the Wet*. Reaction from reviewers was on the whole positive. The reviewer in *The Times* considered the flashback technique 'ingenious' and noted that 'in practice, it works out well and lucidly, with no awkward breaks'. The writer H. E. Bates was even more enthusiastic, believing that Shute's style 'is, in fact, of its kind, masterly' and concluding that 'in its narrative skill, its technical detail and its human values, Shute's novel is quite admirable'. The novel was not published in America until the end of October. Here, the opinions were a little more mixed. The reviewer in the *Chicago Daily Tribune* was clearly not impressed, believing that 'the plot might have been handled well by another writer. In Shute's hands, it is 310 pages of clumsy flashbacks and minute, boring details'. Others were far more positive, believing that 'As always, Shute writes in plain, unadorned prose, packs his books with pluck and poignancy, and handles his flashbacks as easily as he would a basic trainer'. By now, both Shute and his publishers were well used to the views of the critics and buying public often being at odds with one another, and as usual the novel sold well.

The time in England went much the same way as it had in America – a mixture of business and pleasure. On 18 August, Nevil, Frances and Shirley spent the evening with Flora Twort in Petersfield. For Flora and Nevil this would be the last time these two long-time friends would ever meet.

The Norways arrived back in Melbourne in mid-September, tired but relieved that the trip had been free from illness. They were greeted by the prospect of increasingly mild and sunny days, spring having just started in Australia. The people of Melbourne had a lot to look forward to. The annual Royal Melbourne Show had just opened, the Australian Rules Grand Final between Collingwood and Melbourne would take place in front of a sell-out crowd at the Melbourne Cricket Ground on 20 September, and the England cricket team would be touring trying to retain the Ashes trophy. However, above all, Hollywood was coming to Melbourne, but Nevil Norway was far from happy.

In an interview with the press during his stopover in New York, Norway had been asked about the forthcoming filming of *On the Beach*. He displayed a phlegmatic attitude, saying, 'An author is an individualist. To make a movie, changes are inevitable, and an author never likes them very much. He's better off getting along to something creative'. This was sound advice which Norway had usually followed during the previous five film adaptations of his novels. Unfortunately, this was not the case for *On the Beach*, and things were rapidly going from bad to worse.

Having acquired the film rights to the novel, Stanley Kramer had employed John Paxton to write the screenplay. Paxton had both experience and ability, having co-written the screenplay for an earlier Kramer film, *The Wild One*, and received an Academy Award nomination for his screenplay of *Crossfire* in 1948. Although he had no obligation at all to involve Norway in the production of the film, nonetheless Kramer sent him a copy of Paxton's draft script in June 1958. He did not get the response he expected; Norway hated it. His three-page letter and a detailed appendix listed the many issues he had with the screenplay. These ranged from what could be considered as niggling complaints to fundamental disagreements. For instance, he believed Paxton had introduced too much realism into the characters' behaviour by allowing the relationship between Dwight Towers and Moira Davidson to become physical. Norway believed that in 'times of intense stress and disaster people prove to be far stronger than you think they would be, far stronger than they think they would be themselves'. To emphasise this he had deliberately created characters that were better than they may have been in real life in order to highlight the plight of good people facing a disaster they had not deserved. He believed that the proposed screenplay had altered the underlying emotional idea of the book.

In a courteous reply, Kramer asked Norway to 'Have faith. We are doing much of what you want – I trust we shall meet in September in Australia and be able to sweat out the rest'. Norway's response was not conciliatory; beginning 'Since our last correspondence I have been trying to think why I dislike the first Paxton script of *On the Beach* so much' and ending 'I have written twenty-one books, all of them first-class stories. Believe me, I know more about storytelling than Paxton, or you, or anybody else in your organisation. And I'm flat out to help you'. In a short reply, Kramer again politely tried to calm the author down, assuring him that he was certainly looking forward to meeting up in Australia in October. He was clearly hoping that any issues would be more easily resolved face-to-face. Unfortunately this was to be proved a forlorn hope.

While Norway may now have had misgivings about the filming of *On the Beach*, many others saw it as a great opportunity to keep Melbourne on the map after the Olympic Games. At a federal level, although Menzies' initial reaction to a request from the Stanley Kramer Picture Corporation for co-operation with the Royal Australian Navy had been a little lukewarm, the official response when it came was far more positive. The press release from the Acting Minister for the Navy, confirming the co-operation, concluded that the film would 'be shown throughout the English-speaking world and would provide excellent publicity for the Royal Australian Navy and for Australia generally'.

In spite of these many stresses, it seems Norway was able to still keep to a regular writing routine, and by the middle of December, he had written around 20 per cent of what would become *Trustee from the Toolroom*.

Stanley Kramer and the advance technical support team arrived in Melbourne on 8 November. Casting for the film had been completed, with Gregory Peck and Ava Gardner having been contracted to play the lead characters of Dwight Towers and Moira Davidson. Anthony Perkins was to play Peter Holmes, while a newcomer, Donna Anderson, would be his wife, Mary. Peck and Gardner were certainly among the biggest names in Hollywood at that time and generated great interest in the press at both home and abroad. Perhaps one of the most interesting choices for a part in the film was Fred Astaire, who had been surprisingly cast as Julian Osborne (changed from John Osborne in the novel), the scientist with a love for motor racing. Well known, but perhaps reaching the end of his career in musicals, this was to be his first dramatic part. With much of the production planning now in place, the main cast would be arriving in Melbourne on 16 January for an expected twelve-week schedule. With the budget for the film having now grown to nearly $4 million, this was indeed to be a big production.

True to his word, shortly after arriving in Melbourne, Kramer and a number of his senior team visited Norway for dinner at his home in Langwarrin. Kramer was hoping to resolve the issues Norway had with the screenplay before production started. The meeting did not go well, developing into a huge argument between the two, which ended with the usually mild-mannered Kramer storming out. It seems this was the final straw for Kramer, who after all had no obligation to take any notice of Norway as far as the content of the film was concerned. The production of the film went ahead without any further interaction with Norway. In spite of the fact that much of it was shot in locations close to his home, as far as is known, he never went to any of the film sets, from that point distancing himself from the whole venture. It is really not clear why Norway took such great exception to the changes Kramer was proposing. After all, the film version of *A Town Like Alice* had omitted about half of the novel, and yet Norway had accepted this. Whatever the reason, the rift with Kramer was one which would never be healed. A member of the cast who Norway did get on with was Fred Astaire. Despite the issues Norway had with the film, Astaire visited him at Langwarrin on a number of occasions during his time in Melbourne. Astaire later said of his meetings with Norway: 'I had the pleasure of meeting him in Australia and he was very kind to me. I admired him as a person and a writer very much'.

On top of the conflict with Kramer, a series of other smaller problems troubled Norway as the year ended. His Jaguar sports car was stolen with those responsible being caught and jailed, and he had to tell a long-time friend that he could not lend him any more money for the present. As a result, his health began to suffer, and during December he experienced a number of what he later described as dizzy fits. On 18 December 1958, it all finally caught up with him, and he was admitted to the Royal Melbourne Hospital having suffered a suspected stroke.

Not surprisingly, news of Nevil Shute's illness was reported by newspapers in Australia, but such was his name internationally, it also made the front page of the national newspapers in Britain. The initial assessment at the Royal Melbourne Hospital was that he had indeed suffered a stroke, and he was given medication to reduce the risk of further blood clots. Fortunately, the damage caused by the stroke appeared to be limited, with some minor paralysis of the facial and ocular muscles but no paralysis of the limbs. However, as with all stroke victims, there was always a possibility of a second attack. He was therefore kept in hospital over Christmas for treatment and observation. In view of the fact that there was a risk of a recurrent stroke occurring, Frances was keen for Shirley to return home as soon as possible. They knew she was somewhere in Italy but did not know exactly where. Frances therefore asked Dick Casey, the

Minister for External Affairs, if he could help locate Shirley and pass on a message asking her to return home. After a little difficulty, Shirley was found in Rome and she arrived back in Melbourne early on 26 December.

On the last day of the year Nevil was still in hospital but now well enough to compose a three-page letter to Dwye Evans at Heinemann. It was now clear that the stroke had been mild and not paralysed any of his limbs, though the sight in his left eye had been temporarily affected, making it difficult for him to read for any length of time. Before the stroke, Norway had completed about 20 per cent of his latest novel, and he was hopeful of sending a complete manuscript to Watt by June 1959. However, unsure of how quickly he would recover, he was now informing Heinemann that it would be safer for them not to expect a new book for the Christmas trade of 1959. He was already beginning to experiment with a newly acquired tape recorder in hospital, but looking on the most gloomy side he reflected that 'I have a considerable store of memories of active things and curious places to draw on, and although a store like this would become exhausted very soon I think it is quite possible that one or two books might be written through a tape recorder even though my eyesight were to be practically gone'. This was perhaps the first time that he considered his career as a novelist might have to come to a close.

16

The Last Year
January 1959–January 1960

Nevil Norway was released from hospital during the first week of 1959. Both his sight and optimism had begun to recover but he was well aware that he had been lucky, and that he would need to take things easy for the time being. As a result, one of the events he had to miss was the tenth Australian Citizenship Convention, which was held in Canberra on 20 January. Although never afraid to speak his mind, Norway had always been wary about speaking in public on subjects outside of his expertise. As one of Australia's most famous and successful migrants at that time, he had been invited by the Department of Immigration (probably at the suggestion of Dick Casey) to present a paper on *The Future Population of Australia*. Opened by the Governor General, this would probably have been the highest profile public political event that Nevil Norway had ever spoken at.

Unfortunately, still recovering from his stroke, he was unable to attend, and so the chairman of the Australian Broadcasting Commission, Sir Richard Boyer, read Norway's paper in his absence. In a paper which combined the imagination of the novelist with an engineer's analytical thought process, Norway posed the question of what life would be like in a hundred years' time if the population of Australia had grown to 100 million. Considering, in detail, aspects such as food production, water resources, industrialisation and labour, he concluded that not only was such a scenario feasible but also desirable. He ended by suggesting that 'as the population grows towards 100 million as I think it will, I think Australians will grow a little less aggressive and a little less successful, till they take their rightful place on equal terms in comity with the great nations of the world'. After less than a decade in the country, Norway now felt at home enough in Australia to be able to speak at such a high-level gathering on the country's future.

Although restricted in travel and participation in external events, Norway started writing again almost as soon as he was released from hospital. His eyesight was a problem but he hoped this would only be temporary. He was part way through *Trustee from the Toolroom* and was starting to construct a section of the novel set in Tahiti without having visited the location. A stickler for accuracy, he was always reluctant to write about a place he had actually not visited, but on this occasion he had little choice. He therefore wrote to the British Consul in Tahiti requesting very specific information on a wide range of subjects from the timetable of the transport services between Papeete and Honolulu to picture postcards of the harbour and the names of lower-class cafés on the waterfront.

While Norway was trying to take it easy and recover from his stroke during the early months of 1959, much of the rest of Victoria were seemingly totally absorbed with the filming of *On the Beach*. In a letter to Heinemann's Melbourne office, Alexander Frere had noted that 'it must be very exciting for you all to be so close to a piece of Hollywood bally-hoo like this'. Of course, from his perspective as chairman of William Heinemann, what he most hoped for from all the publicity was increased book sales.

Much of the Melbourne press and public could certainly not get enough of the 'Hollywood bally-hoo'. Even before filming had started in earnest on 15 January, every aspect of the film and its stellar cast seemed to be of interest, even down to the problems that Ava Gardner's hairdresser had keeping the star's hair in shape in a humid Melbourne climate! When filming did start, it was not humidity that was the problem, but heat. A heatwave hit the state and the cast found themselves working in temperatures of over 100°F during the first weeks of filming. The high temperatures did not keep the crowds away though. As the production moved from Berwick to Frankston, Canadian Bay, Williamstown and downtown Melbourne, so the excited, cheering and applauding crowds followed. The racing sequence depicting Shute's description of the last Australian Grand Prix was filmed at two locations: Phillip Island and the Riverside International Raceway in California. One of Norway's friends, Alec Menhinick, doubled for Fred Astaire in the full-speed racing sequences filmed at Phillip Island. There were rumours that Nevil Norway, the keen amateur racing driver, was in the crowd during the race meeting filming, but this has never been absolutely confirmed. When the filming of *On the Beach* in Australia finally finished on 27 March, the whole production returned to America to complete short location sequences in California and San Francisco. Philip Davey's book *When Hollywood Came to Melbourne* gives a wonderfully detailed account of nearly every aspect of the making of *On the Beach*. Nevil Shute had indeed bought a great deal of publicity to Melbourne, and it should have been something of which he was very proud. However, his anger about the way he believed Kramer was misrepresenting his novel had not subsided, and as the release of the film itself got nearer, so his misgivings about the whole venture increased.

At the beginning of May, Norway suffered another problem with his health. An attempt by his doctor to reduce the anticoagulant medication he was taking resulted in another minor stroke, the main consequence of which was that his sight was further affected. He also now had some problems with sensitivity in his right hand, making writing very difficult. After his stroke at the end of the previous year, he had been pretty certain that a full recovery would be possible after a brief rest. Now he was less optimistic. At the very least it seemed he would need to stay on anticoagulant medicine for the rest of his life and be restricted to staying around the home taking things quietly for at least the next year. For an almost perpetual traveller like Norway, this must have been very hard to come to terms with.

In addition to his own declining health, he also had to cope with the retirement of a number of people that had been fixed points in his working life for so long. Firstly, he had received news that Ronald Watt was leaving A. P. Watt. Ronald had been Norway's literary agent since his first book had been published in 1926. Staunchly loyal to his friends, Norway had always had full confidence in Ronald and was very reluctant to let anybody else deal with his affairs. His first reaction to the news was that there must have been some dispute in the company, and so he offered to pay for Ronald to fly out to Australia or else reluctantly travel to England himself to resolve the issue. However, following reassurance from Dwye Evans at Heinemann and Watt himself, Norway was eventually persuaded that nothing untoward had taken place, Ronald was simply retiring, and he agreed to give Ronald Watt's replacement a chance. At this time he also learnt that Alexander Frere, another long-time friend, was no longer chairman of William Heinemann – again a change which unsettled him. In this case, though, while Frere had left the board of William Heinemann, he was still chairman of the overall holding company. Finally, his loyal and long-serving secretary Gladys Bessant retired. Having been with him for twelve years, her role was now formally taken on by Heather.

Increasingly aware of his frailty, he was now thinking far more urgently about what would happen to his literary estate after his death, and he wanted Heather to learn more about his business affairs as quickly as she could. Shirley, unable to stay in one place for too long, was already on her way back to England. She planned to help Frances' aged parents move into a house that Nevil had financed the renovation of, before moving on to Vienna to recommence the German language studies she had interrupted when her father had fallen ill.

Although Norway was now having to take things quietly, as a creature of habit his life was still based around the routine that he had followed for so many years: writing in the mornings, going around the farm in the afternoon, and the workshop in the evenings. The farm at Langwarrin, which now consisted of 205 acres, 130 of which had been cleared, was still more of a hobby than a business. The land now supported 68 cows and 300 pigs, but as he himself admitted, the operation was totally uneconomic. He was doing this because he was interested in farming and did not relish living in the middle of an undeveloped block of land.

As he wrote to Dwye Evans, reflecting on his current way of life:

'I still feel a bit lost if I do not sit down at my desk at 9.30 every morning to work till lunch time. It sometime happens at the conclusion of a book that I think 'Now I am going to take two months holiday' but it never works out that way, and I find myself back at my desk in the mornings in a very short time, even though I have nothing in particular to do.'

While he was using his routine to try and assure himself that things were still the same, he was also aware that in reality they were not; in the same letter, talking about the book he was working on, he said that 'if no further illness intervenes I do not see any reason why it should not be in the hands of A. P. Watt & Son in London, and in yours, by the end of September'. Norway kept to his long-trusted routine and by September the manuscript for *Trustee from the Toolroom* was with A. P. Watt. His optimism for the future had also improved, as he and Frances were now planning a trip by sea to Europe in mid-1960. Anticipating that a long stay in London would now prove too stressful, Norway had rented a castle in La Spezia, Northern Italy, for a month. Complete with its own servants, this was intended to provide the relaxed atmosphere in which to continue to recuperate.

Still not keen to take things easy, almost as soon as he had finished the first draft of *Trustee from the Toolroom*, Norway set to work on another project. Concerned by the difficulties most Australian writers had making a living and the lack of opportunities there were for promoting their work outside of the country, he set to work writing a memorandum to the prime minister on ways of improving this situation. Very soon he found that similar problems were faced by Australian artists, sculptors, composers and musicians. He therefore called in the help of experts from these fields such John Tallis, Margaret Sutherland and Robert Hughes, and by the time it was complete, *A Memorandum about Creative Writers, Artists and Composers in Australia with Legislative and Financial Recommendations* had evolved into a detailed document running to fifty pages. Norway sent the *Memorandum* to Robert Menzies on 20 October, acknowledging that while it was 'entirely unsolicited. I have written it because it seems a good idea for an immigrant to put his experience at the disposal of the country that has done so much for him'. Based on his own experience, he believed that an aspiring writer should have a full-time occupation and write in the evening, until writing becomes more profitable than the occupation. Norway was absolutely clear on one point – he did not believe that the way to advance the arts in Australia was by providing subsidies or fellowships to artists.

Apart from a brief polite letter from Menzies expressing agreement with many of Norway's ideas and the hope that they could one day meet to discuss them, little seems to have been actually done with this *Memorandum*. It surfaced again in 1960 and 1961, when mechanisms for supporting the arts in Australia were briefly considered but not followed up. It would not be until 1967 that a body for promoting the arts in Australia was given government approval and the Australia Council for the Arts was formed. It is possible that Norway's *Memorandum* in some way helped start the ball slowly rolling.

In addition to the *Memorandum* on creative writing, Norway also got himself involved in the government's deliberations on copyright law. In 1955, along with seven authors from the Society of Authors, he had been a signatory to a letter published in *The Times* commenting on the Copyright Bill which was being discussed in Parliament in England. In September 1958, the Attorney General of Australia appointed a committee, chaired by Justice J. A. Spicer, to examine whether any changes were now required to the copyright law of Australia. Norway decided to write a written submission and then make a request to present evidence in person to the Spicer Committee. He sent a written submission to the Committee on 18 September which ended with the typically forthright statement 'I have therefore done the best I can with this deplorable document, the Copyright Act 1912-1950. It has left on my mind an impression that it was drafted solely in the interests of the publishers and recording companies, and that the rights and interests of the creative persons have been little considered, if at all'. Perhaps surprisingly, he was invited to appear before the Committee in Canberra on 4 November. He was not optimistic about his presentation to the Committee, commenting that 'I got the impression that my evidence was unwelcome to the Committee as their deliberations were nearly over and what I said was liable to upset the apple cart'. The Spicer Committee completed its report on 22 December 1959, and Norway's misgivings turned out to be justified as none of his suggestions for change made it into the final report's recommendations.

Having completed his involvement with the Spicer Committee, and eager to continue working, Norway returned to his desk to start on a new project. In mid-November, after having briefly experimented with the outline of a play called 'Nativity at Eucla', Norway quickly moved back to familiar territory, starting on a new novel with a working title of '*Incident at Eucla*'.

December was not a good month for Nevil Norway. Although Kramer's film of *On the Beach* was not set for its worldwide premiere until the middle of the month, Norway had attended a private pre-release screening of the film. His opinion of Kramer's interpretation of his novel was certainly not improved by what he saw, as he bluntly described it to be 'the worst film that has ever been made of one of my books, without exception'. Naturally, Norway was on the restricted guest list for the Melbourne premiere of the film, but after initially accepting, he changed his mind and decided not to attend. It was reported that he would provide a written statement giving his reasons for not attending. He had written to a friend that he was preparing this statement with the assistance of his solicitor in order to avoid any legal action. Even if it was completed, the statement was never released, the only printed record seems to be a short quote that 'the film was not a "good portrayal" of his book'.

The worldwide premiere of *On the Beach* took place on the evening of 17 December. In this case, though, it really was worldwide. Kramer and United Artists had pulled out all of the stops by arranging for eighteen of the world's major cities to premiere the film on the same evening. For the first time, a film was simultaneously released on all continents with the stars dispersed accordingly. Fred Astaire, Anthony Perkins and Donna Anderson were at the Los Angeles premiere, while Ava Gardner was in Rome. Perhaps most interestingly of all, Gregory Peck was at the film's premiere in Moscow. Although it was a private screening to a specially invited audience, this was still the first time that an American feature film had ever been premiered in the Soviet Union. Given the content of the film, Kramer and United Artists were a little apprehensive about how the film would be received in Moscow. In the end, though, all went well, with Peck describing the event as 'a memorable evening'.

As a consequence of the time zones, but perhaps justifiably given that it was in many ways the home of *On the Beach*, Melbourne was the first city on 17 December to actually show the film. Around 3,200 specially invited guests attended, including the state premier Henry Bolte and the governor Sir Dallas Brooks, but of course, Norway was not there. He was however remembered by the audience, because when the name Nevil Shute appeared on the film's opening credits, the audience applauded.

The response of the opening night's film critics around the world was generally very positive. The critic of *The Age* in Melbourne, clearly impressed, thought it was 'a film of tremendous power and impact, an emotional experience which leaves you breathless and suspended in a trance-like state hours after leaving it'. More restrained but still positive was the response of Bosley Crowther in *The New York Times*, who thought that 'Mr. Kramer has brilliantly directed a strong and responsive cast' and that it was a 'deeply moving picture'.

The film critic of *The Times* in London was the only one in the mainstream media to comment on way the relationship between Dwight Towers and Moira Davidson had changed between book and film, a change that had so upset Norway. Believing this change to be 'a pity', he nonetheless thought that 'for most part, Mr. Kramer's sincerity and seriousness are everywhere apparent'. In *The Sydney Morning Herald,* the critic thought that 'it is difficult to believe that many of the people who have admired the novel will be offended by the adaptation that scenarist John Paxton has so skilfully made for Kramer'. *On the Beach* was by no means a commercial failure, eventually grossing about $11 million. It was, however, not nominated for any of the major categories at the thirty-second Academy Awards, a year which was dominated by *Ben Hur*. It did, though, receive nominations in the Best Film Editing and Best Dramatic or Comedy Score categories. Since its release, *On the Beach* has become one of the most popular anti-war films of all time, with a message that is still relevant in today's world. In spite of his reservations, it is also a film with which the name of Nevil Shute is still positively associated.

On 20 December, aware of public interest in both the film and the subject, the well-respected British Sunday newspaper *The Observer* published a full-page, appreciative profile of Nevil Shute, titled 'Best-Seller of Best-Sellers'. Having described how Shute usually had to get 'steamed up' about a subject in order to write a book about it, the article concluded that 'Many people will be grateful that this modest, kindly man, who could retire any day he wanted and live comfortably ever after on the wealth he has already earned, got sufficiently "steamed up" about atomic warfare to write "On the Beach".'

As the new decade dawned, Norway was making good progress on his latest novel *'Incident at Eucla'*. The narrator of the story is William Spear, a 59-year-old research metallurgist from Sheffield in England whose wife has just died after a long illness. Encouraged to take a holiday before returning to work, he decides to visit Australia to lay a plaque at the grave of their only son, who had been killed in an aeroplane crash during the war. His son is buried at Ceduna, a small town on the west coast of the Eyre Peninsula in South Australia. After travelling to Fremantle by ship, Spear decides to drive the 1,200 miles from Perth to Ceduna in order to see something of a country that is so new to him. After a drive on an almost empty road in deteriorating weather, he reaches the isolated town of Eucla, which is now little more than a disused telegraph office and small cottage. He finds himself sharing the overcrowded and basic facilities with individuals from a range of different backgrounds, including an Aboriginal stockman and his heavily pregnant wife. Notes that Shute wrote show that he was intending to develop the story into an intriguing nativity theme. He was already well into chapter three and was sure he would have a new novel with his agent by autumn. Although his health had not yet fully recovered, things were improving and there was also a trip to Europe to look forward to in the next six months.

On Tuesday 12 January, he went to his study after breakfast, as usual, to continue writing. As the morning progressed, however, he began to feel unwell, and by lunchtime his condition had deteriorated to such an extent that an ambulance was called. He had suffered a severe stroke and eventually lost consciousness on the way to the Freemasons Hospital in Melbourne. Nevil Shute Norway, engineer and best-selling novelist, died at about 8.30 later that evening. He was not quite 61 years old.

17

Epilogue
January 1960–April 1960

The death of Nevil Shute Norway made the 10.00 pm national news bulletins in Australia, and very soon the press from around the world were on the telephone to his family at Langwarrin wanting information and quotes.

When the newspapers were published in Australia the following morning, naturally the death of one of their most famous citizens made the front pages. Since migrating to the country in 1950, most of his novels had contained an Australian theme, and while some in Britain had suggested this had bordered on propaganda at times, for most in his new country he had been considered a huge asset.

Ten hours later, newspapers across the whole range of the social and political spectrum in Britain were also reporting his death. Under the headline 'Shute, the Master, is Dead' the *Daily Mirror* described him as 'one of the most successful of British best-selling authors' while *The Times* printed an extensive obituary describing him as 'a novelist of intelligent and engaging quality, deservedly popular, and at the same time a notable figure in the aeronautical world'. Two weeks later, 'J.B.O.' contributed an addition to this particular obituary because he felt Norway had 'qualities of character that need to be mentioned if a true picture of him is to be drawn'. He thought that the 'most important, and least known of all, was his unfailing generosity, combined with a wonderful consideration for others and a thoughtfulness for their needs'. The author of this piece was Norway's old housemaster, J. Basil Oldham, who himself had been a recipient of this generosity on more than one occasion.

Over the following days and weeks, many articles were published describing the life and work of Nevil Shute Norway. There were, of course, reflections on his literary output from contemporaries such as J. B. Priestley and Sir Compton Mackenzie, but there was also debate on why Shute, more than most other best-sellers, seemed to be unappreciated by so many literary reviewers. Perhaps one of the most poignant articles during this period was written by Alexander Frere. He had spent his life in the publishing world, and as chairman of William Heinemann he worked closely with many renowned authors, including Graham Greene, John Steinbeck, D. H. Lawrence and Somerset Maugham. He had known Nevil Norway for over twenty years and considered him to be 'supremely, a story-teller' but also 'one of the bravest, most gifted and essentially good human beings it has ever been my fortune to know'.

In keeping with the character of the man, the funeral of Nevil Norway was a private affair. It took place at Springvale Crematorium on 15 January, with attendance limited to family and very close friends and acquaintances, and the media presence kept to a minimum. Norway's coffin was draped in the Australian flag, with the service being led by the Bishop of Melbourne, John. D. McKie. One of those present was R. G. (Dick) Casey, the Minister for External Affairs, who had become a personal friend of the family over the previous years. Norway's body was cremated and his ashes eventually scattered over the Solent, the stretch of water which separates the Isle of Wight from the mainland of England and a place where Norway had spent many happy hours sailing. The service at the crematorium had been preceded by a private service for the family at their home in Langwarrin. While Heather was at both, Frances was not well enough to attend the service at Springvale. Meanwhile, Shirley was still in Vienna, trying to make arrangements to return home.

The following week, a public memorial service was held at St Paul's Anglican Church, Frankston. The service, which was attended by many from his local community who knew him as Nevil Norway the farmer rather than Nevil Shute the author, was also led by the Right Reverend

McKie, who told the congregation 'we are here today to pay a tribute of respect and regard to a famous man'.

With Nevil's death, the key reason keeping the rest of the family in Australia had gone. While the relationship between Frances and Nevil may have had its ups and downs, seven months later she wrote how 'we all still feel like a ship without a rudder'. Life on a small, rather isolated farm in rural Victoria no longer seemed so attractive, and although Frances' father had died at the end of the previous year, her mother and three of her brothers and sisters were still alive. In 1962 she finally moved back to England where she bought a detached thatched cottage in the picturesque coastal Suffolk village of Walberswick. Frances visited Australia again for a short period in 1967 but never returned there again to live, remaining in the UK until her death in 1971.

Heather took her responsibility as a trustee of her father's large and still growing literary estate seriously and continued to live in Toorak, a prosperous suburb of Melbourne. By the beginning of 1963, though, love had intervened. She met Donald Mayfield, a technical representative from America who had been seconded to Australia. They were married, and very soon they moved to America, where she still lives today (2017).

Inheriting her father's love for travel and his spirit of adventure, Shirley did not stay in Australia very long. She was soon back in London, but quickly moved on again, and over the following years she lived in many parts of world, including Thailand, Iowa and Toronto. Like her father she had an interest in the religion and culture of the Far East, and she developed what became a lifelong interest in transcendental meditation. She died while on a visit to India in 2009.

At the end of March, the manuscript that Nevil Norway had finished just before he died was published as usual by William Heinemann in Britain and Australia, and William Morrow in America. Nevil Shute's final novel *Trustee from the Toolroom* begins where Nevil Norway had started his life: Somerset Road, Ealing. The principal character, Keith Stewart, is a mechanical engineer who enjoys making models and writing articles about them in his spare time. He works full-time for the magazine *Miniature Mechanic*, writing about the hobby he loves. His wife works in a local draper's shop, and the childless couple, though not rich, are content with their life. Keith's sister is married to John Dermot, a lieutenant commander in the Royal Navy who has recently been made redundant and has taken the decision to move to Canada. In the late 1950s, Britain imposed foreign exchange controls which severely limited the amount of money a person could take out of the country. In order to overcome this problem, Dermot and his wife decide to sail their yacht to Canada, with their wealth, which has been converted into diamonds, hidden in a metal box which is cemented into the keel of the vessel. While they are on this journey they ask the Stewarts to look after their young daughter Janice, who will then fly to join them when they reach Vancouver. Three and a half months later, the Dermots have reached the south pacific when their yacht is caught up in a severe and unexpectedly savage storm. The yacht is driven into a coral reef off the Tuamotus, where it sinks with John Dermot and his wife being drowned. Keith Stewart learns that his sister and brother-in-law are dead and that they are buried on a uninhabited island in a region he has never heard of. Aware that Janice Dermot's financial security lies in the bottom of the wrecked yacht, a man who has never been outside of the country in his life resolves to somehow find his way there and retrieve the diamonds. A familiar Shute theme emerges, with a rather ordinary man being placed in an extraordinary situation.

The novel generally received positive reviews. Some loved Shute's well-known eye for all kinds of detail, noting that 'the descriptive brilliance never falters and the book is crammed with apparatus; one could never say cluttered, because it all works'. Others just loved the positive aspects of human nature that the story promoted, suggesting that 'It's all rather improbable, this tale ... but it does leave behind the afterglow of human warmth and kindness that has become the trade-mark of this author's career'.

Expecting strong sales, Heinemann set a world record for the first edition of a novel, with a print run of 200,000. The book was chosen at the monthly selection by the Book Club and The Book Society in Britain, and the Book of the Month Club in America. It was soon top of *The Sunday Times* list of best-sellers, and spent five months in *The New York Times* Best Sellers list.

In spite of the fact that *Trustee from the Toolroom* was turning out to be another best-seller, there were still those who were baffled by the success of Nevil Shute. Throughout his career, critics had often complained that his characters were flat, style matter of fact and plots far-fetched. Norway himself had always been modest about his ability, frequently saying that he was just an engineer who happened to write novels. In his autobiography, lamenting the death of his brother, he had written 'if Fred had lived we might have had some real books one day, not the sort of stuff I turn out'. Perhaps the real truth of the matter is that Nevil Shute Norway made a far bigger contribution to twentieth century popular literature than he has often been given credit for.

The Published Works of Nevil Shute

i) Principal Published Works

Nevil Shute's principal published work consists of twenty-three novels, a novella, a play and a volume of autobiography. His first two novels, *Stephen Morris* (written in 1923) and *Pilotage* (written in 1924), were rejected by publishers at the time and so he shelved the manuscripts intending to look at them again one day. In the end this was something he never did, and the original manuscripts were found among his papers after his death. Following some editing, the two stories were published in 1961 as a composite volume with the title *Stephen Morris*.

Also among his papers were two versions of a novella *The Seafarers*. The first of these was published as a serial in the short-lived Australian magazine *Home* in 1948. The second, and longer of the two, was edited and published by Paper Tiger in 2002.

The following gives details of the first publication in the United Kingdom and America of the books of Nevil Shute. In five cases the title in each country was different.

Novels

Marazan, Cassell, London, August 1926.

So Disdained, Cassell, London, August 1928; *The Mysterious Aviator*, Houghton Mifflin, Boston, November 1928.

Lonely Road, Cassell, London, February 1932; William Morrow, New York, March 1932.

Ruined City, Cassell, London, July 1938; *Kindling*, William Morrow, New York, May 1938.

The Published Works of Nevil Shute

What Happened to the Corbetts, William Heinemann, London, February 1939; *Ordeal*, William Morrow, New York, March 1939.

An Old Captivity, William Heinemann, London, March 1940; William Morrow, New York, February 1940.

Landfall: A Channel Story, William Heinemann, London, November 1940, William Morrow, New York, September 1940.

Pied Piper, William Heinemann, London, February 1942; William Morrow, New York, January 1942.

Pastoral, William Heinemann, London, September 1944; William Morrow, New York, August 1944.

Most Secret, William Heinemann, London, August 1945; William Morrow, New York, October 1945.

The Chequer Board, William Heinemann, London, May 1947; William Morrow, New York, March 1947.

No Highway, William Heinemann, London, December 1948; William Morrow, New York, August 1948.

A Town Like Alice, William Heinemann, London, June 1950; *The Legacy*, William Morrow, New York, June 1950.

Round the Bend, William Heinemann, London, June 1951; William Morrow, New York, February 1951.

The Far Country, William Heinemann, London, August 1952; William Morrow, New York, September 1952.

In the Wet, William Heinemann, London, May 1953; William Morrow, New York, April 1953.

Requiem for a Wren, William Heinemann, London, April 1955; *The Breaking Wave*, William Morrow, New York, April 1955.

Beyond the Black Stump, William Heinemann, London, April 1956; William Morrow, New York, August 1956.

On the Beach, William Heinemann, London, June 1957; William Morrow, New York, July 1957.

The Rainbow and the Rose, William Heinemann, London, July 1958; William Morrow, New York, October 1958.

Trustee from the Toolroom, William Heinemann, London, March 1960; William Morrow, New York, March 1960.

Stephen Morris, William Heinemann, London, September 1961; William Morrow, New York, September 1961.

The Seafarers, Paper Tiger, Cresskill, May 2002.

Plays
Vinland the Good, William Heinemann, London, October 1946; William Morrow, New York, October 1946.

Non-Fiction
Slide Rule: The Autobiography of an Engineer, William Heinemann, London, June 1954; William Morrow, New York, May 1954.

ii) Additional Published Works
Although not his normal genre, *Blackwood's Magazine* published two short stories by Nevil Shute: 'The Airship Venture' in 1933 and 'Air Circus' in 1937. In addition, Nevil Shute wrote a foreword for two books (*The Secret War; Once is Enough*), and an introductory chapter for a third (*Independent Company*). During his earlier career as an aviation engineer, and under the name of N. S. Norway, he also wrote two technical papers and a chapter for a book on the future of aviation. Details of all of these can be found in Notes on Sources.

Selections from a Photo Timeline

School Play, The Taming of the Shrew, Oxford Preparatory School, Easter 1913. Nevil Norway, front row, centre. This was his last term at the School.

Members of Oldham's House, Shrewsbury School, 1916. Nevil Norway, back row, centre. The housemaster J. Basil Oldham, front row, left.

Balliol College, Oxford University, 1919. This was Norway's first year as an undergraduate.

The R.100 under construction at Howden Airship Station, 1927.

Selections from a Photo Timeline

The R.100 at the Royal Airship Works, Cardington, prior to its flight to Canada, 1930

AIRSPEED
1931 YEARS OF CONTINUOUS PROGRESS 1937

1931 THE 'TERN' — SAILPLANE HOLDER OF THREE RECORDS **1932** THE 'FERRY' AIR LINER – 30 H.P. / PASSENGER **1933** THE 'COURIER' — FIRST BRITISH MACHINE WITH RETRACTABLE UNDERCARRIAGE **1934** THE 'ENVOY' I — TWIN ENGINED TRANSPORT **1935** THE 'ENVOY' II **1936** THE 'ENVOY' III **1937** THE 'OXFORD' — ROYAL AIR FORCE TRAINER

AIRSPEED AIRCRAFT — used for transport throughout the world.

AIRSPEED AIRCRAFT — have a continuous record of reliable service.

AIRSPEED AIRCRAFT — chosen for Royal Air Force training.

AIRSPEED AIRCRAFT — supplied to H.M. Air Council.

AIRSPEED (1934) LIMITED, THE AIRPORT, PORTSMOUTH, ENGLAND.
Tel.: Portsmouth 2444 (3 lines)

1937 advertisement for Airspeed. This highlights the huge advances the company had made since its formation in 1931.

A charcoal sketch of Nevil Norway by Flora Twort, 1938.

Lieutenant Commander Norway RNVR, 12 May 1944.

Selections from a Photo Timeline

Pond Head House, Hayling Island. The Norways' home from 1941 until 1950 (photo taken 2003).

A publicity photo of Nevil Shute, now a full-time author, 1948.

Nevil, Frances and Heather Norway in the grounds of Pond Head House, 1950.

Nevil Norway in front of the Percival Proctor, which he flew to Australia and back.

Selections from a Photo Timeline

Nevil Norway and Jimmie Riddell (right) at a stopover during their flight to Australia, 1948.

Frances, Heather and Nevil studying a map of Australia in the drawing room at Pond Head House, 1950.

Nevil and Frances a year after arriving in Australia, Mount Eliza, Victoria, 1951.

The Norways' family home in Langwarrin, Victoria, Australia nearing Completion, July 1952. The Norways lived here until 1960.

Selections from a Photo Timeline

Nevil, Frances and Heather Norway on a beach somewhere on the Mornington Peninsula, Victoria, in the late 1950s.

Nevil and Frances Norway leaving Los Angeles after meeting Stanley Kramer, 27 May 1958.

13 January 1960, Melbourne – The Age announces the death of one of Australia's most well-known authors.

Image Credits

Cover	Reproduced by kind permission of the Bauer Media Group
p.259, upper	Reproduced by kind permission of the Headmaster, Dragon School, Oxford
p.259, lower	Reproduced by kind permission of Shrewsbury School
p.260, upper	Balliol Archive Photo 34.24A. Reproduced by kind permission of Balliol College, Oxford University
p.260, lower	Ward Philipson Photo Memories. Reproduced by kind permission of John A. Moreels, M.B.E.
p.261, upper	Reproduced by kind permission of the Airship Heritage Trust
p.261, lower	*Flight*, 24 June 1937. Reproduced by kind permission of Aviation Ancestry
p.262, upper	Flora Twort. Reproduced by kind permission of Petersfield Museum
p.262, lower	Reproduced by kind permission of the Imperial War Museum
p.263, upper	Reproduced by kind permission of John Anderson
p.263, lower	Reproduced by kind permission of the Bauer Media Group
p.264, upper	Reproduced by kind permission of the Bauer Media Group
p.264, lower	Reproduced by kind permission of the Bauer Media Group
p.265, upper	Reproduced by kind permission of the Bauer Media Group
p.265, lower	Reproduced by kind permission of the Bauer Media Group
p.266, upper	Reproduced by kind permission of the Bauer Media Group
p.266, lower	Reproduced by kind permission of the Bauer Media Group
p.267, upper	Reproduced by kind permission of Heather Mayfield

p.267, lower   Reproduced by kind permission of University of Southern California Libraries
p.268   Reproduced by kind permission of Fairfax Syndication, Sydney

Notes on Sources

Prologue

Page xii — 'ten pound Pom'. The colloquial name for someone who migrated from England to Australia under the Assisted Passage Scheme after the Second World War.

Chapter 1 – Foundations

Page 3 — 'He was ... her day'. Georgina Shute published 20 novels between 1889 and 1902 under the pseudonym of G. Norway.

Page 3 — 'Remember that ... of life'. Commonly attributed to Cecil Rhodes. Probably a misquotation of a much longer conversation Rhodes had with Lord Grey. Stead, W. T., (Ed), *The Last Will and Testament of Cecil J Rhodes* (London: William Clowes and Sons, 1902) p. 183

Page 4 — 'we are ... not exist'. Remark to Arthur Balfour in 1899 about the Boer War. Carlton, C., *Warriors: A Military History of the British Monarchy* (Oxford: Routledge, 2003) p. 147

Page 4 — 'last of ... gentlemen's wars'. van Hartesveldt, F. R., *The Boer War: Historiography and Annotated Bibliography* (Westport: Greenwood Publishing, 2000) p. 32

Page 5 — 'Like her...in 1916'. Norway, M. L., *The Sinn Féin Rebellion as I Saw It* (London: Smith, Elder and Company, 1916)

Page 5 — 'Fred's arrival ... an honour'. *The Times*, 1 November 1895, p. 1

Page 6 — 'after nearly ... than Fred'. Shute, N., *Slide Rule* (London: William Heinemann, 1954), p. 21

Page 6 — 'of seeing ... Somerset Road'. *Ibid*, p. 6

Page 7 — 'As late ... boarding schools'. McKibben, R., *Classes and Cultures England 1918 – 1951* (Oxford: Oxford University Press, 1998) p. 237

Page 8 — 'Clarendon nine'. Nine Schools studied as part of the Royal Commission on the Public School 1861–64. McKibben, R., *Classes and*

	Cultures England 1918–1951 (Oxford: Oxford University Press, 1998) p. 235
Page 8	'so intolerable … possible course'. Shute, N., *Slide Rule* (London: William Heinemann, 1954), p. 8
Page 8	'Although Nevil … dining table'. Email from Gay Sturt to Richard Thorn, 8 May 2015
Page 9	'Henry Sturt … rural surroundings'. Email from Gay Sturt to Richard Thorn, 15 July 2015
Page 9	'It is … John Betjeman'. Lycett Green, C., *John Betjeman, Letters, Volume 2* (London: Methuen, 1995), p. 204
Page 9	'On 17 August … in Ireland'. *The Times*, 17 August 1912, p. 6
Page 10	'a liberal … imperialist school'. Norway, M. L., Norway, A. H. and Jeffery, K. (Editor), *The Sinn Féin Rebellion as They Saw It* (Dublin: Irish Academic Press, 1999), p. 91
Page 10	'an insult … Post Office'. *Ibid*, p. 16
Page 10	'the gentleman … of administration'. *The Irish Times*, 18 September 1912, p. 9
Page 11	'For two … South Hill'. Shute, N., *Slide Rule* (London: William Heinemann, 1954), p. 14
Page 11	'I am … to enjoy'. *Ibid*
Page 12	'Norway generously … longer afford'. Oldham, J. B., *Reminiscences*, Unpublished manuscript, British Library, X.512/1360
Page 12	'only fit … serious scholarship'. Obituary of Mr J. B. Oldham, *The Times*, 1 December 1962, p. 10
Page 12	'His School … future novelist'. Dr Mike Morrogh, *Nevil Shute and Shrewsbury School*, Lecture to Members of UK Nevil Shute Society, 26 September 2010. Copy available from Nevil Shute Norway Foundation
Page 12	'all of … very bad'. Shute, N., *Slide Rule* (London: William Heinemann, 1954), p. 22
Page 12	'*VB Shrewsbury*'. Members of Form VB at Shrewsbury School, *VB Shrewsbury* (London: Adnitt and Naunton, 1916)
Page 12	'war to … all wars'. Although this phrase is usually associated with President Woodrow Wilson, it was in common use before he used it. H. G. Wells published a book on the reasons entitled *The War That Will End War* in 1914.
Page 13	'news of … loud cheering'. *The Times*, 5 August 1914, p. 3
Page 13	'One man … miles long'. BBC History, Volunteering and Recruitment <http://www.bbc.co.uk/history/worldwars/wwone/soldiers_stories_gallery_01.shtml>
Page 13	'The general … miss it'. Graham, M., *Oxford in the Great War* (Barnsley: Pen and Sword Books, 2014), p. 24

Notes on Sources

Page 13	'a few ... foreign foe'. *The Irish Times*, 5 August 1914, p. 4
Page 14	'all young ... and enlist'. *The Times,* 5 August 1914, p. 3
Page 14	'What are ... your duty?'. *Daily Express,* 5 August 1914, p. 5
Page 14	'over the top'. Term used in WW1 to describe soldiers climbing out of their trenches to advance across no man's land towards the enemy positions.
Page 15	'Lord Kitchener ... his sympathy'. Telegram to A. H. Norway from the War Office, 7 July 1915, National Archives, WO 339/31653
Page 15	'He has ... in Despatches'. Rugby School, *Memorials of Rugbeians who Fell During the Great War Vol. 2* (Rugby: Rugby School, 1917)
Page 15	'I have ... forward his'. *Ibid*
Page 16	'About to ... Light Infantry'. Email from Dr Mike Morrogh, Shrewsbury School to Richard Thorn, 28 May 2014.
Page 16	'the most ... in Dublin'. The History of the Hibernian Hotel <http://arrow.dit.ie/cgi/viewcontent.cgi?article=1003&context=hibhot>
Page 17	'behaved in ... most impartially'. Norway, M. L., Norway, A. H. and Jeffery, K. (Editor), *The Sinn Féin Rebellion as They Saw It* (Dublin: Irish Academic Press, 1999), p. 17
Page 17	'Arthur had ... that year'. Norway, A. H., *Naples Past and Present* (New York: Frederick A. Stokes, 1901)
Page 18	'For this ... of Jerusalem'. *The Irish Times,* 15 June 1916, p. 8
Page 18	'which we ... the world' . Norway, M. L., Norway, A. H. and Jeffery, K. (Editor), *The Sinn Féin Rebellion as They Saw It* (Dublin: Irish Academic Press, 1999), p. 41
Page 18	'the impression ... in Ireland'. *The Irish Times,* 22 January 1917, p. 4
Page 19	'I was ... my parents'. Shute, N., *Slide Rule* (London: William Heinemann, 1954), p. 25
Page 19	'I was ... two years'. *Ibid*
Page 19	'In May ... in Dublin'. Woods, J. L., (1916) 'Easter week in Dublin', *The Salopian*, Vol. 25, No. 12 , 20 May 1916
Page 19	'for the .... difficult circumstances'. Norway, M. L., Norway, A. H. and Jeffery, K. (Editor), *The Sinn Féin Rebellion as They Saw It* (Dublin: Irish Academic Press, 1999), p. 89
Page 19	'N. S. Norway ... Cert. A.' Dr Mike Morrogh, *Nevil Shute and Shrewsbury School,* Lecture to Members of UK Nevil Shute Society, 26 September 2010. Copy available from Nevil Shute Foundation
Page 20	'By the ... or missing'. Written answer to the House of Commons by the prime minister, 23 December 1915 See <http://hansard.millbanksystems.com/written_answers/1915/dec/23/figures-announced-by-prime-minister>
Page 21	'On the ... Honourable Order'. Information provided by the Central Chancery of the Orders of Knighthood, St James's Palace, London

Page 22	'a new ... before me'. Shute, N., *Slide Rule* (London: William Heinemann, 1954), p. 33

Chapter 2 – University

Page 24	'For instance ... to university'. Analysis of information from Dawson, H. N., *Shrewsbury School Register Vol II* (Shrewsbury: Wilding and Son, 1964)
Page 24	'Whatever the ... for entry'. See Anderson, J., *Parallel Motion* (Kerhonkson: Paper Tiger Inc, 2011) pp. 26–30 for a detailed record of Norway's application and admission to Balliol College
Page 24	'his fearful stammer'. *Ibid*, p. 27
Page 24	'However following ... military service'. Shute, N., *Slide Rule* (London: William Heinemann, 1954), p. 33
Page 25	'ordinary' and 'humdrum', having 'excelled at nothing'. *Ibid* p. 35
Page 25	'Certainly the ... notable alumni'. See <http://archives.balliol.ox.ac.uk/Past%20members/remalum.asp>
Page 26	'discharged his ... and fidelity'. 145355/20, Application for Superannuation from Arthur H. Norway, General Post Office, 11 July 1920
Page 26	'formalities of ... happily absent'. St Martin's Letter Bag, *St Martin's Le Grand Magazine*, 1921, pp. 101-103
Page 27	'This wood ... and these'. Shute, N., *Slide Rule* (London: William Heinemann, 1954), p. 47
Page 28	'He was ... which graduated'. Howatson, A. M., *Mechanicks in the Universitie: A History of Engineering Science at Oxford* (Oxford: University of Oxford, 2008), p. 69
Page 28	'with a ... for Balliol'. Shute, N., *Slide Rule* (London: William Heinemann, 1954), p. 35

Chapter 3 – Aeroplanes

Page 31	'rarely can ... to come'. *The Times*, 1 January 1923, p. 17
Page 31	'Retrieve the ... their predecessors'. *Daily Mirror*, 1 January 1923, p. 7
Page 31	'The Year of Convalescence'. *Ibid*, p. 7
Page 32	'By 1918 ... a month'. Edgerton, D., *England and the Aeroplane: Militarism, Modernity and Machines*, 2nd Ed. (London: Penguin, 2013), p. 22
Page 32	'Although now ... the war'. Fearon, P., (1974) 'The British airframe industry and the state 1918–1935', *Economic History Review*, 27 (2), pp. 236–251
Page 32	'As a ... were there'. Anon, (1923), 'Editorial', *Flight*, 15 (7), p. 88
Page 33	'Given all ... in business'. Brancker, W. S., (1923) 'The position of air transport today', *Flight*, 15 (7), pp. 91 – 94

Notes on Sources

Page 33	'The proposed ... Atlantic liner'. Anon (1923) 'The proposed airship line between Spain and South America', *Flight*, 15 (21), pp. 276 – 278
Page 34	'In winter ... people warm'. Sharp, C. M., *D.H. A History of de Havilland*, 2nd Ed. (Shrewsbury: Airlife, 1982), p. 72
Page 34	'In 1922 ... road transport'. Brancker, W. S., (1923) 'The position of air transport today', *Flight*, 15 (7), p. 92
Page 34	'shakeout'. Edgerton, D., *England and the Aeroplane: Militarism, Modernity and Machines, 2nd Ed.* (London: Penguin, 2013), p. 37
Page 34	'At the ... of £98,580'. Sharp, C. M., *D.H. A History of de Havilland*, 2nd Ed. (Shrewsbury: Airlife, 1982), p. 85
Page 35	'just plain ballast'. Shute, N., *Slide Rule* (London: William Heinemann, 1954), p. 52
Page 36	'Advertised fees ... once qualified'. Anon, (1923) 'Training R.A.F. reserve pilots', *Flight*, 15 (29), pp. 416 – 417
Page 36	'The Bookshop ... Flora Twort'. Munro-Faure, A., *Flora Twort: A Petersfield Artist*, (Hampshire: Hampshire County Council, 1995), p. 4
Page 37	'Sometime late ... Square, Petersfield'. Shute, N., (1923) *No. 1, The Square, Petersfield*, Unpublished Story, MS 2199, Papers of Nevil Shute Norway, National Library of Australia, Canberra
Page 38	'in giving ... the book'. Letter from N. S. Norway to the Incorporated Society of Authors, Playwrights and Composers, 27 April 1923. Additional Manuscripts MS 56763, Archives and Manuscripts, British Library
Page 38	'our reader ... and discussion'. Letter from Ronald Boswell, Bodley Head Ltd to N. S. Norway, 12 July 1923. Additional Manuscripts MS 56763, Archives and Manuscripts, British Library
Page 38	'In a ... second novel'. Letter from N. S. Norway to Methuen Ltd, 3 September 1923. Additional Manuscripts MS 56763, Archives and Manuscripts, British Library
Page 38	'a very poor book'. Shute, N., *Slide Rule* (London: William Heinemann, 1954), p. 53
Page 38	'four men ... between them'. Cobham, A. J., edited by Derrick, C., *A Time to Fly* (London: Shepheard-Walwyn, 1978), p. 48
Page 39	'it hardly ... strong plot.' Letter from H. Aubrey Gentry, Cassell and Co. Ltd to N. S. Norway, 1 July 1924. Additional Manuscripts MS 56763, Archives and Manuscripts, British Library
Page 39	'He became ... November 1924'. Norway, N. S., (1924) 'The case for the revival of the water channel', *Journal of the Royal Aeronautical Society*, Vol. 28, pp. 647–652
Page 40	'with some regret'. Shute, N., *Slide Rule* (London: William Heinemann, 1954), p. 54
Page 40	'I knew ... that time'. *Ibid*, p. 53

Chapter 4 – Airships

Page 42	'perhaps the ... ever designed'. Morpurgo, J. E., *Barnes Wallis* (London: Ian Allan, 1981), p. 92
Page 43	'What became ... and Australia'. *The Times,* 31 March 1922, p. 14
Page 44	'The initial ... airships themselves'. House of Lords debate on Airship Policy, 21 May 1924. See <http://hansard.millbanksystems.com/lords/1924/may/21/airship-policy>
Page 44	'Airships are ... it were'. Stopes-Roe, M., *Mathematics With Love* (Basingstoke: Macmillan, 2005), p. 140
Page 44	'to Service ... naval reconnaissance'. House of Lords debate on Airship Policy, 21st May 1924 See <http://hansard.millbanksystems.com/lords/1924/may/21/airship-policy>
Page 44	'Finally, on ... the R.100'. National Archives, London, AIR 2/262, Contract with Airship Guarantee Company for construction of a rigid airship
Page 45	'Given that ... Socialist Ship'. Anderson, J., *Airship on a Shoestring* (London: New Generation Publishing, 2014), p. 21
Page 45	'Our Wonderful ... the Future'. *Daily Express,* 19 November 1924, p. 1
Page 45	'Great Britain ... airship service'. *Ibid*
Page 45	'The Labour ... paragraph statement'. *The Daily Mirror,* 7 November 1924, p. 14
Page 45	'it was ... melting pot'. Swinfield, J., *Airship,* (London: Conway, 2012) p. 129
Page 46	'I designed ... ship myself'. Morpurgo, J. E., *Barnes Wallis* (London: Ian Allan, 1981), p. 149
Page 46	'I like ... for him'. Stopes-Roe, M., *Mathematics With Love* (Basingstoke: Macmillan, 2005), p. 158
Page 47	'In the ... and overworked'. Shute, N., *Slide Rule* (London: William Heinemann, 1954), p. 58
Page 47	'In the ... original features'. Morpurgo, J. E., *Barnes Wallis* (London: Ian Allan, 1981), p. 116
Page 48	'a derelict ... of Crayford'. Shute, N., *Slide Rule* (London: William Heinemann, 1954), p. 60
Page 49	'the new ... untested assumptions'. National Archives, London, CAB 24/175/9, Cabinet Memorandum: Airship Policy
Page 49	'I have ... be entertained'. *Ibid*
Page 49	'the *Shenandoah* ... present strength'. *The Sydney Morning Herald,* 7 September 1925, p. 9
Page 49	'I never ... to that'. *The East Hampshire Post,* 26 February 1981, p. 27
Page 50	'I want ... of that'. Letter from Nevil Norway to Flora Twort, 28 September 1925, Petersfield Museum Collection

Notes on Sources

Page 50 — 'I shall be ... say no'. *Ibid*

Page 50 — 'For two ... that way?'. Letter from Nevil Norway to Flora Twort, 30 September 1925, Petersfield Museum Collection

Page 52 — 'Perhaps this ... marry him'. Letter from Nevil Norway to Flora Twort, Undated – Circa 1926, Petersfield Museum Collection

Page 53 — 'the preponderant ... social engagement'. McKibben, R., *Classes and Cultures England 1918–1951* (Oxford: Oxford University Press, 1998) p. 516

Page 53 — 'Looking at ... and espionage'. *The Sunday Times,* 21 June 1925, p. 10

Page 53 — 'Norway had ... publish *Marazan*'. Letter from E. Aubrey Gentry, Cassell and Company to N. S. Norway, 23 February 1926. Additional Manuscripts MS 56763, British Library

Page 53 — 'anything and ... literary diet'. Shute, N., (c. 1949/50) 'My Week', Unpublished text of a speech, Nevil Shute Papers – Additions, Syracuse University Libraries, New York

Page 53 — 'The only ... adventure stories'. Shute, N., *Slide Rule* (London: William Heinemann, 1954), p. 110

Page 54 — 'Maybe overdoing ... every clause'. Letter from N.S. Norway to Cassell and Company, 11 March 1926. Additional Manuscripts MS 56763, British Library

Page 54 — 'Since then ... loyal friend'. Shute, N., *Slide Rule* (London: William Heinemann, 1954), p. 65

Page 54 — 'It had own ... anything published'... 'As for ... unvarnished truth'. *The Draconian,* January 1927, p. 6471

Page 55 — 'This first ... a story'. *The Aberdeen Press and Journal,* 7 September 1926, p. 2

Page 56 — 'The design ... Deacon'. Anderson, J., *Airship on a Shoestring* (London: New Generation Publishing, 2014), pp. 48–88; Deacon, K., *The Men and Women Who Built and Flew the R.100* (Howden: Langrick Publications, 2008) pp. 9–20

Page 56 — 'Saturday: Mr ... to Sherburn'. Anon, (1927) 'Light plane clubs', *Flight,* 19 (17), p. 261

Page 56 — 'The less ... taxiing in'. Anon, (1927) 'Light plane clubs', *Flight,* 19 (26), p. 446

Page 57 — 'By the ... achieve this'. Letter from Nevil Norway to Flora Twort, 17 June 1927, Petersfield Museum Collection

Page 58 — 'why the ... that space' ... 'though the ... at all'. *The Saturday Review of Literature,* 13 September 1928, p. 649

Page 58 — 'Although only ... aspiring novelist'. *The Times Literary Supplement,* 8 December 1928, p. 491

Page **58** — 'so far ... without examination'. National Archives, London, AIR 5/982,

	R.100: Arrangements for Flight to Canada, Air Ministry Minute, 25 May 1928
Page 58	'the greatest ... years afterwards'. Shute, N., *Slide Rule* (London: William Heinemann, 1954), p. 84
Page 58	'had the ... commercial sense'. *Ibid*, p. 84
Page 59	'I have ... this character'. Morpurgo, J. E., *Barnes Wallis* (London: Ian Allan, 1981), p. 150
Page 59	'Mrs Burney ... my children'. Swinfield, J., *Airship*, (London: Conway, 2012) p. 149
Page 59	'all to keep Burney out'. *Ibid* p. 151
Page 60	'He was ... Aeronautical Society'. *The Yorkshire Post*, 26 February 1929, p. 28
Page 60	'During 1929 ... the Future'. Burney, C. D., *The World, the Air and the Future* (London: Alfred A Knopf, 1929)
Page 61	'*The Times* ... the event'. *The Times*, 15 October 1929, p. 20
Page 61	'*The Times* ... the event' Anon, (1929) 'Launch of R. 101', *Flight*, 21 (42), pp. 1110–1112
Page 61	'A week ... had flown'. Anon, (1929) 'R. 101', *Flight*, 21 (41), pp. 1088–1095
Page 61	'Fortunately all ... was complete'. National Archives, London, AIR 5/971, R.100: Progress reports from the Airship Guarantee Company, January to November 1929

Chapter 5 – Success and Failure

Page **64**	'As early ... the day'. *The Western Morning News and Mercury*, 26 November 1929, p. 7
Page 64	'As early ... the day'. *The Courier and Advertiser*, 2 December 1929, p. 6
Page 64	'at 6 o'clock ... of vantage'. *The Hull Daily Mail*, 16 December 1929, p. 5
Page 65	'In addition ... and Norway'. Anderson, J., *Airship on a Shoestring* (London: New Generation Publishing, 2014), p. 210
Page 65	'It was ... our mistakes'. Shute, N., *Slide Rule* (London: William Heinemann, 1954), p. 84
Page 66	'To us ... old-time envy'. *The Hull Daily Mail*, 16 December 1929, p. 4
Page 67	'*The Times* ... Dennistoun Burney'. *The Times*, 17 December 1929, p. 14
Page 67	'*The Times* ... Dennistoun Burney'. *The Daily Mirror*, 17 December 1929, p. 20
Page 67	'The following ... London area'. Anon, (1929) 'H.M. Airship R.100', *Flight*, 21 (51), p. 1323
Page 67	'He later ... his life'. Shute, N., *Slide Rule* (London: William Heinemann, 1954), p. 95

Notes on Sources

Page 68	'Therefore on ... an end'. Morpurgo, J. E., *Barnes Wallis* (London: Ian Allan, 1981), p. 174
Page 68	'In fact ... these flights'. Anderson, J., *Airship on a Shoestring* (London: New Generation Publishing, 2014), p. 207
Page 69	'It was ... advice given'. National Archives, London, AIR 5/982, R.100: Arrangements for Flight to Canada, Notes of Meeting with D.A.D., 28 July 1930
Page 69	'In addition ... of 100'. Anderson, J., *Airship on a Shoestring* (London: New Generation Publishing, 2014), pp. 213 and 216
Page 69	'Wallis could ... airship contraption'. Morpurgo, J. E., *Barnes Wallis* (London: Ian Allan, 1981), p. 177
Page 69	'It seemed ... of death'. National Archives, London, AIR 5/982, R.100: Arrangements for Flight to Canada, Form of Indemnity, Flight of R.100
Page 69	'Sir Dennis ... Air Ministry'. *Ibid*, Notes of meeting with Secretary of State for Air, 23 May 1930
Page 69	'Reports suggested ... in England'. *Ibid*, Loose Minute, 21 July 1930
Page 69	'Other though ... their research'. Horry, R., (2010) 'Botany of the air', *Viewpoint*, No. 92, pp. 8–9
Page 70	'Norway kept ... Aeronautical Society'. Norway, N.S., (1931) 'R.100 Canadian flight, 1930', *Journal of the Royal Aeronautical Society*, Vol. 35, Issue 245, pp. 401–414
Page 70	'almost staggering'. *Ibid*, p. 404
Page 70	'sleep all ... normal breakfast'. *Ibid*, p. 404
Page 70	'Burney also ... the flight'. Burney, C. D., (1930) 'Empire air communications', *United Empire*, Vol. 21, pp. 135–142
Page 70	'shot off ... frame 2'. Norway, N.S., (1931) 'R.100 Canadian flight, 1930', *Journal of the Royal Aeronautical Society*, Vol. 35, Issue 245, p. 408
Page 70	'large enough ... bus through'. *Ibid*, p. 407
Page 70	'as the ... the world'. *The Times*, 1 August 1930, p. 14
Page 71	'It is ... in Montreal'. Countryman, B., *R100 in Canada*, (Ontario: Boston Mills Press, 1982), p. 69
Page 71	'I would ... for good'. Norway, N. S., (1931) 'R.100 Canadian flight, 1930', *Journal of the Royal Aeronautical Society*, Vol. 35, Issue 245, p. 411
Page 72	'tea was ... without tea'. *The Times*, 18 August 1930, p. 12
Page 72	'Found a ... of it'. Swinfield, J., *Airship*, (London: Conway, 2012) p. 271
Page 72	'got away with it'. Shute, N., *Slide Rule* (London: William Heinemann, 1954), p. 110
Page 73	'On the ... Bromley, Kent'. *The Times*, 13 September 1930, p. 1
Page 73	'Five years ... children themselves'. Letter from Nevil Norway to Flora Twort, 28 September 1925, Petersfield Museum Collection

Page 73	'It seems … of September' Shute, N., *Slide Rule* (London: William Heinemann, 1954), pp. 138–139
Page 74	'essentially an … first time'. *The Times,* 4 October 1930, p. 10
Page 74	'The bureaucracy … had crashed'. National Archives, London, AIR 2/444, Issue of Permit to Fly for H.M. Airship R. 101, Air Ministry Note, 13 October 1930
Page 74	'The written … never completed'. Simon, J., *Report of the R.101 Inquiry* (London: H.M.S.O, 1931), pp. 56–57
Page 75	'seemed strangely … cast off'. *The Daily Express,* 6 October 1930, p. 2
Page 75	'After an … watch-keeping routine'. Simon, J., *Report of the R.101 Inquiry* (London: H.M.S.O, 1931), p. 73
Page 76	'Finally, on … Euston Station'. *The Times,* 11 October 1930, p. 12
Page 77	'Nobody from … the Inquiry'. Shute, N., *Slide Rule* (London: William Heinemann, 1954), p. 144
Page 77	'One of … to India'. National Archives, London, AIR 2/444, Issue of Permit to Fly for H.M. Airship R. 101, Air Ministry Minute, 2 October 1930
Page 77	'In later … the Certificate' Orange, V., *Dowding of Fighter Command* (London: Grub Street Publishing, 2008), p. 62
Page 77	'It is … she could'. Simon, J., *Report of the R.101 Inquiry* (London: H.M.S.O, 1931), p. 95
Page 78	'At a … Cardington closed'. National Archives, London, CAB 23/68, Cabinet Papers 31 August 1931
Page 78	'An airship … in 2016'. *Lincolnshire Echo,* 4 December 1931, p. 1
Page 78	'the airship venture'. Shute, N., (1933) 'The Airship Venture', *Blackwood's Magazine*, 233 (1411), pp. 599–627
Page 78	'it is … to go'. *The Times,* 19 November 1931, p. 13
Page 78	'the decision … rather doubt'. Shute, N., *Slide Rule* (London: William Heinemann, 1954), p. 149

Chapter 6 – Entrepreneur

Page 79	'For instance … 45.5 per cent respectively'. Garside, W. R., *British Unemployment 1919–1939* (Cambridge: Cambridge University Press, 1990), p. 13
Page 80	'In comparison … the country'. *Ibid,* p. 10
Page 80	'The Prime … difficulties'. *The Times,* 1 January 1931, p. 14
Page 80	'the one … of difficulties'. *Ibid,* p. 13
Page 80	'deal immediately … with unemployment'. 1929 Labour Party General Election Manifesto See <http://www.labour-party.org.uk/manifestos/1929/1929-labour-manifesto.shtml>
Page 80	'By January … were growing'. National Archives, London, CAB 23/66, Cabinet Papers and Minutes for 21 Jan 1931

Notes on Sources

Page 81   'Despite the ... the Company'. National Archives, London, AVIA 2/636, Memorandum from Sir Eric Geddes, Chairman, Imperial Airways to H. M. Government

Page 81   'At the ... to 20,000'. Anon, (1930) 'The British aircraft industry', *Flight*, 22 (47), pp. 1265–1369

Page 81   'no major ... the 1950s'. Edgerton, D., *England and the Aeroplane: Militarism, Modernity and Machines*, 2nd Ed. (London: Penguin, 2013), pp. 37–38

Page 82   'we have ... anything else'. *The Times*, 1 January 1931, p. 18

Page 82   'had become ... those days'. Shute, N., *Slide Rule* (London: William Heinemann, 1954), p. 150

Page 83   'as the ... his time'. Clabby, J. F., *Brigadier John Tiltman: A Giant Among Cryptanalysts* (Fort George G. Meade: National Security Agency, 2007), p. 4

Page 83   'both beautiful and efficient'. Shute, N., *Slide Rule* (London: William Heinemann, 1954), p. 151

Page 84   'Therefore on ... were proposing'. Letter from A. Hessell Tiltman to Sir Alan Cobham, 22 October 1930, File X006-0170/001/024001, RAF Museum, Colindale

Page 84   'Finally on ... his services'. Letter from Nevil Norway to Sir Alan Cobham, 7 December 1930, File X006-0170/001/037/001, RAF Museum, Colindale

Page 85   'While Norway ... potential backers'. Note on the Company's Proposed Building Programme. A. H. Tiltman, 1930, File X006-0170/001/024001, RAF Museum, Colindale

Page 85   'During the ... extreme happiness'. *The Times*, 16 February 1931, p. 9

Page 86   'The newly ... Tern glider'. Middleton, D. H., *Airspeed: The Company and its Aeroplanes* (Lavenham: Terence Dalton Ltd, 1982), p. 9

Page 86   'Finally on ... raise finance'. *The Financial Times*, 13 March 1931, p. 5

Page 87   'Norway was ... and courage'. Tiltman, H., (1966) 'Looking Backwards', *Journal of the Royal Aeronautical Society*, Vol. 70 (No. 661), pp. 143–145

Page 87   'The local ... the neighbourhood'. *The Yorkshire Post*, 24 March 1931, p. 10

Page 87   'I am ... on Tuesday'. Letter from Nevil Norway to Sir Alan Cobham, 22 April 1931, File X006-0170/001/037/001, RAF Museum, Colindale

Page 88   'as having ... petrol tank'. Anon, (1932) 'The Airspeed Ferry', *Flight*, 24 (16), pp. 317–320

Page 88   'Typical of ... 38 minutes'. *The Hull Daily Mail*, 25 August 1931, p. 8

Page 89   'a dead loss'. Shute, N., *Slide Rule* (London: William Heinemann, 1954), p. 170

Page 90   'With the ... by itself'. *The Aberdeen Press and Journal*, 4 February 1932, p. 2

Page 90	'Mr. Shute writes ... discerning hand'. *The New York Times Book Review*, 20 March 1932, p. 23
Page 91	'The AS. 4 Ferry ... single fatality'. Taylor, H. A., *Airspeed Aircraft Since 1931* (London: Putman and Company Ltd, 1970), p. 35
Page 91	'Cobham estimated ... joy rides'. Cobham, A., (1966) 'Blazing the Trail', *Journal of the Royal Aeronautical Society*, Vol. 70 (No. 661), pp. 268–269
Page 92	'were more interested in selling than in building'. Tiltman, H., (1966) 'Looking Backwards', *Journal of the Royal Aeronautical Society*, Vol. 70 (No. 661), pp. 143–145
Page 92	'Less than ... of 71'. *The Times*, 14 June 1932, p. 1
Page 92	'In many ... and Nevil'. Norway, M. L., *The Sinn Féin Rebellion as I Saw It* (London: Smith, Elder and Company Ltd, 1916)
Page 93	'An exception ... May 1933'. Shute, N., (1933) 'The Airship Venture', *Blackwood's Magazine*, 233 (1411), pp. 599–627
Page 94	'The Directors ... voluntary liquidation' *The Financial Times*, 24 July 1934, p. 12
Page 95	'reckless and ... to dishonesty'. Shute, N., *Slide Rule* (London: William Heinemann, 1954), p. 202
Page 95	'After the ... wrong reasons'. *The Financial Times*, 5 September 1934, p. 5
Page 95	'On 22 September ... finally began'. Cobham, A. J., edited by Derrick, C., *A Time to Fly* (London: Shepheard-Walwyn, 1978), pp. 175–176
Page 96	'Although not ... its lifetime'. Anon, (1934) 'Aeronautical Engineering Training', *Flight*, 26 (1345), pp. 1036–1037
Page 96	'the greatest ... of aviation'. *The Daily Mirror*, 20 October 1934, p. 1
Page 97	'Sitting observing ... budding novelist'. *The Times*, 11 December 1935, p. 4
Page 97	'Radio Drama ... of Silence'. *The Daily Mirror*, 5 December 1934, p. 1
Page 98	'Since 1935 ... manufacturer's activity'. National Archives, London, CAB 24/255, Memorandum on the German Air Programme, 13 May 1935
Page 98	'try to ... husband should'. Shute, N., *Slide Rule* (London: William Heinemann, 1954), p. 240
Page 99	'In October ... *Air Circus*'. Shute, N., (1937) 'Air Circus', *Blackwood's Magazine*, 242 (1464), pp. 433–472
Page 99	'I am ... happy relationship.' Middleton, D. H., *Airspeed: The Company and its Aeroplanes* (Lavenham: Terence Dalton Ltd, 1982), pp. 106–107
Page 99	'the first shock to my pride'. Shute, N., *Slide Rule* (London: William Heinemann, 1954), p. 246
Page 100	'In November ... first time'. *The Times*, 24 November 1938, p. 23

Notes on Sources

Chapter 7 – Peace and War

Page 104	'MGM listed ... to start'. *The Observer*, 4 February 1940, p. 12
Page 104	'a fixed and invariable rule'. 'My Week', Unpublished article, circa 1950. Additions, Nevil Shute Papers, Syracuse University, New York
Page 105	'it was ... brought out'. *The New York Times Book Review*, 9 March 1938, p. 19
Page 105	'that coming ... any good'. *The New York Times Book Review*, 17 April 1938, p. 19
Page 105	'who look ... Nevil Shute' ... 'if he ... distinguished hear after'. *The Observer*, 17 July 1938, p. 6
Page 106	'peace with honour'. *The Times*, 1 October 1938, p. 12 and p. 14
Page 106	'However by ... the Luftwaffe'. National Archives, London, CAB 24/255, Memorandum on the German Air Programme, 13 May 1935
Page 106	'he considered ... some thought'. Anon, (1939) 'Airspeed's Annual', *Flight*, Vol. 35, No. 1575, p. 231
Page 106	'subjects which ... to approach'. Letter from N.S. Norway to David Martin, 11 January 1960. Additions, Nevil Shute Papers, Syracuse University, New York
Page 107	'His departure ... the service'. *The Times*, 3 January 1939, p. 12
Page 108	'A year ... Great Britain'. National Archives, London, CAB 24/269, Air Raid Precautions – Householders' Handbook, 31 March 1937
Page 108	'if I ... face together'. Shute, N., *What Happened to the Corbetts* (London: William Heinemann, 1939), p. 235
Page 109	'an astonishing ... best-seller *Kindling*'. *The New York Times Book Review*, 26 March 1939, p. 93
Page 109	'A large ... to happen'. *The Saturday Review of Literature*, 26 March 1939
Page 109	'He later ... or breathe'. Shute, N., *Slide Rule* (London: William Heinemann, 1954), p. 2
Page 110	'With typical ... to submarines'. National Archives, London, AVIA 8/422, Scheme for New Type of Aero Engine: Proposals by Sir Dennis Burney, 1936–1941
Page 110	'Not a ... have appeal'. National Archives, London, ADM 179/137, Combined Naval and Air Staff Requirements for Gliding Torpedoes, 1939–1940
Page 111	'Having just ... off war'. Shute, N., (1940) 'The Young Captives', *Wings: The Literary Guild Magazine*, March 1940, pp. 5–8
Page 111	'At 4.15 pm ... from Poland'. National Archives, London, CAB 23/100, Cabinet Papers and Minutes for 2 September 1939
Page 111	'that this ... with Germany'. The transcript of Neville Chamberlain's declaration of war can be found at http://www.bbc.co.uk/archive/ww2outbreak/7957.shtml?page=txt

Page 112	'In his ... a week'. National Archives, London, CAB 68/1/4, Home Security Report No. 1, 12 September 1939
Page 113	'the great ... together well' ... 'its parts ... and unusual'. *The Saturday Review of Literature,* 2 March 1940, p. 11
Page 114	'the characters ... highly effective'. *The Sunday Times,* 7 April 1940, p. 7
Page 114	'While the ... less successful'. *The Observer,* 17 March 1940, p. 6
Page 114	'Norway, who ... Dennis Burney'. National Archives, London, ADM 179/137, Combined Naval and Air Staff Requirements for Gliding Torpedoes, 1939–1940
Page 115	'The unpublished ... this work'. MS 2199, Papers of Nevil Shute Norway, National Library of Australia, Canberra
Page 115	'an elderly yachtsman'. Shute, N., *Slide Rule* (London: William Heinemann, 1954), p. 3
Page 117	'extraordinarily interesting ... delightfully told'. *The Sunday Times,* 8 December 1940, p. 5
Page 117	'The present ... the future' ... 'a good ... genuinely moving'. *New Statesman and Nation,* 7 December 1940, p. 574
Page 119	'Unfortunately, the ... *Dads Army*'. *Dads Army* Series 5 Episode 12 'Round and Round Went the Great Big Wheel', First broadcast 22 December 1972, BBC1
Page 119	'The history ... *Parallel Motion*'. Pawle, G., *The Wheezers & Dodgers* (Barnsley: Seaforth Publishing, 2009). A reprint of *The Secret War* originally published by George Harrap and Co. Ltd., 1956
Page 120	'The history ... *Parallel Motion*'. Anderson, J., *Parallel Motion* (Kerhonkson: Paper Tiger Inc, 2011) Chapter 7 for a detailed record of Norway's work with IAAWD and DMWD.
Page 120	'for goodness ... age group'. *The East Hampshire Post,* 26 February 1981, p. 27
Page 120	'Commander Charles ... former secretary'. Smith, J., *Nevil Shute,* (Cresskill: Paper Tiger Inc, 2002) p. 47
Page 120	'Goodeve in ... the DMWD'. Pawle, G., *The Secret War* (London: George G. Harrap & Co. Ltd., 1956) p. 119.
Page 121	'Pied Piper ... are sure fire'. *Time,* 12 January 1942, p. 76
Page 121	'a most ... probable setting' ... 'It is ... certainly please'. *The Saturday Review of Literature,* 10 January 1942, p. 9
Page 122	'This process ... a Norway'. *The Sunday Feature* 'Set Square', First broadcast 9 February 1997, BBC Radio 3
Page 122	'has been ... his duties'. National Archives, London, ADM 340/367, RNVR Officer Service Records, William North – Edward O'Connor
Page 122	'Although most ... never published'. Ministry of Information, Series 1,

	MS2199, Papers of Nevil Shute Norway, National Library of Australia, Canberra
Page 123	'The result ... Normandy Landings'. Ministry of Information, Series 1, MS 2199, Papers of Nevil Shute Norway, National Library of Australia, Canberra
Page 123	'He also ... Australia, Canberra'. Ministry of Information, Series 1, MS 2199, Papers of Nevil Shute Norway, National Library of Australia, Canberra
Page 123	'at a period of ... that it wasn't'. Letter from N.S. Norway to David Martin, 11 January 1960. Additions, Nevil Shute Papers, Syracuse University, New York
Page 123	'rather a trivial little book' ... 'written in a hurry'. Smith, J., *Nevil Shute*, (Cresskill: Paper Tiger Inc, 2002) p. 58
Page 123	'as live ... given us'. *The Times Literary Supplement*, 23 September 1944, p. 461
Page 123	'a good ... Novel writing' ... 'six months ... bomber base'. *The New York Times*, 25 August 1944, p. 11
Page 124	'relief to ... love story'. *Daily Herald*, 27 September 1940, p. 2
Page 124	'very, very wrong'. Shute, N., Foreword in Pawle, G., *The Secret War* (London: George G. Harrap & Co. Ltd., 1956) p. 119.

Chapter 8 – Home and Abroad

Page 125	'today we ... In Europe' ... 'until that ... normal habits'. *The Times*, 1 January 1945, p. 8
Page 127	'the people ... Far East'. National Archives, London, CAB 66/58/20, Morale and Welfare in the Far East, 20 November 1944
Page 127	'At the ... for 1945'. *Motion Picture Daily*, 11 December 1944, p. 10
Page 128	'This time ... should start'. *The Times*, 5 April 1945, p. 8
Page 128	'fearsome temper' ... 'was quite frequently enraged'. Nevil Shute Norway Foundation <http://www.nevilshute.org/Reminisces/ShirleyNorway1.php>
Page 128	'was not ... Calcutta gossip'. Letter from N. S. Norway to G. Grafton Greene, 30 April 1945. MS 2199, Papers of Nevil Shute Norway, National Library of Australia, Canberra
Page 129	'stories of ... of detail'. Telegram from G . Grafton Greene to N. S. Norway, 26 May 1945. MS 2199, Papers of Nevil Shute Norway, National Library of Australia, Canberra
Page 129	'must face ... out here'. Letter from N.S. Norway to G. Grafton Greene, 30 May 1945. MS 2199, Papers of Nevil Shute Norway, National Library of Australia, Canberra
Page 129	'a fine ... of Rangoon'. *Ibid*

Page 129	'In the ... in London'. Letter from N. S. Norway to G. Grafton Greene, 24 June 1945. MS 2199, Papers of Nevil Shute Norway, National Library of Australia, Canberra
Page 130	'Socialist government ... the country' ... 'would have ... of Gestapo'. Hennessy, P., *Never Again*, (London: Jonathan Cape, 1992) p. 82
Page 130	'First atomic ... hits Japan'. *The Times*, 7 August 1945, p. 4
Page 131	'technical genius'. *Ibid*
Page 131	'His day ... 7.30pm'. 'My Week', Unpublished article, circa 1950. Additions, Nevil Shute Papers, Syracuse University, New York
Page 131	'a quite ... unloving father' ... 'gave her ... and wrong'. *The Sunday Feature* 'Set Square', First broadcast 9 February 1997, BBC Radio 3
Page 132	'to perpetuate ... the war'. Letter from N. S. Norway to David Martin, 11 January 1960. Additions, Nevil Shute Papers, Syracuse University, New York
Page 132	'best formed books'. *Ibid*
Page 132	'partly laboured and fragmentary'. ... 'Mr Shute ... of tones'. *The Times Literary Supplement*, 18 August 1945, p. 389
Page 133	'Mr. Shute ... his talent'. *Evening Standard*, 17 August 1945, p. 6
Page 133	'as a ... gruesomely effective'. *The New York Times*, 26 October 1945, p. 17
Page 133	'Having completed ... in 1948'. Shute, N., (1948) 'The Seafarers', *Home*, 4 December 1948, 18 December 1948 and 1 January 1949
Page 133	'Just over ... finally published'. Shute, N., *The Seafarers*, (Cresskill: Paper Tiger Inc, 2002)
Page 134	'Norway had ... metal fatigue'. Pugsley, A., (1966) 'Airships', *Journal of the Royal Aeronautical Society*, Vol. 70 (No. 661), p. 49
Page 135	'one of ... in history'. Shute, N., *Vinland the Good* (London: William Heinemann, 1946), Preface
Page 135	'a journey ... the side'. *Ibid*
Page 135	'as true ... to produce'. *Ibid*
Page 136	'It had ... racial prejudice'. 'On Stirring Up Hornets' Nests', Unpublished Speech, Additions, Nevil Shute Papers, Syracuse University, New York
Page 136	'Norway had ... in 1945'. White, W., *A Rising Wind*, (New York: Doubleday, Doran and Company, 1945)
Page 137	'embarrassingly slight' ... 'a heavyweight ... lightweight novel'. *Time*, 31 March 1947, p. 112
Page 137	'a rather ... parts warrants'. *The Times Literary Supplement*, 24 May 1947, p. 249
Page 137	'despite our vaunted liberalism, our strident soap-box screams for tolerance, no American could have written The Chequer Board'. *The Saturday Review of Literature*, 3 May 1947, p. 17

Notes on Sources

Page 138	'On 5 March 1947 ... left her'. Entry in Flora Twort Diary, 5 March 1947, Petersfield Museum, Hampshire
Page 138	'There was ... was injured'. Anderson, J., *Parallel Motion* (Kerhonkson: Paper Tiger Inc, 2011) p. 173
Page 138	'There is ... great fun'. *The Chicago Defender*, 29 May 1947, p. 15
Page 139	'standing amid ... shaking hands'. *Chicago Sunday Tribune*, 29 June 1947, Pt. 4, p. 4
Page 139	'In the ... this country'. *The New Statesman and Nation*, 26 July 1947, pp. 71-72
Page 139	'I have ... easier times'. Orwell, G., *It Is What I Think 1947-1948* (London: Secker & Warburg, 1999) p. 258
Page 140	'I know ... books alone'... 'An unsuccessful... foreign exchange'. Letter from N. S. Norway to John Pudney, 7 November 1947. John Pudney Papers, Series 2, Box 3, Folder 11, Harry Ransom Humanities Research Centre, University of Texas at Austin.
Page 141	'I found ... labelled hut'. *World Books Broadsheet,* February 1952, pp. 1–2
Page 141	'He did ... *Blind Understanding*'. Unpublished manuscript *Blind Understanding,* MS 2199, Papers of Nevil Shute Norway, National Library of Australia, Canberra
Page 142	'Ten years ... World War'. *The Guardian*, 18 February 2000, p. 24
Page 143	'The characterisation ... damn quick'. Letter from R. P. Watt to Louisa Callender, Heinemann, 5 April 1948. Nevil Shute Norway Author File, Random House Group Archive, Rushden
Page 144	'Such was ... both sides'. Letter from A. S. Frere, William Heinemann Ltd to R. E. Staple, BOAC, 21 September 1948. Nevil Shute Norway Author File, Random House Group Archive, Rushden
Page 144	'if any ... Nevil Shute'. *The Observer*, 5 December 1948, p. 3
Page 144	'this is ... so far' ... 'it is ... literary significance'. *The Bookman*, November 1948, pp. 1–2
Page 145	'The Book Society ... in 1948.' *The Observer*, 1 January 1950, p. 7

Chapter 9 – Australia and Back

Page 146	'Marjorie of ... With Star'. *Daily Express*, 23 September 1948, p. 1
Page 146	'Mrs Dobson ... for £5 5s'. *Ibid*
Page 146	'The trip ... rubber dinghy'. Letter from N. S, Norway to A. Dwye Evans, William Heinemann Ltd, 14 July 1948. Nevil Shute Norway Author File, Random House Group Archive, Rushden
Page 148	'the trip ... getting somewhere'. Riddell, J., *Flight of Fancy* (London: Robert Hale Ltd, 1950) p. 38
Page 149	'quite seriously ... his Viking'. Entry in Flight Log, 3 October 1948.

	MS 2199, Papers of Nevil Shute Norway, National Library of Australia, Canberra
Page 149	'getting somewhere'. Letter from N. S, Norway to A. Dwye Evans, William Heinemann Ltd, 12 October 1948. Nevil Shute Norway Author File, Random House Group Archive, Rushden
Page 149	'U. Prajnananda ... Methodist Minister'. *The Age*, 6 December 1941, p. 14
Page 150	'Although there ... a monk'. Castro, S. J., (2013) 'Critics of Meher Baba: Paul Brunton and Rom Landau', See <http://stephenjcastro.blogspot.com/2013/01/paul-brunton-and-meher-baba-in-search.html>
Page 150	'Dismal feeling ... the blue'. Riddell, J., *Flight of Fancy* (London: Robert Hale Ltd, 1950) p. 130
Page 151	'Like many ... new material'. *Northern Standard*, 26 November 1948, p. 3
Page 152	'a beautiful little town' ... 'one might ... happy life'... 'the coast ... ever seen'. Entry in Flight Log, 11 December 1948. MS 2199, Papers of Nevil Shute Norway, National Library of Australia, Canberra
Page 152	'the name ... it right' ... 'Nevil is ... recover soon'. Riddell, J., *Flight of Fancy* (London: Robert Hale Ltd, 1950) pp. 140–141
Page 152	'He still ... is genuine'. Entry in Flight Log, 8 December 1948. MS 2199, Papers of Nevil Shute Norway, National Library of Australia, Canberra
Page 154	'Author Makes Mercy Flight'. *Cairns Post*, 21 December 1948, p. 5
Page 155	'a colossally ... elite attended'. Entry in Flight Log, 25 December 1948. MS 2199, Papers of Nevil Shute Norway, National Library of Australia, Canberra
Page 155	'British Author ... Surf Victims'. *Queensland Times*, 28 December 1948, p. 1
Page 155	'absurd customs regulations'. *The Daily News*, 22 January 1949, p. 18
Page 155	'an ugly ... of drunks' ... 'the 10 ... of time'. Entry in Flight Log, 30 December 1948. MS 2199, Papers of Nevil Shute Norway, National Library of Australia, Canberra
Page 156	'was spoilt ... the city'. Entry in Flight Log, 1 January 1949. MS 2199, Papers of Nevil Shute Norway, National Library of Australia, Canberra
Page 156	'large number of drunks, with lots of noise and confusion'. Riddell, J., *Flight of Fancy* (London: Robert Hale Ltd, 1950) p. 162
Page 157	'could have ... at home' ... 'that in ... anywhere else'. *The Australian Women's Weekly*, 21 January 1949, p. 17
Page 157	'another unbelievable ... and rudeness'. Riddell, J., *Flight of Fancy* (London: Robert Hale Ltd, 1950) p. 168
Page 157	'I am ... dreary towns'. Entry in Flight Log, 21 January 1949. MS 2199,

Notes on Sources

Page 158	Papers of Nevil Shute Norway, National Library of Australia, Canberra 'one of … for Nevil'… 'his journey immense distance'. Riddell, J., *Flight of Fancy* (London: Robert Hale Ltd, 1950) p. 245
Page 158	'very sad … start work'. Entry in Flight Log, 14 March 1949. MS 2199, Papers of Nevil Shute Norway, National Library of Australia, Canberra
Page 158	'I'll probably … wind landing'. Letter from N. S, Norway to A. Dwye Evans, William Heinemann Ltd, 12 October 1948. Nevil Shute Norway Author File, Random House Group Archive, Rushden
Page 159	'Riddell's would … a foreword'. Riddell, J., *Flight of Fancy* (London: Robert Hale Ltd, 1950)
Page 159	'Norway's flight … his death'. Flight Log from England to Australia, MS 2199, Papers of Nevil Shute Norway, National Library of Australia, Canberra
Page 159	'On his … and skiing'. *The Guardian*, 18 February 2000, p. 24

Chapter 10 – Exasperation

Page 161	'The result … Frances Norway'. Stevenson, D., (1949) 'Models and Fiction', *The Model Engineer*, Vol. 100 (No. 2487), pp. 93–94 and 97
Page 161	'A month … northern Queensland'. *Townsville Daily Bulletin*, 18 April 1949, p. 2
Page 162	'His working … draft manuscript'. Author's notes for *A Town Like Alice*. MS 2199, Papers of Nevil Shute Norway, National Library of Australia, Canberra
Page 162	'Norway though … 50 years time'. Anon., (1958) 'Shute Shoots Back', *Books and Bookmen*, Vol. 3, No. 12, p. 11
Page 163	'1950 was … of decision'. *The Sunday Times*, 1 January 1950, p. 1
Page 165	'Petrol consumption … a month'. National Archives, London, CAB 128/12, Cabinet Papers and Minutes for 22 March 1948
Page 165	'Let Us … Through Together'. Labour Party manifesto, 1950. See <http://www.politicsresources.net/area/uk/man/lab50.htm>
Page 165	'With the … petrol allowance'. Letter from N. S. Norway to the Ministry of Fuel and Power, 17 January 1950. X902/2404, General Reference Collection, British Library
Page 166	'the continual … restraints induce'. Letter from N. S. Norway to the Ministry of Fuel and Power, 27 January 1950. X902/2404, General Reference Collection, British Library
Page 166	'the inconvenience … transport daily'. Letter from the Ministry of Fuel and Power to N. S. Norway, 9 February 1950. X902/2404, General Reference Collection, British Library
Page 166	'bound by … my work' … 'in consequence … and popular'. Letter

	from N. S. Norway to the Ministry of Fuel and Power, 13 February 1950. X902/2404, General Reference Collection, British Library
Page 166	'in a ... unconventional ways' *Ibid*
Page 167	'As a ... be British'. Hammerton, A. J. and Thomson A., *Ten Pound Poms* (Manchester: Manchester University Press, 2005)
Page 167	'predominantly European ... and culture'. Jupp, J., *The English in Australia* (Cambridge: Cambridge University Press, 2004) p. 132
Page 168	'On 21 April ... the country'. Letter from N. S., Norway to A. Dwye Evans, William Heinemann Ltd, 21 April 1950. Nevil Shute Norway Author File, Random House Group Archive, Rushden
Page 168	'rather fancied ... Cairn's way'. *The Australian Women's Weekly*, 29 April 1950, p. 17
Page 168	'I found ... Gulf Country'. *World Books Broadsheet,* February 1952, pp. 1–2
Page 169	'pushes one ... to page'. *The Sunday Times*, 11 June 1950, p. 1
Page 169	'lacked Buchan's ... the mysterious'. *Daily Herald*, 14 June 1950, p. 6
Page 169	'there is ... your novels'. Letter from A. Dwye Evans, William Heinemann Ltd to N. S. Norway, 22 November 1950. Nevil Shute Norway Author File, Random House Group Archive, Rushden
Page 170	'a fan'. Letter from N. S. Norway to A. Dwye Evans, William Heinemann Ltd, 25 April 1950. Nevil Shute Norway Author File, Random House Group Archive, Rushden
Page 170	'At a ... deemed indecent'. *The Irish Times*, 14 October 1950, p. 3
Page 170	'Over dinner ... be published'. *The Sunday Times*, 16 July 1950, p. 5

Chapter 11 – A New World

Page 174	'We led ... a head!'. Hammerton, A. J. and Thomson A., *Ten Pound Poms* (Manchester: Manchester University Press, 2005) p. 103
Page 174	'On its ... at sea'. *The West Australian*, 8 February 1950, p. 2
Page 175	'He now ... in Australia'. *The West Australian*, 16 August 1950, p. 13
Page 176	'British to his bootstraps'. Starr, G., 'Menzies and Post-war Prosperity' in Nethercote, J, R, *Liberalism and the Australian Federation* (Sydney: Federation Press., 2001) p. 183.
Page 176	'You've got ... over you'. Martin, A. W., 'Menzies, Sir Robert Gordon' in *Australian Dictionary of Biography*. See <http://adb.anu.edu.au/biography/menzies-sir-robert-gordon-bob-11111>
Page 176	'Under what ... current novel'. *The Manchester Guardian*, 24 June 1950, p. 6
Page 176	'everybody was ... his face'. Letter from N. S. Norway to Alan Cobham, 23 April 1951. X006-0170/001/037/001, RAF Museum, Colindale
Page 176	'everyone and ... happen next'. *The Argus*, 21 August 1950, p. 7

Page 176	'Novelist's Wife … Except His!'. *The Age*, 21 August 1950, p. 5
Page 177	'a Victorian community overseas'. Briggs, A., *Victorian Cities* (London: Penguin Books, 1990) p. 277
Page 180	'whenever I … very odd'. Letter from N. S. Norway to A. S. Frere, William Heinemann Ltd, 20 December 1950. Nevil Shute Norway Author File, Random House Group Archive, Rushden
Page 181	'*Round the Bend* … moderately entertaining'. *The New York Times*, 2 March 1951, p. 23
Page 182	'Invited to … than himself'. *The Age*, 1 May 1951, p. 5
Page 182	'He wrote … developing country'. Letter from N. S. Norway to Kilham Roberts, Society of Authors, 19 March 1951. British Library MSA183
Page 182	'their affairs … complete chaos'. Letter from N. S. Norway to A. Gyde, William Heinemann Ltd, 16 May 1951. Nevil Shute Norway Author File, Random House Group Archive, Rushden
Page 182	'For instance … uneasy amalgam'. *The Observer*, 10 June 1951, p. 7
Page 183	'does not … his mission'. *The Daily Telegraph*, 15 June 1951, p. 6
Page 183	'a roar of rage'. *The Australian Women's Weekly*, 1 August 1951, p. 26
Page 184	'*No Highway* … it got'. *The Observer*, 5 August 1951, p. 6
Page 184	'Norway received … home again'. *The Dandenong Journal*, 7 November 1951, p. 16

Chapter 12 – Flying a Different Flag

Page 185	'I really … the world' … 'I do … anywhere else'. Letter from N. S. Norway to Alan Moorehead, 28 February 1952. MS5654, Papers of Alan Moorehead, National Library of Australia, Canberra
Page 186	'Fantastic prices … own function'. *The Argus*, 1 January 1952, p. 2
Page 187	'The news … war again'. Letter from N. S. Norway to Dwye Evans, William Heinemann Ltd, 1 December 1950. Nevil Shute Norway Author File, Random House Group Archive, Rushden
Page 187	'I want … happier circumstances'. *The Australian Women's Weekly*, 23 July 1952, p. 13
Page 188	'apologising to … of advertising'. Letter from N. S. Norway to Arnold Gyde, William Heinemann Ltd, 7 February 1952. Nevil Shute Norway Author File, Random House Group Archive, Rushden
Page 188	'as if … invisible barrier'… 'many still … the news' … 'many seen crying'. *The Argus*, 19 February 1952, p. 3
Page 188	'Queen of … of Australia'. Proclamation by Sir William McKell, 7 February 1952. National Archives of Australia, Record A6382
Page 189	'On 11 February 1952 … the summer'. National Archives, London, CAB 128/24, Conclusions of Cabinet Meeting, 11 February 1952
Page 189	'In *The Times* … page four'. *The Times*, 18 February 1952, p. 4

Page 190	'It was ... first place'. *The Elizabethan,* Toorak College Magazine, July 1953. pp. 8–9
Page 190	'While this ... *Sydney Morning Herald*'. *The Sydney Morning Herald*, 12 May 1952, p. 2
Page 190	'Norway had ... asking Riddell'. Pocock, T., *Alan Moorehead* (London: Pimlico, 1991) pp. 218–219
Page 191	'they got along splendidly'. McCamish, T., *Our Man Elsewhere – In Search of Alan Moorehead* (Carlton: Black Inc, 2016) p. 171
Page 192	'Nevil's kind ... in Dajarra'. *National Link-Up News*, 15 November 2010, p. 6
Page 192	'While Nevil ... a Norway'. Letter from L. H. Penhall to the Director of Native Affairs, 21 August 1952. F984, Aboriginal Half Caste Population Records – Walter Norway, National Archives of Australia, Canberra
Page 192	'At the ... *Rum Jungle*'. Moorehead, A., *Rum Jungle* (London: Hamish Hamilton, 1953)
Page 192	'This evocative ... good reviews'. *The Sunday Times*, 11 October 1953, p. 5
Page 192	'They now ... a year'. *Barrier Miner*, 5 June 1952, p. 9
Page 194	'too much ... intending migrants'. *The Times*, 2 August 1952, p. 6
Page 194	'propaganda on ... Communist books'. *The Spectator*, 1 August 1952, p. 170
Page 194	'the sort of ... of his birth'... 'the pictures ... are farcical'. *The Listener*, 7 August 1952, p. 235
Page 194	'all the ... human book'. *Punch*, 27 August 1952, p. 297
Page 195	'that the ... hindering them'. Letter from N. S. Norway to Dwye Evans, William Heinemann Ltd, 17 October 1952. Nevil Shute Norway Author File, Random House Group Archive, Rushden
Page 195	'Nevil Shute ... for Australia'. *The Argus*, 16 August 1952, p. 13
Page 195	'three trade ... Government department'. *Ibid*, p. 13
Page 195	'could have ... English readers'. *The Age*, 16 August 1952, p. 16
Page 195	'Mr. Nevil Shute ... almost irresistible'. *The Mercury*, 30 August 1952, p. 11
Page 195	'an absorbing tale ... and love'. *Saturday Review*, 12 September 1952, p. 39
Page 196	'In the end he ... book published'. Callinan, B. J., *Independent Company* (Melbourne: William Heinemann Ltd, 1953)
Page 196	'Also on ... West Australia'. *The Times*, 10 October 1952, p. 6
Page 197	'I can ... anywhere else'. Letter from N. S. Norway to Alan Moorehead, 28 February 1952. Papers of Alan Moorehead, MS 5654, National Library of Australia

Page 198	'Like others ... To Delhi'. Sharp, C. M., *D.H. – A History of de Havilland* (Shrewsbury: Airlife Publishing Ltd, 1982) p. 317
Page 199	'unhesitatingly announced ... without interruption'. *Daily Express*, 4 May 1953, p. 4
Page 200	'Fiction deals ...the world'. Shute, N., *In the Wet* (London: William Heinemann, 1953), Author's Note
Page 200	'which is going to make a lot of people very angry. Many will say it should have never been written'. *Daily Sketch*, 4 May 1953, p. 7
Page 200	'disgruntled hobbledehoy of a tale'. *The Sunday Times*, 3 May 1953, p. 5
Page 200	'unctuous and ... little vulgar'. *The Observer*, 3 May 1953, p. 9
Page 200	'a work of ... ill-timed impertinence' ... 'Shute's use ... Majesty the Queen'. *The Listener*, 7 May 1953, p. 773
Page 200	'certainly a ... undisguised propaganda' ... 'compels me ... the end' *The Daily Telegraph*, 8 May 1953, p. 8
Page 200	'did not ... since developed'. Letter from A. S. Frere to E. E. Bartholomew, William Heinemann Ltd, 19 May 1953. Nevil Shute Norway Author File, Random House Group Archive, Rushden
Page 200	'Five years ... bad taste'. Anon., (1958) 'Shute Shoots Back', *Books and Bookmen*, Vol. 3, No. 12, p. 11
Page 201	'permitted a commercial that was in the worst possible taste, a description of a car as the Queen of the Road'. *The New York Times*, 3 June 1953, p. 47
Page 201	'To some ... a way'. House of Lords Sitting, 23 June 1953 <http://hansard.millbanksystems.com/lords/1953/jun/23/the-coronation-american-television>.
Page 202	'This situation ... our own'. *The Sydney Morning Herald*, 12 August 1953, p. 2
Page 202	'The year ... of oil'. *The West Australian*, 5 December 1953, p. 2

Chapter 13 – The Future and the Past

Page 204	'the most ... any visitor'. *The Sydney Morning Herald*, 4 February 1954, p. 1
Page 205	'This one ... *Brisbane Telegraph*'. *Brisbane Telegraph*, 19 February 1954, p. 12
Page 206	'Tomorrow she is all ours!'. *The Argus*, 23 February 1954, p. 1
Page 206	'Our Undoubted Queen'. *The Argus*, 24 February 1954, p. 7
Page 206	'It was ... in Australia'. *The Age*, 15 March 1954, p. 2
Page 206	'This health ... being recorded'. Notes for a Nevil Norway lecture '*On Autobiographies*', circa mid-1950s. Additions, Nevil Shute Papers, Syracuse University, New York
Page 207	'The *Saturday Review* ... Aircraft company'. *Saturday Review*, 5 June 1954, pp. 36–37

Page 208	'On 20 April ... stop this'. *The Sydney Morning Herald*, 20 April 1954, p. 1
Page 208	'that for ... Airship R.101'. *Flight*, 5 March 1954, p. 8
Page 209	'a wretched ... it brilliantly'. *The Observer*, 27 June 1954, p. 9
Page 209	'while another ... to be learned'. *The Times Literary Supplement*, 2 June 1954, p. 419
Page 209	'Either Mr. Shute ... about it'. *Flight,* 19 September 1954, p. 466
Page 209	'Although, he ... for them'. Masefield, P. G and Gunston, B., *Flight Path* (Shrewsbury: Airlife Publishing Ltd, 2002) p. 105
Page 210	'had led ... with it'. Masefield, P. G., *To Ride a Storm* (London: William Kimber & Co Ltd, 1982) pp. 204–205
Page 210	'a great ... English Press'. Letter from B. N. Wallis to N. S. Norway, 9 August 1954. Cambridge University Library, Department of Manuscripts and University Archives, Vickers Ltd: Records, MS Vickers Doc 780
Page 210	'sufficiently acquainted ... right judgment'. *Ibid*
Page 210	'thought it ... still living'. *Ibid*
Page 210	'Norway replied ... caused him'. Letter from N. S. Norway to B. N. Wallis, 19 August 1954. Cambridge University Library, Department of Manuscripts and University Archives, Vickers Ltd: Records, MS Vickers Doc 780
Page 210	'it seemed ... those days'. Letter from N. S. Norway to A. H. Tiltman, June 1954. POMRC 2004/234, Portsmouth Museum
Page 211	'this small ... hundred miles'. Letter from N. S. Norway to Alan Moorehead 22 July 1954. Papers of Alan Moorehead, MS 5654, National Library of Australia
Page 211	'as always ... to use'. Letter from N. S. Norway to A. Dwye Evans, William Heinemann Ltd, 9 July 1954. Nevil Shute Norway Author File, Random House Group Archive, Rushden
Page 212	'Frances told ... of November'. *The Sun-Herald*, 4 July 1954, p. 29
Page 212	'They had ... of horses'. *The Argus*, 15 May 1954, p. 15
Page 212	'During his ... La Grande resident'. *La Grande Observer,* 25 August 1954, p. 1
Page 213	'Not surprisingly ... the Inquiry'. *Daily Express*, 20 October 1954, p. 2

Chapter 14 – Novelist, Farmer and Racing Driver

Page 215	'Even holiday ... metropolitan area'. *The Argus*, 3 January 1955, p. 3
Page 216	'The feeling ... in January'. *The Age*, 19 January 1955, p. 12
Page 216	'On 17 February ... hydrogen bomb'. *The Times,* 18 February 1955, p. 8
Page 216	'The Frere's ... J. B. Priestley'. *The Argus*, 8 March 1955, p. 12
Page 217	'unrivalled journalistic ... of narrative'. *The Illustrated London News*, 4 June 1955, p. 1028

Notes on Sources

Page 217	'Shute's qualities ... of fact' ... 'laborious and unconvincing'. *The Times Literary Supplement*, 29 April 1955, p. 215
Page 218	'an ardent ... new country' ... 'because of ... complete sincerity'. *The Age,* 12 February 1955, p. 1
Page 218	'from every ... bad book'. *The Argus*, 14 May 1955, p. 15
Page 218	'a very ... intelligent story'. *Daily Boston Globe,* 10 April 1955, p. A31
Page 218	'A skilled ... Hitchcocky suspense'. *Time*, 18 April 1955, p. 118
Page 218	'In the ... Tennant Creek'. *The Age*, 11 July 1955. p. 3
Page 220	'The fact ... at 30'. Letter from N. S. Norway to Alec Menhinick, 5 May 1953. The Menhinick Archive, Nevil Shute Norway Foundation Website , <http://www.nevilshute.org>
Page 220	'The film ... miss it'. *Daily Express*, 3 March 1956, p. 6
Page 221	'On 1 March ... Marshall Islands'. *The Times*, 25 May 1954, p. 8
Page 221	'The theme ... in 1954'. *La Grande Observer,* 7 February 1957, p. 1
Page 222	'was written ... customary aplomb' ... 'it is ... good theme' *The Observer,* 13 May 1956, p. 12
Page 223	'a professionally ... disguised film-script'... 'the best novel its author has written for some time'. *The Daily Telegraph*, 4 May 1956, p. 8
Page 223	'a contrived ... of work' ... 'the insipid ... the mouth' *The Times Literary Supplement*, 25 May 1956, p. 309
Page 223	'the ending ... the reading' ... 'some North-westerners ... the story'. *The Oregon Statesman*, 22 September 1956, p. 4
Page 223	'an appealing ... two cultures'. *The New York Herald Tribune Book Review*, 12 August 1956, p. 2
Page 223	'The official ... 8 August'. *The Australian Women's Weekly*, 8 August 1956, p. 33
Page 224	'When it ... great success'. *The Argus*, 21 September 1956, p. 9
Page 224	'despite having ... the morning'. *The Sunday Feature* 'Set Square', First broadcast 9 February 1997, BBC Radio 3
Page 224	'The working ... Phillip Bay'. Author's notes for *On the Beach*. MS 2199, Papers of Nevil Shute Norway, National Library of Australia, Canberra
Page 224	'He also ... the manuscript'. Letter from N. S. Norway to Major General Frank Kingsley Norris, 5 October 1956. *Ibid*
Page 224	'This was ... with Norris'. Norris, F. K., *No Memory for Pain* (Melbourne: Heinemann, 1970) p. 237
Page 225	'he didn't ... the oldest'. See <http://www.delarue.net/norway.htm>
Page 225	'On the ... of 103,000'. Posey, C. A., *The Olympic Century XVI Olympiad* (Toronto: Warwick Press Inc, 1996)
Page 225	'Shute ... in 1959'. Smeeton, M., *Once is Enough* (London: Rupert Hart-Davis Ltd, 1959)

Page 226	'Years later … outgoing individual'. Email from Bruce Kirby to Richard Thorn, 13 May 2016

Chapter 15 – Armageddon, Conflict and Decline

Page 228	'On the … Honours List'. *The Sydney Morning Herald,* 1 January 1957, p. 1
Page 228	'our economic … become clear'. *The Argus*, 1 January 1957, p. 4
Page 228	'from Stettin … the Continent'. Gilbert, M., *Churchill – A Life* (London: William Heinemann Ltd, 1991) p. 866
Page 229	'On the 20 … Soviet Union'. *The New York Times*, 21 January 1957, pp. 1 and 3
Page 229	'Fours days … late spring'. *The New York Times*, 25 January 1957, p. 22
Page 229	'The third … since 1952'. The Commonwealth of Australia, *The Report of the Royal Commission into British Nuclear Tests in Australia, Volume 2* (Canberra: Australian government Publishing Service, 1985) Appendix G
Page 229	'As far … nuclear weapons'. Taylor, R. and Pritchard, C., *The Protest Makers* (Oxford: Pergamon Press, 1980) pp. 5–7
Page 229	'at present … nuclear weapons'. H.M.S.O., *Defence – Outline of Future Policy,* (London: H.M.S.O, 1957) p. 2
Page 231	'this is … a whimper'. Shute, N., *On the Beach* (London: William Heinemann, 1957)
Page 231	'Of course … this one'. *Cumberland Evening News,* 14 November 1957, p. 11
Page 231	'The mainstream … and unrepresentative'. *The Times Literary Supplement*, 14 June 1957, p. 361
Page 231	'scientific work … Australian Navy'. *The Sunday Times*, 2 June 1957, p. 7
Page 231	'quietly and … and subdued colours' … 'by far … considerable achievement'. *The Daily Telegraph*, 7 June 1957, p. 13
Page 231	'skilfully muted and restrained' … 'both moving and horrifying'. *The Listener*, 13 June 1957, p. 972
Page 231	'an austere … become real'. *The Chicago Daily Tribune*, 4 August 1957, p. B1
Page 231	'it is … inadequate characterisation'. *The New York Times*, 24 July 1957, p. 23
Page 232	'Winston Churchill … to Eisenhower'. Lees-Milne, J., *A Mingled Measure: Diaries 1956-1972*(London: John Murray Publishing Ltd, 2000) p. 54
Page 232	'I cannot … the story'. Letter from N. S. Norway to R. G. Casey, 7 June 1957. Papers of Richard G Casey, NAA:M1129/Norway N S, National Archives of Australia, Canberra

Notes on Sources

Page 232	'the most ... a century'. Brians, P., *Nuclear Holocausts: Atomic War in Fiction 1895–1984* (Kent: Kent State University Press, 1987) p. 13
Page 232	'arguably Australia's ... important novel'. Haigh, G., (2007) 'Shute the Messenger', *The Monthly*, June, pp. 42–53
Page 233	'By 10 September ... the novel'. *The Age*, 10 September 1957, p. 4
Page 233	'A fellow ... in Britain'. Priestley, J. B., (1957) 'Britain and the Nuclear Bombs', *New Statesman*, Vol. 54, No. 1390, pp. 554–556
Page 234	'the properly ... the country' ... 'not a democratic procedure'. Letter from N. S. Norway to Alfred M. Dickie, 27 February 1959. Papers of Richard G. Casey, NAA:M 1129/Norway N S, National Archives of Australia, Canberra
Page 234	'In early ... in Britain'. Letter from N. S. Norway to R. G. Casey, 11 December 1957. Papers of Richard G. Casey, NAA:M1129/Norway N S, National Archives of Australia, Canberra
Page 234	'Casey replied ... been sustainable'. Letter from R. G. Casey to N. S. Norway, 16 December 1957. Papers of Richard G. Casey, M 1129, National Archives of Australia, Canberra
Page 235	'nowhere could ... in Melbourne'. *The Australian Women's Weekly*, 22 April 1958, p. 47
Page 237	'ingenious'... 'in practice ... awkward breaks'. *The Times*, 31 July 1958, p. 11
Page 237	'is, in fact ... kind, masterly' ... 'in its narrative ... is quite admirable'. *The Sunday Express*, 10 August 1958, p. 6
Page 237	'the plot ... boring details'. *Chicago Daily Tribune*, 26 October 1958, p. B18
Page 237	'As always ... basic trainer'. *Time*, 27 October 1958, p. 98
Page 238	'An author ... something creative'. *The New York Times*, 22 June 1958, p. 8
Page 238	'in times of ... be themselves'. Letter from N. S. Norway to Stanley Kramer, 14 July 1958. Stanley Kramer Papers, Collection 161, Charles E Young Research Library, UCLA
Page 238	'Have faith ... the rest'. Letter from Stanley Kramer to N. S. Norway, 18 July 1958. Stanley Kramer Papers, Collection 161, Charles E Young Research Library, UCLA
Page 238	'Since our ... so much' ... 'I have written ... help you'. Letter from N. S. Norway to Stanley Kramer, 21 August 1958. Stanley Kramer Papers, Collection 161, Charles E. Young Research Library, UCLA
Page 238	'In a short ... in October'. Letter from Stanley Kramer to N. S. Norway, 28 August 1958. Stanley Kramer Papers, Collection 161, Charles E. Young Research Library, UCLA
Page 239	'be shown ... Australia generally'. Press Release from F M Osborne,

	19 August 1958. Film On the Beach-Cooperation of the RAN, A463, 1958/2449, National Archives of Australia, Canberra
Page 239	'True to ... in Langwarrin'. Davey, P. R., *When Hollywood Came to Melbourne* (Melbourne: Philip R. Davey, 2009) p. 15
Page 240	'A member ... Fred Astaire'. Email from Heather Mayfield to Richard Thorn, 12 May 2015
Page 240	'I had ... very much'. *The Age*, 14 January 1960, p. 5
Page 240	'Not surprisingly... in Britain'. *Daily Express,* 22 December 1958, p. 1
Page 241	'I have ... practically gone' . Letter from N. S. Norway to A. Dwye Evans, William Heinemann Ltd, 31 December 1958. Nevil Shute Norway Author File, Random House Group Archive, Rushden

Chapter 16 – The Last Year

Page 243	'as the ... the world'. Norway, N. S., (1959) 'The Future Population of Australia', *Australian Citizenship Convention*, 20–22 January, Canberra
Page 243	'He therefore ... Water front'. Letter from N. S. Norway to British Consul, Tahiti, 2 February 1959. Nevil Shute Norway Foundation <http://www.nevilshute.org/Misc/letterfromnevilshutefeb59.pdf>
Page 243	'it must be ... like this'. Letter from A. S. Frere to Val Arnott, William Heinemann Ltd, 16 December 1958. Nevil Shute Norway Author File, Random House Group Archive, Rushden
Page 243	'Even before ... Melbourne climate'. *The Age*, 15 January 1958, p. 8
Page 245	'I still feel ... to work till ... back at ...though I have nothing in particular to do'. Letter from N. S. Norway to A. Dwye Evans, 1 July 1959. Nevil Shute Norway Author File, Random House Group Archive, Rushden
Page 246	'if no ... of September'. *Ibid*
Page 246	'entirely unsolicited ... for him'. Letter from N. S. Norway to R. G. Menzies, 20 October 1959. Suggestions for Encouragement of Australian Writers, Artists, Sculptors and Composers, NAA: A463, 1965/2870, National Archives of Australia, Canberra
Page 247	'In 1955 ... In Parliament'. *The Times*, 14 November 1955, p. 5
Page 247	'I have ... at all'. N. S. Norway Submission to the Spicer Committee, NAA: A432, 1958/2338, National Archives of Australia, Canberra
Page 247	'I got ... apple cart'. Letter from N. S. Norway to Robert Hughes, 5 November 1959. Papers of Robert Hughes, MS 10935, State Library Victoria, Melbourne
Page 247	'The Spicer ... report's recommendations'. *Report of Copyright Law Committee* (Canberra: Commonwealth of Australia, 1959)
Page 248	'the worst ... without exception'. Smith, J., *Nevil Shute,* (Cresskill: Paper Tiger Inc, 2002) p. 150
Page 248	'He had ... legal action'. *Ibid* p. 150

Page 248	'the film was not a good portrayal of his book'. *The Age*, 18 December 1959, p. 1
Page 248	'a memorable evening'. Davey, P. R., *When Hollywood Came to Melbourne* (Melbourne: Philip R. Davey, 2009) p. 200
Page 249	'a film ... leaving it'. *The Age*, 18 December 1959, p. 2
Page 249	'Mr. Kramer ... responsive cast' ... 'deeply moving picture'. *The New York Times*, 18 December 1959, p. 34
Page 249	'a pity' ... 'for most' ... 'everywhere apparent'. *The Times*, 16 December 1959, p. 3
Page 249	'it is difficult ... for Kramer'. *The Sydney Morning Herald*, 18 December 1959, p. 7
Page 249	'Many people ... "On the Beach".' *The Observer*, 20 December 1959, p. 7
Page 250	'Notes that Shute ... Nativity theme'. Unfinished manuscript, *Incident at Eucla*, MS 2199, Papers of Nevil Shute Norway, National Library of Australia, Canberra

Chapter 17 – Epilogue

Page 251	'one of ... best-selling authors'. *Daily Mirror*, 13 January 1960, p. 19
Page 251	'a novelist ... aeronautical world'. *The Times*, 13 January 1960, p. 15
Page 251	'qualities of ... him is to be drawn' ... 'the most important ... for their needs'. *The Times*, 28 January 1960, p. 16
Page 252	'supremely, a story-teller' ... 'one of the bravest ... fortune to know'. *The Sunday Times*, 19 January 1960, p. 18
Page 253	'we are ... famous man'. *The Age*, 21 January 1960, p. 3
Page 253	'we all still feel like a ship without a rudder' Letter from F. M. Norway to A. Dwye Evans, 7 August 1960. Nevil Shute Norway Author File, Random House Group Archive, Rushden
Page 254	'the descriptive ... all works'. *The Guardian*, 1 April 1960, p. 8
Page 254	'It's all ... this tale ... but it does leave behind ... of this author's career'. *The New York Times Book Review*, 3 April 1960, p. 4
Page 255	'if Fred had ... I turn out'. Shute, N., *Slide Rule* (London: William Heinemann, 1954), p. 21

A Select Bibliography

i) Primary Sources

MS 2199, Papers of Nevil Shute Norway, National Library of Australia, Canberra
Acquired by the Library in 1968, this collection consists of manuscripts of published works, unpublished literary manuscripts, and a small number of miscellaneous documents such as Norway's flight log for his trip from England to Australia and an unpublished film script.

Nevil Shute Papers, Syracuse University Libraries, New York
In 1971, Syracuse University were given an approved microfilm copy of the collection in Canberra. This material has since been supplemented by additional primary material such as notes for lectures and speeches, and some secondary material such as copies of early published short stories.

Nevil Shute Author File, Random House Group Archive and Library, Rushden, UK
William Heinemann became part of the Random House Group in 1997. The Group's Archive and Library at Rushden contains an author file for Nevil Shute. This consists of letters between Norway and staff at Heinemann, some press cuttings and sales information. The period covered is principally 1949 to 1963.

Nevil Shute's American publisher William Morrow is now an imprint of HarperCollins Publishers. An author archive for Nevil Shute cannot be located.

A Select Bibliography

Nevil Shute's first four novels were published in the United Kingdom by Cassell and Company. The Company is now part of the Orion Publishing Group and no archive can now be found related to either Shute or the publication of these novels.

ii) Secondary Sources

Anderson, J., *Parallel Motion: A Biography of Nevil Shute Norway* (Kerhonkson: Paper Tiger, 2011)

Anderson, J., *Airship on a Shoestring* (London: New Generation Publishing, 2014)

Charlesworth, M., *J B Oldham of Oldham's Hall* (East Horrington: Greenbank Press, 1996)

Cobham, A. J. and Derrick, C. (Editor), *A Time to Fly* (London: Shepheard-Walwyn, 1978)

Countryman, B., *R100 in Canada* (Ontario: Boston Mills Press, 1982)

Davey, P. R., *When Hollywood Came to Melbourne* (Melbourne: Philip R. Davey, 2009)

Deacon, K., *The Men and Women Who Built and Flew the R.100* (Howden: Langrick Publications, 2008)

Devitt, D. (Editor), *A Diversity of Dragons* (Bath: Desmond Devitt, 2003)

Foy, M. T. and Barton, B., *The Easter Rising* (Stroud: The History Press, 2011)

Gifford, C., *Nevil Shute: A Bibliography* (Adelaide: Auslib Press, 1988)

Haigh, G., (2007) 'Shute the Messenger', *The Monthly*, June 2007, pp. 42–53.

Howatson, A. M., *Mechanicks in the Universitie* (Oxford: University of Oxford, 2008)

Levy, B., *Beyond the Beach: The Wit and Wisdom of Nevil Shute* (Mendham: BLS Publishing, 2012)

Martin, D., (1960) 'The Mind that Conceived On the Beach', *Meanjin*, Vol. 19, No. 2, pp. 193–200.

Middleton, D. H., *Airspeed* (Lavenham: Terence Dalton, 1982)

Moorehead, A., *Rum Jungle* (London: Hamish Hamilton, 1953)

Morpurgo, J. E., *Barnes Wallis: A Biography* (London: Ian Allan, 1981)

Munro-Faure, A, *Flora Twort: A Petersfield Artist* (Portsmouth: Hampshire County Council, 1995)

Norway, M. L., Norway, A. H. and Jeffrey, K., *The Sinn Féin Rebellion as They Saw It* (Dublin: Irish Academic Press, 1999)

Pawle, G., *The Secret War* (George G. Harrap: London, 1956)

Riddell, J., *Flight of Fancy* (London: Robert Hall, 1950)

Sharpe, C. M., *D.H.: A History of de Havilland* (Shrewsbury: Airlife, 1982)

Shute, N., *Slide Rule* (London: William Heinemann, 1954)

Stopes-Roe, M., *Mathematics with Love* (Basingstoke: Macmillan, 2005)

Smith, J., *Nevil Shute* (Cresskill: Paper Tiger, 2002)

Swinfield, J., *Airship: Design, Development and Disaster* (London: Conway, 2012)

Taylor, H. A., *Airspeed Aircraft Since 1931* (London: Putnam, 1970)

The Nevil Shute Norway Foundation

The principal aim of the Foundation is to further public awareness in the life and writings of Nevil Shute Norway. The Foundation has its genesis in a Nevil Shute internet book club which was formed in late 1996. This group suggested that a small gathering should be organised to mark the then approaching one hundredth anniversary of Shute's birth. This 'small gathering' quickly grew into a formal Centennial Symposium which was held in Albuquerque, New Mexico in January 1999. Attended by over 120 delegates from five countries, those present included Shute's two daughters and their family.

Since then, the Nevil Shute Norway Foundation has developed into a dynamic not-for-profit international organisation which hosts a range of national and international conventions and workshops devoted to Shute's work; maintains lending libraries in the UK, USA and Australia; supports the Shute Memorial Library in Alice Springs; assists in the development of educational programmes related to Shute's writing; publishes a monthly newsletter; funds an annual Nevil Shute Excellence in Aviation Scholarship; and maintains a web site. The link for the Foundation's website is:

http://www.nevilshute.org

The website contains an extensive range of photographs, documents and articles and is an excellent resource for anyone interested in finding out more about the life and work of Nevil Shute Norway.

Acknowledgements

When I began work on this book, it was with some trepidation that one of the first people I contacted was John Anderson. John is President of the Nevil Shute Norway Foundation, a biographer of Norway, and an acknowledged authority on all things Shute. I need not have worried. From that first contact John has been a source of unlimited enthusiasm and advice, always eager to assist and keen to share any new information he comes across. He also read through various drafts of the manuscript, and offered many useful comments for improvements.

The number of people alive today who actually knew Nevil Norway is rapidly dwindling. His surviving daughter Heather Mayfield has been fully supportive and diligently responded to what at times must have seemed my never-ending stream of questions. Others who generously shared their memories of Norway were Angela Groves, Lisa Greenwood, Ruth Greenwood, Bruce Kirby and Virginia McKenna.

I am massively indebted to Margaret Halton and Alex Stephens at A. P. Watt/United Agents and the Trustees of the Estate of Nevil Shute Norway, for giving permission to quote from the published books, unpublished writing and letters of Nevil Shute Norway. I wish to acknowledge and thank the many archivists, librarians and researchers who have helped my search for material and provided information. I am particularly indebted to Daniel Albon, formerly RAF Museum, London; Scotia Ashley, Kate Bossen, Tighearnán Kelly and Emily Witt, National Library of Australia; Katy Ball, Portsmouth Museum; Jessica Black, University of Melbourne; Natalie Elliott, Toorak College; Paul Gansky, formerly Harry Ransom Center; Geoffrey Goodall, Melbourne; Rex Hobson, Royal Victorian

Acknowledgements

Aero Club; Bruce Kay, National Archives of Australia; Professor Shoshana Knapp, Virginia Tech; Aisling Lockhart, Trinity College Dublin; Sarah Minney, Consultant Genealogist; Oliver Mahony, Lady Margaret Hall, Oxford University; Nicholas Mays, News International; Dr Mike Morrogh, formerly Shrewsbury School; Valérie Nolk, St Paul's School, Colet Court; Mary O'Sullivan, the Irish Film Classification Office; Dr Kathrin Pieren, formerly the Petersfield Museum; Diane Richard, Mosaic Research; Brian Riddle, National Aerospace Library; Michael Riordan, St John's and the Queen's Colleges, Oxford University; David Rymill, Hampshire Records Office; Gay Sturt, the Dragon School, Oxford; and Graham Thompson, Royal Museums Greenwich. To any I have missed, my sincere apologies.

My long-time friend and academic colleague Professor Peter Sydenham has, as always, been an immense help. Whether it was though our weekly Skype discussions or by never ever complaining when I started rambling on about Shute yet again, I am grateful to him. Three other long-time friends, Professor Bob Green, Professor Ashu Sharma and Dr Christopher Beck, also helped in their different ways with advice and by offering comments at various stages of the book's development.

Martin Toseland and Richard Sheehan provided expert advice and comment on various versions of the draft manuscript, all of which was gratefully accepted. In spite of the assistance I have received from so many, I am naturally solely responsible for any errors that remain.

Finally, but most importantly, I wish to thank my wonderful wife Danusia. Without her total support, constant encouragement and always sound judgement, this book would have remained a long unfulfilled ambition.

Richard Thorn
January 2017

About the Author

Richard Thorn is a former Head of Computing and Engineering at the University of West London; Victoria University, Melbourne and the University of Derby. A Professor of Measurement Systems, he has published a number of books on measurement science and engineering during his career, but a biography of Nevil Shute was always waiting in the background.

Index

Aeroplanes
    AS.1 Tern 85, 86, 88, 89
    AS.4 Ferry 88, 91
    AS.5 Courier 90, 93, 96
    AS.6 Envoy 94
    AS.10 Oxford 98
    AS.51/52/53/58 Horsa 89
    Bristol Type 75 33
    D.H. Comet 1 34, 190, 198, 213
    D.H. 88 Comet 96
    D.H. 9/9a 34
    D.H 10a 41
    D.H. 34 24
    D.H. 89 98
    Percival Proctor Mk. V 141, 146, 147, 159, 179, 196
    Shackleton-Murray SM1 92
Air Circus 99, 258
Aircraft Manufacturing Company (Airco) 25 – 27
Airship Guarantee Company 40, 41-78
Airship Venture, The 93, 258
Airships
    LZ120 41
    R.38 47

R.80 42
R.100 44-78
R.101 44-78
U.S.S. Shenandoah 49
Airspeed (1934) Ltd 95-100
Airspeed Aeronautical College 96
Airspeed Ltd 85-94
Alington, Rev. Cyril 11, 15, 19, 24
Anderson, Donna 239, 248
Anderson, Sir John 112
Annakin, Ken 163
Assisted Passage Scheme 167, 175, 180
Astaire, Fred 239, 240, 244, 248
Attlee, Clement 130, 139, 146, 165, 169
Australian Citizenship Convention 242
Australian Women's Weekly 124, 156, 168, 196, 183, 187, 195
Baldwin, Stanley 45, 60
Balliol College, Oxford University 24, 28
Bates, H. E. xiii, 237
Baxter, Anne 121
Beach Assault 122
Bessant, Gladys 131, 170, 245
Betjeman, Sir John 9, 124, 169, 183, 200

Beyond the Black Stump 221-223
Bishop, Major Percy 74
Bishop, Ronald 34
Blackwood's Magazine 39, 93, 99
Blind Understanding 141
Bolte, Henry 248
Bookshop, The 36
Booth, Squadron Leader R. S. 64, 69
Boyer, Sir Richard 242
Brahms, Maria 36
Brancker, Sir W. Sefton 74
Breaking Wave, The 218
Brooks, Sir Dallas 248
Bryan, Dora 184
Burney, Sir Charles Dennistoun 42-49, 55-61, 67, 69, 70, 71, 77, 110, 115
Callinan, Lt.–Colonel Bernard 196
Calwell, Arthur 167
Campaign for Nuclear Disarmament, The 230, 233
Casey, Richard (Dick), G. G. (later Baron) 208, 232, 234, 240, 252
Chamberlain, Neville 106, 111
Chequer Board, The 132, 136-137
Churchill, Winston 106, 114, 126, 130, 165, 189, 228, 232
Clarendon Nine 8
Clarke, Dr Marcus 152, 154
Cobham, Sir Alan John 27, 34, 38, 43, 84-96, 99, 180, 209
Colmore, Squadron Leader Reginald 46, 74
Corfton Road, Ealing 7
Craneswater Park, Southsea 93
Cunningham, John 36
Dalrymple, Ian 127
Davey's Bay Yacht Club 179, 211

Davies, Captain G. O. C. 122
Dawson, Sir Trevor 76
de Havilland Aircraft Company 27, 34, 35
de Havilland, Sir Geoffrey 26, 27
Department of Miscellaneous Weapons Development 119-124
Dietrich, Marlene 184
Displaced Persons Scheme 179, 194
Diving Doravane, The 110
Doravane, The 110, 114
Dowding, Air Vice Marshall Hugh 77
Dry Hole, The 216
du Maurier, Daphne 145
Easter Week in Dublin 19
Eastwood (née Heaton), Phoebe 192
Edwards, Herbert James 'Ringer' 153, 161, 169
Egerton, Sir Reginald 9
Eliot, T. S. 231
Ellison, A. E. 92
Evans, A. Dwye 121, 149, 158, 168, 169, 187, 211, 241, 245
Far Country, The 193-196
Fellowes, Group Captain Peregrine 46
Fenton, Enid Laura 28
Films
 A Town Like Alice 169, 218-220, 223
 Landfall 117, 163
 Lonely Road/Scotland Yard Commands 97
 No Highway/No Highway in the Sky 143, 184
 On the Beach 233, 235, 238, 243, 244, 248
 Pastoral 124, 127
 Ruined City 103

Index

The Pied Piper 120, 121
Finch, Peter 218, 220, 223
Flight of Fancy 159
Frere, Alexander 144, 216, 243, 245, 252
Gadsden, Major General Frederick 5, 11
Gardner, Ava 239, 243, 248
George, David Lloyd 43, 80
Geysel-Vonck, J. G. 157, 161, 169
Gilstrap, Dr Clarence 212, 219, 221
Goodeve, Commander Charles F. 116, 120
Grabowsky-Atherstone, Lt.-Commander Noel 72
Gray, Edward 135
Great Panjandrum, The 119
Greene, Graham 121, 133, 216, 252
Greene, G. Grafton 128
Greenwood, Fred 192, 219
Greenwood, Ruth 192
Griffin, Marion 178
Griffin, Walter Burley 178
Grimthorpe, Lord 84, 86, 95, 98, 99
Guided Feet, The 132
Hailgate, Howden 51
Hardingham, Robert 39
Hassall, Ian 122, 182
Heaton, Arthur 85
Helena Road, Southsea 97
Herbert, Sir A. P. 54, 216
Hewitt, A. E. 86
Hoare, Sir Samuel 45, 49
Hughes, Robert 246
Hyde-White, Wilfred 184
In the Wet 199-202
Incident at Eucla 247, 249
Independent Company 196
Inspectorate of Anti-aircraft Weapons and Devices 116-119

Jaguar XK140 220, 225, 240
Jenkin, Prof. Charles Frewen 24, 25
Johns, Glynis 184
Johnson, Amy 36, 39
Kindest Goanna, The 216, 221
Kindling 104, 105
Kingsley Norris, Major General Frank 224
Kirby, Bruce 226
Kitchener. Field Marshall Horatio 12, 15, 16
Korda, Sir Alexander 127
Kramer, Stanley 234-235, 238-240, 244, 248, 249
La Grande, Oregon 212, 213, 216, 219, 221
Lame Ducks Fly, The 115
Landfall: A Channel Story 116
Langstone Tower 112, 115, 116
Langwarrin, Victoria 179, 184, 192, 193, 245
Laski, Marghanita 194
Last Days on Earth, The 231
Last Year, The 230
Lee, Jack 220
Legacy, The 168
Lonely Road 90-91
Lynam, C.C. 8
MacDonald, Ramsay 44, 45, 60, 76, 80, 106
MacKenzie, Sir Compton 253
MacMahon, James 18
MacMillan, Harold 13
Maralinga 229
Marazan 52-55
Masefield, Sir Peter 209, 210

309

McAuliffe, Reg 152
McCrae, John 15
McDowall, Roddy 121
McKenna, Virginia 218, 220
McKie, Bishop John D. 252, 253
McLean, Sir Robert 59, 68, 69
Meager, Captain George 64
Melbourne Club, The 216
Menhinick, Alec 227, 244
Mental Flight, The 134
Menzies, Sir Robert Gordon 169, 175, 186, 188, 189, 207, 208, 239, 246
Merrijig Hotel, The 180
Ministry of Information 126
Model Engineer, The 161
Moorehead, Alan McCrae 142, 190, 197, 211
More, Kenneth 184
Most Secret 121, 132, 133
Mount Eliza, Victoria 178
Murray, Lee 92
Mysterious Aviator, The 57
Nalder, F. S. 16
Nathan, Sir Matthew 17
National Aviation Day 88, 91, 95, 99
Nativity at Eucla 247
No Highway 142-145
Norway, Arthur Hamilton
    awarded New Year's Honour 21
    character and personality 5, 17, 18
    controversy surrounding his appointment to Dublin 9
    obituary in *The Times* 107
    political views 10
    view of colleagues on his retirement 26
Norway, Frances Mary (née Heaton)
    engagement to Nevil Norway 73
    family background 57
    life after Nevil Norway's death 253
    marriage to Nevil Norway 86
    relationship with husband 73, 89, 104, 138, 219
    view of Australia 167
Norway, Frederick Hamilton
    character and personality 6
    death 14, 15
    effect of his death on parents 15, 16, 18
    military service 14
    relationship with Nevil 6
Norway (now Mayfield), Heather Felicity
    birth 92
    advice to father on book 143
    arrival in Australia 180
    life after Nevil Norway's death 253
    marriage 253
    role as Nevil Norway's Executor 253
    role as Nevil Norway's secretary 219, 245
Norway, Mary Louisa (née Gadsden)
    account of the Easter Rising 19
    character and personality 5, 11, 92
    death 92
    family background 5
Norway, Nevil Shute
    becoming a racing driver 220, 225
    beginning association with Cassell and Company 53
    beginning association with William Heinemann Ltd 107
    beginning association with William

Index

Morrow and Company 90
birth 3
character and personality 6, 12, 23, 59, 73, 107, 121, 128, 130, 138, 140, 155, 165, 178, 182, 183, 185, 191, 205, 209, 224, 238, 244, 251, 252
contact with the literary establishment 215
controversy of *In the Wet* 200
controversy over his Will 235
coping with declining health 244
criticism of the R.101 project 209, 210
death 250
difficulties at first school 8
difficulties in finding a publisher 38, 39
difficulties with bureaucracy 118, 121, 128, 155, 176
dispute with the Ministry of Fuel and Power 165, 166
dispute with Stanley Kramer 238-240
doing a Norway 122, 175
ending association with Cassell and Company 107
engagement to Frances Heaton 77
experience as a private pilot 36
experience as a screen writer 127
experience as a war correspondent 122, 128
experience of the Easter Rising 17-19
finding a first publisher 53
first engagement 28
health issues 109, 118, 184, 219, 240, 244

influence of Oxford Preparatory School 8, 9
introduction to the aviation industry 25
marriage 86
Norway as a poet 12, 27
obituary in *The Times* 251
opinion of America 139, 166, 202
opinion of Australia 183, 185, 197, 214
opinion of Barnes Wallis 58
opinion of Canada 71
opinion of Dennistoun Burney 58
reasons for moving to Australia 168, 175
reasons for using pseudonym 54
relationship with Frances Heaton 73, 89, 104, 138, 219
relationship with Flora Twort 36, 49, 52
relationship with Hessell Tiltman 26, 39, 82, 87, 99, 210
relationship with J Basil Oldham 11. 19, 252
relationship with the media 189
reputation for predicting the future 213
stammer 7, 8, 20, 23, 109
support for a multi voting system 199
working day as an author 104
working for the Ministry of Information 128, 129
Norway, Shirley Anne
birth 97
death 253
godmother 52

311

life after Nevil Norway's death 253
opinion of *On the Beach* 224
overseas travel 235, 240, 245, 252, 253
view of move to Australia 167, 197
Norway, Walter 191
Octaplane, The 110
Old Captivity, An 113, 114
Oldham, James Basil 11, 252
Old Mill, Langstone 112
On the Beach 230-232
Once is Enough 226
Ordeal 108
Orwell, George 117
Other Side, The 121
Oxford and Cambridge Club, The 116, 128, 156, 178, 198
Oxford Preparatory School 8, 54
Pastoral 123-124
Paxton, John 238, 249
Pearce, Patrick 17
Peck, Gregory 239, 248
Perkins, Anthony 239, 249
Petrov Affair, The 207
Pied Piper 120, 121
Pilotage 39, 40
Piuro 29
Pond Head House 118, 168, 170
Preminger, Otto 121
Price, Major Ivon 17
Priestley, John Boynton 53, 107, 144, 216, 233, 252
Pudney, John 140
Pugsley, Professor Alfred 134
Rainbow and the Rose, The 236, 237
Ranelagh Club, The 178
Ranelagh Estate 178

Reed, Carol 127
Rendlesham Avenue, Ranelagh Estate 178
Requiem for a Wren 216-218
Richmond, Lt. Colonel Vincent 46, 75, 210
Riddell, James (Jimmie) 142, 146-159
Rising Wind, A 136
Roberts, Dr Harry 37
Robertson, Sir Macpherson 96
Rope, Squadron Leader F Michael 46, 75
Round the Bend 180, 181
Roxbee-Cox, Dr Harold 47
Royal Airship Works 44, 63, 65, 78
Rugby School 8, 10, 11
Ruined City 104, 105
Rum Jungle 192
Runagate 111, 170
Sandys, Duncan (later Baron) 229
Scott, Major George H. 46, 65, 67, 69, 75
Seafarers, The 133
Second Front 122
Secret War, The 119
Shackleton, William 92
Sherriff, R. C. 202
Shrewsbury School 11, 16, 19
Shute, Georgina 3
Slide Rule 206, 207, 208, 209
Smeeton, Miles 225, 226
Smith, Arthur L 24
Snow, C. P. 169
Snowy Mountains Hydro-Electric Scheme 179
So Disdained 57, 58
Somerset Road, Ealing 3, 5, 6, 253
South Hill House, Dublin 11, 16

Index

Southwell, Evelyn 12
Spicer, Justice J. A. 247
SS Strathnaver xii, 168, 170, 173-176
St. Leonard's Club, York 60, 73, 85, 86
St. Paul's Preparatory School, Hammersmith 7
Stephen Morris 37-39
Stewart, James 184
Stodart, Squadron Leader David 96
Streamline Cars Ltd 110
Sturt, Henry 8, 9
Sturt, Oliver 25, 28
Sutherland, Margaret 246
Swinnerton, Frank 105
Syme, Ian 211
Tallis, John 246
Tank Landing Craft 122
Teed, Major Philip 51
Temple, John E. 46, 47, 52
Thomas, George Holt 25, 27
Thomas, Sir Miles 144, 199
Thomson, Lord Christopher Birdwood 44, 45, 60, 72, 74
Tiltman, Alfred Hessell 26, 27, 39, 61, 82-100, 210
Tiltman, John 83
Toorak College 185, 190, 197
Toraplane, The 110, 111, 114
Town Like Alice, A 168-170
Trebetherick, Cornwall 9
Trustee from the Toolroom 253, 254
Tuxen, Saxil 178
Two Gentlemen of Soho 216
Twort, Flora Caroline 36, 37
U. Prajnananda 150, 162
Ulm, Charles T. P. 97
Vinland the Good 135, 136

Wagstaff, Hester 36
Walker, Charles Clement 26, 35, 40
Wallis, Barnes Neville (later Sir) 42-48, 58-61, 65, 67, 68, 119, 210
Watt, A. P. 54
Watt, Ronald Pollock 54, 57, 90, 97, 103, 143, 231, 244
Weston, Dr Dillon 69
What Happened to the Corbetts 108
White, Walter 136, 138
Wigham Richardson, George 100, 106
Wilson, Charlie 179, 183, 192
Woods, John Lowe 19
Woolley, Monty 121
World the Air and the Future, The 60
Worrall, Captain Harry 91
Wright, Orville 32
Wright, Wilbur 32
Yorkshire Aeroplane Club 51, 52, 56, 84, 91